DAYS AND NIGHTS AT

Costello's

DAYS AND NIGHTS AT

JOE McCARTHY

LITTLE, BROWN AND COMPANY   BOSTON / TORONTO

FIRST EDITION

The quote on pages 20–21 from the obituary of A. J. Liebling in the January 11, 1964 issue of *The New Yorker* is reprinted by permission; © 1964 The New Yorker Magazine, Inc.

The quote on page 33 from George Frazier's column on *duende* is reprinted courtesy of The Boston Globe.

LIBRARY OF CONGRESS CATALOGING IN PUBLICATION DATA

McCarthy, Joseph W.
  Days and nights at Costello's.

  1. United States—Biography. 2. McCarthy,
Joseph W. 3. Costello's Restaurant. I. Title.
CT220.M26 920'.073 80-16082
ISBN 0-316-55373-5

BP

Designed by Janis Capone

*Published simultaneously in Canada
by Little, Brown & Company (Canada) Limited*

PRINTED IN THE UNITED STATES OF AMERICA

CONTENTS

DAYS AND NIGHTS AT

Costello's

INTRODUCTION

THE FREELANCER'S LIFE CAN BE A RAGTAG ONE, scrambling from one assignment to another, trying to keep each magazine's editors happy while writing the best possible piece you can. And trying to make ends meet. But it has its compensations, too, and I have had more than my share, not the least of which have been the fascinating people I have written about. Think about it: getting to know John F. Kennedy, Harry Truman, Clare Boothe Luce, Jimmy Durante, Clark Gable, Mary Martin, Henry Ford II, and myriad other personalities who have really had important or at least very public roles to play in our times. Not a bad job at all for a guy who grew up in the Cambridge far removed from Harvard. It's certainly been rewarding. Some people even find it interesting enough to have asked me to share with others!

In fact, my friend and editor Ned Bradford suggested in 1972 that I write a memoir of my life as a freelancer.

I resisted . . . and maybe when you get through with this book you will wish I has shown greater resistance . . . but in the end I decided I could write a book, a *kind* of memoir that might be entertaining and fun for the reader.

Anyhow, since I have never been the story, but rather the storyteller, this is going to be a memoir with everybody at the center but me. After all, my professional life has really been that of a guy who goes out, interviews and hangs out with people, listens well, and waits for those special moments that amuse, expose character, or give new perspectives on people, and then writes it down, like the story of Gable's doves. . . .

1

COSTELLO'S

WHEN I GAVE UP A JOB AS A MAGAZINE WRITER in 1948 to become a freelance (or unemployed) writer of books and magazine articles, all the freelance writers I knew told me that I was crazy. I had started before Pearl Harbor as a writer, but, in the army of World War II, I became an editor on the staff of *Yank*, the enlisted men's weekly, to escape from service as a private in a pack artillery battalion. In the pack artillery, training for mountain or jungle warfare, we had to disassemble a 75-millimeter howitzer into six parts and pack it on the backs of six mules. Then we walked, each of us leading one of the mules. Editing was better than that. But, two years after the war, I found myself still editing and I wanted to get back to writing, even though I had a wife and three small children to support.

I was lucky. My first important magazine assignment, from *Life*, was to write an account of a New York City policeman's four-to-midnight tour of duty in a radio patrol car on the streets of East Harlem, one of the roughest precincts in the city. I had proposed a detailed report on the variety of people and various happenings that a policeman encounters during a night on the beat, hoping, of course, that the usual, but interesting, routine incidents – such as family troubles, fights between neighbors, childbirths, fires, barroom brawls – would be topped off by an extra-special or unusual occurrence. Jim Murphy, the patrolman who agreed to be the subject (or hero) of our piece, assured me that we would have no trouble finding such a big event. He pointed out that it was May and the warm spring weather was crowding the streets with people in the evenings. "Up here in East Harlem," Murphy said, "when a crowd gathers, anything can happen."

I spent a week with Murphy and his partner and paperwork recorder, another young patrolman named Peter Fitzpatrick, while they covered a sector of the Twenty-third Precinct between 96th and 106th streets, from Fifth Avenue to the East River, including a stretch of upper Madison Avenue, the Great White Way of Puerto Rican Harlem, so notorious for street fights that the police watched it constantly. *Life* assigned a staff photographer, Tony Linck, to travel with us and take pictures. After a few nights, I had all of the basic ingredients for a good story. I had watched Murphy settle an argument between a woman and a young man about the ownership of a dog, listened to him talk a teenaged boy out of trying to beat up his father for mistreating his mother, and saw him comfort an expectant mother in the throes of birth pains until the ambulance arrived. After he broke up a noisy fight between a husband and wife and tried to calm their three frightened small children, the wife turned on Murphy and berated him for butting into her family's privacy. We drove at dangerous speed through traffic to answer an emergency call from a sixth-floor apartment on East 98th Street. The emergency turned out to be a blown-out electric fuse in the basement of the building. The woman in the apartment handed Murphy a new fuse and said to him, "Will you change it for me? My little girl will take you down to the cellar and show you where the fuse box is." Murphy stared at the woman for a moment, and started to say something to her. Then he gave up and followed the little girl downstairs to the basement.

By Friday, I had everything that I needed except the big dramatic happening to give the story an exciting climax. "Friday is always a wild night around here," Murphy said as we started the four-to-midnight tour. "You'll get something big tonight for sure." But nothing unusual happened. "Don't worry," Murphy said to me reassuringly when we returned to the station house at midnight. "Tomorrow is Saturday. Saturday night is always a rough night." Saturday night turned out to be the quietest night of the whole week, not only in East Harlem, but, as we could hear from the calls on the police car's radio, all over the entire island of Manhattan.

"I can't understand it," Murphy said. "Well, tomorrow night is a Sunday night. I can't promise you much on a Sunday night, but Fitz and I will be here tomorrow, same time, same place, and if you want to take another shot at it, we'll be glad to have you with us."

Sunday evening also started quietly, but soon after dark all hell broke loose on upper Madison Avenue.

Murphy and Fitzpatrick rushed to a carnival grounds at East 108th Street where two other patrolmen from their precinct were surrounded by an angry mob. There had been a stabbing. One of the policemen, Abe Prince, had caught the knifer as he ran from the scene and was struggling to hold him. The other patrolman, George Colligan, was trying to help the victim, whose left cheek was slashed so deeply from his ear to the corner of his mouth that his back teeth could be seen through the open wound. The excited gathering crowd, seeing a fallen victim on the ground beside two policemen, assumed that he had been attacked by the cops and was closing in on Prince and Colligan when Murphy and Fitzpatrick arrived and saved them by driving their patrol car straight into the middle of the mob, scattering it in all directions. Then Murphy and Fitzpatrick covered Prince and Colligan while they got the victim into an ambulance and took the prisoner away to the station house to be booked.

Twenty minutes later we were driving east along 108th Street. The patrol cars in those days had only two seats. I was riding with Murphy, while Fitzpatrick and Tony Linck, with his camera, followed us in my car, driven by Bob Thompson, a friend of mine who had volunteered his services as a chauffeur for the evening. Murphy stopped at a red light on Madison Avenue. We saw a young man, a tall and good-looking Puerto Rican, running toward us. The front of his shirt was stained with blood. He grasped the door handle on Murphy's side of the police car, and gasped, "I'm stabbed. Get me to a hospital."

Murphy shouted at him, "You can't get in on this

side! Go around the car and get in on the other side!"

The young man's head slumped to his chest. "I can't . . . make it," he said. He fell slowly to the street, still holding on to the door handle. Murphy pulled his hand away from the handle, opened the door, and got out to drag him around the car to the other door. Fitzpatrick was trying to hold back the noisy crowd that was forming. Murphy and Fitzpatrick lifted the man into the seat of the patrol car and slammed the door. Murphy jumped in behind the wheel and drove away fast, with the siren screaming, down Madison Avenue to the emergency entrance of the Flower and Fifth Avenue Hospitals on East 106th Street. The rest of us followed close behind him in my car. Murphy and Fitzpatrick carried the bleeding young man into the emergency operating room. Linck was busy snapping pictures of the whole scene. The nurse in the operating room had just helped to remove from the same table the man who had been stabbed at the carnival.

"What's this?" she said to Murphy.

"Another stabbing," he said.

"My God," the nurse said. "What are they *doing* out there tonight?"

The nurse began to open a can of plasma. She handed another can of plasma to Murphy. "Here," she said. "You can be working on this one." As the nurse opened the can, twisting a key around its top rim, she bent over the man on the table, looking at his face. She turned away from him and said to Murphy, "Never mind that can. He's gone."

To the newspaper reporters covering New York's police headquarters that night, the killing of the young

Puerto Rican, Ramon Soler by name, was just a routine incident in East Harlem. There was only one paragraph about it in one of the next day's newspapers. But for Tony Linck and me, being on the scene and watching the police work on the case, it provided a climactic ending for our detailed account of Murphy's busy night on the beat. Linck snapped a picture of Murphy questioning Soler's wife, who had seen the stabbing. We went with Murphy to the scene of the crime, a bar on Madison Avenue, where he picked up the manager of the place, the suspect's brother, and brought him back to the hospital, then turned him over to the detectives who had just arrived to work on the case. Murphy had to undress Soler's body, which was still on the table in the emergency room: he had to turn in the clothing with his written report on the homicide. Murphy's sergeant, who was watching, said to him, "You don't need to bother taking off his socks."

When Murphy and Fitzpatrick drove back to the station house it was almost midnight, their quitting time. They heard that the suspected killer had already been picked up in The Bronx and was being questioned in the detective squadroom upstairs. "The brother must have talked," Murphy said. We went to the detectives' room, where Linck managed to snap a picture of Murphy sitting beside the captured suspect. One more picture, taken outside in the street twenty minutes later, illustrated the ending of our story of Murphy's night on the beat. It showed Murphy and Fitzpatrick leaving the station house in civilian clothes, their night's work done.

The next morning I talked on the phone with Robert Coughlan, who was then *Life*'s articles editor.

"Linck's pictures are terrific," he told me. "If you don't get your story in here quick, they'll run the pictures in next week's issue without a story." I sat down immediately and wrote the story, a long one, about eight thousand words, in a day and a half, without revising or retyping or changing a page of it. It wrote itself without much help from me. *Life* ran a full-page advertisement about the article in the *New York Times*, with a big picture of the handsome Jim Murphy standing beside his patrol car on a deserted stretch of Second Avenue in the early dawn light. That lucky story got me off to a good start as a freelance writer; during the next fifteen years, until television began to eat up the big national magazines like *Life*, *Look*, *The Saturday Evening Post*, and the old original and thickly paged *Holiday*, I had plenty of work to do.

A few days after the *Life* article was published, I walked into Tim and Joe Costello's barroom on Third Avenue. As usual, John McNulty was sitting at the bar. He beckoned to me. Unlike many other writers on *The New Yorker* at that time, such as his friend Joseph Mitchell, who fretted and worried over his marvelous pieces of reporting for many months before turning them in, McNulty was a great believer in getting a story done fast. When he talked about writing, McNulty would often tell the Irish joke about a prolonged wake that dragged on for a week, with the dead man's friends returning night after night for reminiscing and drinking. Finally, on the last night before the funeral, a mourner approached the open casket and touched his deceased friend fondly on the cheek. He drew back in surprise and said to the widow, "Why, Mary, he feels *hot!*" The exhausted widow said, "Hot or cold, he goes out of here in the morning."

McNulty said to me, "I'm going to ask you something, and I want you to tell me the truth. How long did it take you to write that piece for *Life* about the cop in East Harlem?"

"A day and a half," I said.

McNulty beamed. "Ah-ha!" he said. "That's what I like to hear! Hot or cold, it goes out of here in the morning!"

There was never another barroom anywhere like Costello's during those years of the thirties, forties, and fifties, when McNulty was hanging out there and writing stories about the place. Its walls were decorated with comic murals sketched by James Thurber, another steady customer, depicting battle scenes in the eternal war between men and women. Above the mirror behind the bar there was a walking stick, broken into two pieces, a memento of an argument that Ernest Hemingway started one night when he was drinking in Costello's with John Steinbeck and John O'Hara. Hemingway claimed that O'Hara's walking stick was not genuine Irish blackthorn, as O'Hara contended. To prove his point, Hemingway broke the stick on his own head. "When you call up Costello's," Eddie Condon, the jazz guitarist, said at that time, "somebody like Burl Ives or Charles Addams or Oliver St. John Gogarty answers the phone."

Gogarty, the Dublin physician and writer who was the prototype of Buck Mulligan, the medical student in James Joyce's *Ulysses*, spent a lot of time in Costello's during his later retirement years. One afternoon there I listened to him describing a visit that Joyce paid to his Dublin home after he had established a prosperous practice as an ear-nose-throat specialist. "He looked around at my lovely house and its lovely gardens," Gogarty said, "and then he turned to me with that sneering smile of his, and he said, 'Ah, Oliver, is this your revenge on mankind?'" Tim Costello's most treasured possession was a typewritten copy of a poem about a bawdy-house madam, composed by an obscure Scottish bard in the early eighteenth century and dictated from memory by Gogarty in Costello's shortly before he died in 1957.

The two Costello brothers were totally unlike each other; Tim was tall, courtly, and eloquent while Joe was short, tough, and gruff. They often battled and did not speak to each other for weeks. Both of them were roguish wits with a lively and erudite interest in literature and journalism and they both hated phony and pretentious intellectuals. One night a stranger at the bar tried to promote a serious discussion about Picasso. Tim stared at him for a moment and said, "What I'd like to see is a man who could draw like Casey, a fellow who used to hang out here. One winter day, the chef turned on the oven in the kitchen when the cat was sleeping inside. Casey drew a picture of the beast heading for the door to soak itself in the snow outside. It was a hell of a picture but he tore it up. He claimed he hadn't gotten the expression right." The Picasso man paid his check and went away.

Tim could recite from memory the original, unexpurgated, Scottish-dialect version of Robert Burns's

"John Anderson My Jo." He was once described in a *Manchester Guardian* article as an authority on Samuel Johnson. "He packs more enthusiasm, penetration and detail into his knowledge of Johnson than any Harvard professor ever did," the *Guardian* said. Tim loathed James Boswell, whom he regarded as a sponger. "If I could have had him in here," Tim said of Johnson, "I'd have given him a quiet table at the back, all by himself, away from all those terrible hangers-on." Tim could quote Johnson's remarks for an hour at a stretch. One of his favorites was the Doctor's reply when a bore asked if he believed that Ben Jonson had written Shakespeare's plays. "I don't know, sir," Johnson said, "but if he didn't, he missed a splendid opportunity."

Because many of Tim's customers and closest friends were writers, editors, or artists at *The New Yorker* – Thurber, John McNulty, A. J. Liebling, Joseph Mitchell, Philip Hamburger, John McCarten, Charles Addams, Kip Orr, and Fred Packard among others – many of his observations and reflections turned up in that magazine's "Talk of the Town" columns. When it was announced that the old Third Avenue elevated train structure was to be torn down, *The New Yorker* reported Costello's disapproval. "The El gave you something to lean against if you were overcome by a sudden moment of weakness or insecurity," Tim said. "We need something to replace it. If I was Mayor of New York, I'd put a railing all along the curb of Third Avenue from Astor Place to the Harlem River. Wouldn't it be grand to hold on to while making up your mind where next, uptown or downtown?"

Many of the stories recalled about Costello's reflect

the barroom's air of easy and casual but strict dignity. One afternoon Tim noted with disapproval that a man at the bar was trying hard to catch the eye of a girl who was sitting alone several stools away from him. Costello didn't put up with such goings-on. Casually, Tim approached the fellow, pretending to be wiping the bar, and leaned over and muttered to him softly, "See here now, O'Brien, there'll be no neck-arching in this saloon this afternoon." On another day, when Sam Goldwyn's movie version of *Guys and Dolls* was opening on Broadway, a publicity man came into Costello's with a group of the gorgeous Goldwyn Girls who were appearing as dancers in the picture. Tim soberly looked over the bevy of exquisite beauties and said to them, "The lot of you should be home sewing." Then he walked back to the end of the bar to sit with his cup of tea.

One night Ed Feingersh, a magazine photographer, brought Marilyn Monroe into Costello's and sat with her in one of the booths. The regular customers paid little attention to the film queen, but Tim's curiosity was aroused. He beckoned Feingersh to the bar and said to him, "Tell me, who is that girl you have with you?"

Feingersh said, "Marilyn Monroe."

Costello, sure he was being put on, flushed red with anger. "Damnit!" he said, "when I ask you a civil question, at least you could give me a civil answer!"

The big attraction of Costello's was its conversation, memorable and quotable for years afterward. Along with Thurber, McNulty, Liebling, Mitchell, Gogarty, and Steinbeck, the regular clientele and frequent visitors included such talkers as cartoonist Walt Kelly, Vincent

Sheean, the foreign correspondent, playwright Brendan Behan, and Bud Freeman, the great jazz saxophonist.

Brendan Behan could talk eloquently on any subject that just occurred to him and he had a store of entertaining memories. One night in Costello's, Behan recalled Louis Armstrong's arrival in Dublin during a European tour. A reporter asked him what he thought of Dublin.

"Dublin?" Louis said. "What's Dublin?"

On another night, Behan became embroiled in an argument with Walt Kelly that ended in a fistfight. After the protagonists were separated and calmed down, Behan apologized and said that the whole misunderstanding was his fault. "Your fault?" Kelly said. "What did you do?"

"I was born," Behan said remorsefully.

Another exchange at the bar that delighted Tim and Joe took place after a long argument about the rights of organized labor. John Steinbeck was defending labor. The spokesman for management was Sergeant Bill Potter, a bank manager in Elizabeth, New Jersey, in civilian life, who was then doing military service as business manager of *Yank*. *Yank*'s main editorial office was on East 42nd Street, two blocks from Costello's, so many soldiers attached to *Yank*, myself included, spent much of their time in Costello's. Sergeant Potter had never read anything except balance sheets and bank statements. He had never heard of John Steinbeck or such Steinbeck books as *The Grapes of Wrath* or *Of Mice and Men*. The sergeant listened impatiently to Steinbeck's final plea for the working man and then he held up his hand and delivered the crusher.

"Mr. Steinbeck," Potter said, "I don't know what kind of a business you're in, but you don't know anything about people."

Like "21," and many of the older eating and drinking places in New York, Costello's started during Prohibition as a speakeasy, upstairs on the corner of Lexington Avenue and 44th Street. Tim and Joe were then not long off the boat from Ireland, where they were born next door to their father's draper's shop in the small town of Ferbane in County Offaly. Before he came to this country, Tim spent "ten glorious years in Dublin" working as a driver of hired automobiles and becoming involved in the war against the British and the civil war of the early 1920s. "Did you ever read the Bible?" he once asked me. "I read it one time when I was in jail in Ireland, and it isn't a bad book at all."

Tim and Joe looked back on the repeal of Prohibition and the passing of their speakeasy with regret. "It was much nicer running a speakeasy than running a public bar," Tim said. "You could let in who you liked, and keep out the ones you didn't like. We only had to keep open three bottles at a time, one Scotch, one rye, and one gin. It was good Scotch, too, and we sold it for seventy-five cents a drink and made money on it."

With the repeal of the Eighteenth Amendment, the Costello brothers opened up at 701 Third Avenue, on the southeast corner of 44th Street, where they remained throughout World War II and for a few years after it. There they became famous as the only publicans in the city with original drawings by James Thurber on their walls. When a tiff with the landlord forced the Costellos to leave the corner location and move next door to 699 Third Avenue, panic seized their followers: it was assumed that the cherished Thurber murals would have to be left behind on the walls of the old place. To everyone's surprise, the new place opened with the same familiar sketches in their usual places above the booths opposite the long bar.

"It was pure luck," Tim said at the time. "When we went into the corner store in 1934, the man who was fixing it up talked us into using sheets of wallboard instead of putting on new plaster, and that's what Jim Thurber drew his pictures on. So when we moved out, we took down the sheets of wallboard and carried them with us. Thurber drew pictures on the walls of the speakeasy, too, but those were on plaster so we had to leave them there. One picture that he did in the speakeasy was a masterpiece. He did it in 1933 when the banks were closing, after Roosevelt took office, and he called it 'The Run on the Bank.' By God, it was wonderful. It had hundreds of men, women, and children, all running like mad, some of them with no clothes on. In the foreground there was this little fellow with a stiff collar and bow tie, staring at all of them with his mouth open. He doesn't know what's going on, and he's trying to figure out what all the excitement's about. It's a shame we had to leave it behind us."

The Thurber murals that the Costello brothers were able to preserve for posterity were sketchy line drawings that faded in later years. In 1972, ten years after Tim's death, a group of *Yank* artists, assembled by Art Weithas, the wartime magazine's art director, retouched and restored the figures of the battling men and women in the murals but the captions beneath the drawings remain today only in the memories of older customers. Under one sketch, showing a woman tackling a male football player, Thurber wrote, "Mount Holyoke 11, Yale 3." On another panel, where a man is shouting at a bedraggled and tipsy Thurber female, he was saying, "Quit acting like Katharine Cornell. All you've got is spinster's booze gloom." There is also a cocktail party scene where one woman is talking to another woman. In the now-faded original line of dialogue she is saying, "My husband went upstairs to bed about a year ago and was never seen again."

As much as Tim and Joe Costello admired Thurber, both of them had a much warmer and deeper admiration for Abbott Joseph Liebling and John McNulty. Liebling and McNulty were both learned and extremely well read, with no intellectual airs about them; they both greatly enjoyed talking with cab drivers, merchant seamen, horse players, retired railroad men, cops, and bookies, so it was only natural that they both enjoyed hanging around in Costello's where there was such a variety of types. If Costello's had been strictly a literary hangout, or a New York version of the Mermaid Tavern—as many people who didn't go there assumed it to be—Liebling and McNulty would have avoided the place. In fact, most of the short stories about Third Avenue that McNulty wrote for *The New Yorker*, and later collected in a book entitled *Third Avenue* which he dedicated to Tim and Joe, were about happenings that he saw or heard about in Costello's, and none of the characters in McNulty's stories are writers or artists.

I never met anybody with a wider variety of passionate

interests, or a wider frame of reference, than Joe Liebling. Only Liebling would, or could, describe Archie Moore, the heavyweight boxer, as "a late-maturing artist, like Laurence Sterne and Stendhal." The anonymous writer of Liebling's obituary in *The New Yorker* well described him by listing some of the things found in his office on the day that he died, late in 1963:

> . . . unsorted, unfiled, within reach, scattered and heaped on his desk, tables, chairs, shelves, and air-conditioner, and, in some cases, hanging at odd angles on his walls, were such items as the latest *Annual Report of The New-York Historical Society*, a 1927 biography of Boss Tweed, two lithographs of jockeys, a drawing of Bob Fitzsimmons just after he defeated Jack (Nonpareil) Dempsey for the middle-weight championship of the world in 1891, Robert Aron's "Histoire de la Libération de la France," the *American Racing Manual*, a volume on "The Theory and Practice of the Preparation of Malt and the Fabrication of Beer," Harold Nicolson's "The Congress of Vienna," a month of issues of the Las Vegas *Sun*, General Freiherr von Bernhardi's "Cavalry in War and Peace," three volumes of Pierce Egan's "Boxiana," the 1955 edition of *Guide Bleu Algérie-Tunisie*, a Christmas card from "The Officers and Men of the First Infantry Division," the third volume of Stendhal's "Journal," the November 28th edition of the Miami *Labor Tribune*, and the collected works of Albert Camus. Those items came close to making up a summary of Liebling's passionate interests, among which were New York, Paris, North Africa, England, boxing, military theory, horse racing, newspapers, labor, food, medieval history, Broadway life, Stendhal, Camus, Colonel Stingo, Pierce Egan, Stephen

Crane, and Ibn Khaldun. These were some of his subjects, and he knew them all thoroughly; he was the most protean of scholars. An immense variety of people and things gave Liebling delight, and he was impatient to pass along his delight to everybody else, in his writings. He wrote about only what he cared about deeply; there was no searching for material, no writing for writing's sake. . . .

This last quality—writing on only what he cared about deeply—was the thing that distinguished Liebling from most other writers, who generally will write about anything that will earn them a few bucks, whether they care about it or not. Not Liebling. Even when he was hard up financially, which was often, he would not think of writing about something that didn't interest him. He could not understand how any writer could write only for money. Joe Mitchell once told us in Costello's about going out to lunch with Liebling and another *New Yorker* writer, who had just had a big and popular but second-rate novel about the Old South published. When the three men got into the elevator at *The New Yorker*, the novelist said, "I just sold my book to the movies for fifty thousand dollars." Liebling said nothing, but Mitchell could see that he was getting livid. The three men got out of the elevator and walked over to Sixth Avenue, none of them saying anything. Then the novelist said, "Isn't it a shame that they're tearing down these nice old buildings along here?" Liebling turned on him, furious, and shouted, "They ought to tear down *all* these damned old buildings! They're good for nothing and they're an eyesore!"

Liebling and Harold Ross, the founder and editor of

The New Yorker, whom Joe deeply admired, shared an intense distaste for the "group journalism" system developed by Henry Luce at *Time* magazine. If *Time* decides to do a story on a United States senator, for instance, a team of girl researchers, and correspondents in Washington and in the senator's hometown, interview the senator and people who know him and dig up a mass of information about him. Their research is written out in detail and handed to a writer-editor, who then writes the story, usually without ever having seen or talked to the senator. Both Liebling and Ross felt strongly that a writer should do all of his own research and interviewing himself, with no help from anybody. Shortly after World War II, John Hersey wrote a long and detailed article for *The New Yorker* about the bombing of Hiroshima, based on interviews with several survivors. Ross and William Shawn, then his managing editor and later his successor as editor, decided to publish all of Hersey's article in one issue of the magazine with nothing else in that issue, no fiction, no cartoons, no theater or book reviews that might dilute the long Hiroshima report's dramatic impact. The appearance of that whole issue of *The New Yorker* devoted exclusively to Hersey's article created quite a stir among readers and in the publishing business. *Time* decided to do a story on it in its Press section. A girl researcher made an appointment to interview Ross about the article at his office. Inasmuch as *The New Yorker*'s office is only a few blocks from *Time*'s office, the writer assigned to the story decided to go along to see Ross while the researcher talked with him. The writer sat and listened, without saying a word, while

Ross politely answered the researcher's questions. Then, with the interview completed, the *Time* people got up to leave. Ross saw them to the door, where the writer spoke for the first time. He asked Ross, "How long did it take Hersey to write this piece?" Ross's reply delighted Liebling, who told it all over town.

"Ross looked the writer over from his head to his feet," Liebling said. "Then he said to him, 'I don't know, but he wrote every goddamned word of it himself.'"

John McNulty was another man who found delight in an immense variety of people and things. While he was playing "My Gal Sal" on a piano, McNulty would recite in time with the music the names of all the presidents of the United States in the order of their succession to that office. Tim Costello enjoyed recalling one time when McNulty disappeared from his job at the *New York Daily News* for several days. Finally, the city editor received a telegram from him in Galesburg, Illinois, which said, "Please send me fifty dollars and my middle initial. I want to join the local Elks." There was one memorable night in Costello's when McNulty returned from a writing stint in Hollywood, bursting with funny stories about Groucho Marx and Barry Fitzgerald, who had become his closest friends in California. He told about attending a formal dance in a producer's home, where he and Groucho and their wives were fox-trotting happily to a Cole Porter tune when somebody requested a sudden change to Johann Strauss's 1868 waltz, "Tales of the Vienna Woods." Groucho glided past the McNultys and said to John, "Not a word of this to the ladies, McNulty, but we've

just gotten word that Napoleon has escaped from Elba."
Another favorite of McNulty's was Groucho's reply
when a Roman Catholic priest said to him in an elevator
at the Plaza, "Aren't you Groucho Marx? You're my
mother's favorite comedian." Groucho said, "I didn't
know you fellows were allowed to have mothers."

McNulty spent so much time in Hollywood with
Barry Fitzgerald that he acquired, and kept for the
rest of his life, some of Fitzgerald's mannerisms and
Irish brogue. He told about Fitzgerald's hatred for the
unending California sunshine and his yearning for the
clouds and rain of Ireland. "Barry would look up,
squinting, at the bright sun in the clear blue sky,"
McNulty said, "and then he would shake his head in
disgust and mutter, 'Oh, my God, how much longer
d'ye think this is going to last?'"

McNulty had a boundless curiosity about everybody
and everything. One evening when he was eating dinner
alone in a restaurant on East 72nd Street, he started
reading the small print on the label of a Tabasco sauce
bottle, which said that Tabasco is a pepper sauce manu-
factured by a family named McIlhenny in New Iberia,
Louisiana. Two days later, McNulty was on a train,
traveling to New Iberia to find out about Tabasco and
the McIlhennys. A few weeks later he wrote an excel-
lent article about them for *The New Yorker*. When he
became an admirer of Alfred Vanderbilt's great three-
year-old racehorse, Native Dancer, he made arrangements to spend a night in a room in the colt's barn at
Belmont Park. That piece had as its closing line the
kind of authentic and exactly recorded spoken words
that only McNulty seemed to catch and remember. He

describes a groom in the Vanderbilt stable pausing to admire Native Dancer as the big star returns from a workout, and then, turning back to work with his curry-comb on another three-year-old, saying reassuringly, "You a good horse, too."

In the semifictional, or largely factual, stories that McNulty wrote about goings-on in Costello's, he referred to Tim as "the boss." In one story, he told about a Sunday afternoon when Tim became fascinated by the elegant manners of two down-and-out derelicts who wandered into the saloon looking for a hand-out. One of them wore a battered straw hat that obviously had been fished out of a trash can. To everybody's astonishment, Tim treated them to the best sherry in the house. After they left, Tim tried on his own hat and stared at himself in the mirror behind the bar. "I wish to God," McNulty quoted him as saying, "I could get my hat to set on my head the way that hat set on that bum. Now didn't it have a hell of a jaunty look to it?"

"I remember it well," Tim said when I reminded him of the story several years later. "McNulty entitled the story 'Two Bums Here Would Spend Freely Except for Poverty,' and that was exactly what I told him at the time. I told him those two fellows would have gladly spent a thousand dollars if they had it.

"McNulty used to write a lot of stories about a bartender we had here named Paddy, but there was one story about Paddy he didn't write. One day I'm sitting here, down at this back end of the bar having my cup of tea and I'm watching, out of the corner of my eye, Paddy down at the other end of the bar becoming very annoyed with two bums he's waiting on. After a while Paddy comes back to where I'm sitting. He's muttering under his breath, and he's rubbing the bar so hard with his bar rag I'm afraid he's going to put his fist through the mahogany. So I ask him what's the matter.

"'Tim,' he says to me, 'there's one thing on this earth I can't endure.'

"'What's that, Paddy?' I says.

"'Human beings!' he says."

There was a ripple of happy excitement in Costello's on the day in 1949 when McNulty came in to announce that he was going to make a trip to Ireland. Like me, he was born in Massachusetts and had never seen Ireland or the sky over it, as the saying goes, but he had spent so much time with the Costellos and Barry Fitzgerald and other Irish-born people that he had come to talk, think, and act like one of them. "A small, jaunty man, best described as Irish of face and manner," the *New York Times* once wrote of McNulty. He shared the Costello brothers' scorn for such sentimental Irish blather as the Blarney Stone, Mother Machree, elves, and leprechauns. McNulty used to say, "Only people with Vincent as a middle name write about leprechauns." Tim would tear Mother Machree to shreds whenever the opportunity was available. "Nobody ever mentions Father Machree," Tim often said. "The poor man was probably working himself to the bone, trying to hold the family together, while Mother Machree was sitting around all day, gabbing with the neighbor women, and the dishes all piled up in the sink."

Still, the Costellos would sometimes get misty-eyed about Ireland, usually when Burl Ives sang for them (almost invariably on Saint Patrick's Day) the ballad about Kevin Barry, who was hung just before the 1916 Easter Rising. One of Tim's favorite cartoons, which he displayed behind the bar, showed a Saint Patrick's Day parade in Atlanta, Georgia, back in the 1920s. In the sketch, thousands of white-robed and hooded Ku Klux Klansmen are massed along the sidewalks of Peachtree Street, watching silently a procession that consists of two black musicians, one blowing a trumpet and the other beating a drum, with one small and solitary Irishman, bedecked with shamrocks and green ribbons, marching proudly behind them. I remember one Saint Patrick's Day when Tim was determined to stay on the wagon, as he did most of the time, because naturally the seventeenth of March was always the busiest working day in the year for the Costellos. When my wife and I elbowed our way through the big crowd at the bar late in the day, we met Tim and saw that his resolution had gone to pot.

"What happened?" I asked.

"Well," Tim said unsteadily, "I was doing fine until I decided to go over to Fifth Avenue and watch some of the Saint Patrick's Day parade. I'm standing there on the sidewalk, and who do I see come marching up the avenue, leading one of the bands of pipers, but an old fellow I know who must be at least eighty years old. He's wearing a tall silk hat, with green ribbon wrapped around it, and he's waving an old blackthorn stick. I took one look at him, and the next thing I knew I was in the Men's Bar at the Biltmore, stinking drunk and buying drinks for everybody in the house."

McNulty was a wonderful title picker. When he broke

the news about his planned trip to Ireland, he already had the title for the story that he was planning to write about it if all went well—"Back Where I Had Never Been." The trip was suggested by John's wife, Faith, much to his astonishment, after he came into some extra money unexpectedly from the sale of a story to a movie company. When McNulty sought Tim's advice about plans and preparations for the trip, he was told, first of all, to buy himself a heavy raincoat with a detachable woolen lining. Second, Tim warned him that Ireland was not all Mother Machree.

"I don't want it to be Mother Machree," McNulty said. "I hope there'll be very little of Mother Machree on this trip."

"A minimum of Mother Machree is what you mean, a minimum of Mother Machree," Tim said. "Will you do as I tell you and go get a warm raincoat?"

The McNultys had a memorable trip to Ireland and John wrote an account of its highlights for *The New Yorker*, a story that Irish people would describe as "lovely." At one point, John wrote, "Children recite in Ireland, and sweetly, too. And people take long walks, and they sit by the fire and talk without a radio going, and do all the other things we used to do but don't seem to do any more." He told about searching in County Kerry for an old Gaelic storyteller. "In Waterville, I spoke to the barmaid in the Butler Arms Hotel about this matter," he said. "That's a good way to begin any quest in Ireland, I learned—speak to the barmaid about it." The barmaid directed him to a local folklore scholar named Tadg Murphy, who took him to an eighty-one-year-old Gaelic-speaking storyteller, whose eyes, according to McNulty, were "as young as if he were twenty-five." In his article, McNulty described the storyteller spinning a long tale about a fisherman who cursed the sea because its bad storms had kept him away from his home while his wife and child were dying. The sea, in revenge, drowned the fisherman and then, after he was buried, sent monstrous waves to his grave and carried away his coffin.

A few days after McNulty's account of his trip to Ireland appeared in *The New Yorker*, I met him strolling along Fifth Avenue, wearing a new tweed jacket that he had obviously bought in Dublin. I complimented him on the story, and mentioned that I had found his report on the Gaelic storyteller in Kerry especially interesting.

"Confidentially," McNulty said, "the storyteller was an old bore. When I got back here to New York, I went to the public library, got a book of Irish folk tales, and copied one of them."

Thirteen years later, six years after McNulty's death, I found myself in Waterville, staying at the Butler Arms Hotel. I went to the bar and asked the barmaid, a pretty red-haired woman named Angela Curley, for a martini. While she was mixing the drink, I asked her if she remembered a man from New York named John McNulty.

"I do indeed," she said. "He came in here asking where he could find a storyteller. I sent him to Tadg Murphy, and Tadg Murphy took him to visit a storyteller near Ballinskelligs, and he wrote about it in his magazine."

I told Miss Curley what McNulty had told me, about the storyteller being a bore and about how he used a story from a book in the New York Public Library. Miss Curley stopped wiping the glass that she was drying and looked at me for a moment.

"You must remember that the storyteller spoke only Irish, or Gaelic, as you call it," she said. "Mr. McNulty couldn't understand a word that he was saying. In any case, Mr. McNulty is now dead and Tadg Murphy is dead. But the storyteller is still alive."

Another one of Tim's favorite customers was George Frazier, who wrote for *Life* and *Esquire* and later became a popular newspaper columnist in his hometown, Boston, but continued to live in an apartment on East 81st Street in New York where there were three names on his mailbox: Spade, Archer, and Frazier. Spade and Archer, of course, were the fictional detectives Sam Spade and Lew Archer. I once asked Frazier why he lived in New York while working for the *Boston Globe*. "I can't live in any city where you can't find a decent restaurant open after three o'clock in the morning," he said. Earlier he had lost a well-paid job as a columnist for the *Boston Herald* because he was spending all of his time carrying on a romance in Fort Wayne, Indiana. He was a man of peculiar work habits and had once turned in a column entirely in Latin. After making a comeback on the *Globe*, Frazier was briefly fired again because he was dictating his columns over the telephone from East 81st Street and seldom mentioning anybody or anything in Boston. He was rehired by the *Globe* after one of his admiring readers hired a plane and flew it over Schaefer Stadium in Foxboro during one of the New England Patriots' crowded Sunday football games, towing a sign that said, "Globe Fears Freedom & Fired Frazier."

In Costello's one evening somebody asked Tim jokingly if he was related to Lou Costello of the Abbott and Costello comedy team. Frazier, who was listening, said, "For years I've been wondering which one of them is Costello. Or which one is Abbott? I still don't know which is which."

A man who was sitting next to Frazier said, "That's easy. The one with the mustache is Costello."

Frazier thought that over for a moment and said, "I don't think either one of them has a mustache."

"Oh, yes," the man said. "The little one."

"The little one?" Frazier said. "Which one is the little one?"

"The little one," the man said, "is the one with the mustache."

Frazier was so fascinated by this dialogue that he later entitled a book of his magazine pieces *The One with the Mustache Is Costello.*

Tim and Joe liked to get Frazier reminiscing about jazz musicians he had known. George was one of the first modern jazz critics; back in the early 1930s, when he was still an undergraduate at Harvard and there was little jazz music criticism published in this county, he wrote about American jazz musicians for a small magazine in Paris called *Jazz-Tango-Dancing*. During the big-band era in the late 1930s, Frazier was a critic for

Downbeat, where he stirred up a sensation by writing, "Martha Tilton stinks." Around that time I spent a weekend in New York and visited a small bar off Times Square, where a trio of black jazz musicians were performing. During a break, I asked one of them if he knew George Frazier. The musician stared at me in amazement, turned to the other two members of the trio, and said, "This is the first sonofabitch who ever asked me if I knew somebody and I *knew* him!" It was Frazier who told about Eddie Condon's remark when the guitarist was in a hospital, suffering from a pancreatic illness and being fed whiskey rectally. Condon looked back over his shoulder at the nurse who was injecting the liquor and said to her, "See what the boys in the ward will have." Another one of Frazier's favorite quotations was Tyree Glenn's remark about a lady jazz pianist: "Her hands are bigger than seventeen dollars' worth of spareribs in 1931." Tim often asked Frazier to repeat a story about Wingy Mannone, the one-armed trumpet player, who arrived in New York from California on a freezing cold day and hurried to a haberdashery to buy a glove for his chilled hand. The man in the store refused to sell Mannone a single glove; he explained that his gloves were sold only in pairs. Incensed, Mannone bought a pair and then shouted at the haberdasher, "Gee, you New York guys really put it on people from out of town, don't you?"

Frazier was a handsome and debonair fellow, who fussed about his clothes and usually wore a carnation in his lapel. He insisted that the buttonhole on his lapel had to be one-sixteenth of an inch wider than the customary width, and, on the underside of the lapel, there had to be a small loop of braid to hold the stem of his flower in place. One day, back in the 1930s, Frazier went to Zareh's, a men's clothing store on State Street in Boston, and announced to my brother Luke, who was working there at the time, that he had to buy a white linen suit.

"Why a white linen suit?" Luke asked.

"I just bought a Packard touring car," George said. "You can't drive to Cape Cod for a weekend in the summertime in a Packard touring car with the top down unless you're wearing a white linen suit."

After he became a columnist in Boston, Frazier discovered, or pounced upon, a reference in an essay by Kenneth Tynan to *duende*, a Spanish word meaning a certain inimitable quality of high style or stylish manner of behavior or performance. George spent most of the rest of his life talking and writing about *duende* and who had it and who didn't have it. "Billie Holliday had *duende*," he would way, "but Ella Fitzgerald doesn't. Gene Kelly is a great dancer but he doesn't have *duende*. Fred Astaire is loaded with it. Tim Costello has it when he puts on his hat. It's just a battered old hat but when Tim puts it on, he endows it with excellence. Remember Mary Martin, straddling a chair on a bare stage in *One Touch of Venus* and singing 'That's Him'? That's *duende*. It's Franklin Roosevelt wearing that old Naval cape at Yalta, and it's Sidney Greenstreet in *The Maltese Falcon*, lower lip protruding, thumbs hooked in his vest pockets, as he said, 'By Gad, sir, I do admire you!'"

Frazier drew a line of distinction between *duende*, or style, and class. "Style was Joe DiMaggio drifting under a towering fly, so leisurely, so gracefully," he once wrote, "but class was what he had when he barred Peter Lawford from Marilyn Monroe's funeral." Frazier listed among those conspicuously lacking *duende* Joan Crawford, Adolphe Menjou, Sandra Dee, Glenn Ford, Sal Mineo, and Andy Williams. Those who had it, in his estimation, included Willie Mays, Peter Ustinov, Johnny Unitas, Robert Mitchum, Bette Davis, James Cagney, Cary Grant, and, of course, Humphrey Bogart, who was Frazier's favorite film actor. George was deeply impressed by a framed bill from the Algonquin Hotel, for damages in one of its rooms during a scrap between Bogart and his third wife, Mayo Methot, which Bogart displayed on a wall in his Hollywood home.

Frazier, who was proud of being a Harvard graduate, died appropriately at Mount Auburn Hospital in Cambridge, Massachusetts, near the Harvard Yard, on June 14, 1974, the day of Harvard's commencement exercises. Shortly before his death, a nurse came to him, asking to make a blood test. George said he didn't want a blood test. "But you must have a blood test," the nurse said. "You came here because you're sick, didn't you?"

"No," George said. "I came here for the Yale game."

By that time, most of the regular patrons whom George had admired at the old Costello's, along with Tim and Joe themselves, were already long gone. I had the good fortune to spend a few days with Tim during his last visit to County Offaly, his birthplace in Ireland, shortly before his death in 1962. When I arrived, I found him in good spirits, sitting on the glassed-in porch of the County Arms Hotel in the medieval town of Birr. It soon became obvious that Costello, at the

County Arms, was being treated as a much more important guest than General Douglas MacArthur ever was at the Waldorf Astoria.

"Sit down here and have a drink," Tim said to me. "I remember one time in Dublin when a bartender said to Oliver Gogarty, 'Doctor, will you have a small or a large whiskey?' Gogarty said, 'There's no such thing as a large whiskey.' After a while I'll get the porter to take you to your room, and show you where the bath is, but you won't need a bath while you're here because in Ireland nobody ever gets dirty. I've done you a great favor, bringing you up here into the midlands where the tourists don't usually come. This is an interesting part of the country. Tomorrow I'll take you to the house in Ferbane, a few miles from here, where I was born and raised, and I'll show you what a peat-burning fire looks like. I'll show you Birr Castle and the ruins of the monastery at Clonmacnois on the River Shannon, where the monks were studying and teaching literature and art in the Dark Ages, back in 545 A.D. Think of that, will you? Only five hundred years after Christ, and they had a school going here in Offaly. Birr Castle was built in the Middle Ages by the Carrolls. You know Charles Carroll of Carrollton?"

"The signer of the Declaration of Independence?" I said.

"Not only did he sign it," Tim said, "he was the only one who signed and put his address after his name. He said he wanted the British to know where they could come and get him if the Revolution flopped. Well, his people built the castle here in Birr. In 1620, the British took it away from them because they were

Catholics, and drove them to America, and gave the castle and all the land around here to an English family named Parsons, the earls of Rosse, who are now Princess Margaret's in-laws. No wonder Charles Carroll jumped into the American Revolution with such eagerness. Drink up your drink and we'll have dinner. The mushrooms here are great. They grow in the open fields, not in caves like the mushrooms in America."

The next day, Tim and his son, Young Tim, who was with him, drove with me in a hired car to Ferbane, where he showed me his family's home and introduced me to his sister Margaret, who was still living there alone. Then we went to the ruins of Saint Ciaran's sixth-century monastery at Clonmacnois and later in the day, back in Birr, we had tea with Miss Kathleen Cavanagh, proprietress of a local vegetable shop and an avid, knowledgeable student of Irish history, whom Tim greatly admired. "I'm sixty-nine years old," Miss Cavanagh said. "Never deny thy age, and the gods will never put a wrinkle in thine face." While she talked about the Irish fighting in a resistance to British rule for seven hundred years—"But we survived, and our star is only beginning to rise!"—Tim's eyes filled up and two tears rolled down his cheeks.

That was the last time I saw Tim in good form. A few months later in New York he died from a heart ailment. The day before he died, Johnny Gallagher, his daytime bartender, came to the hospital to visit him. "Now listen to me, and do what I tell you," Tim said to Johnny. "When I die, I don't want you closing the place or any of that nonsense. Keep the business open as usual, and don't be giving away free drinks of my whiskey to every Tom, Dick, and Harry who comes in to sympathize with you."

A year later Joe Liebling died. Joe Mitchell spoke at his funeral.

"Tim Costello once referred to Joe as 'that good, kind, brave, decent man,'" Mitchell said of Liebling. "In the last two days, I have recalled a multitude of examples of Joe's goodness. I will refer to only one, and to that only because, for some reason that I don't understand, it haunts me. We had been up to the Red Devil Restaurant for lunch. It was one of those times when he was in bad shape physically; his right hand was red and swollen from gout, and his feet were giving him trouble. Also, he was apprehensive about an income-tax matter, and he was having doubts about something he was writing. At lunch, he had been talking about Stephen Crane, and evidently this had put something in his mind. All of a sudden, as we were walking back to the office, he asked me to go with him to a flower store on Madison Avenue. Joe had an amazing variety of friends, and one of them was an elderly woman who was living in a nursing home in the Bronx. Joe liked her for two reasons. As a young woman, she had been a friend of Stephen Crane. Also, although she was crippled and couldn't get around and had outlived all her old friends and was pretty much alone in the world, she still had a great appetite for life and could find pleasure and delight in things as commonplace as a cup of tea. We went into the flower store and Joe ordered a dozen red roses to be sent to her. We started out of the store. The woman had lived in France for many years long ago and loved France, and Joe must have thought of that. He went back and asked the man to put six blue irises in among the roses. Then we went on down to the office, and, walking beside him, I thought of a line in Yeats. I felt that he 'was blessèd and could bless.'"

The building that housed Costello's on Third Avenue was torn down by a new owner in 1974. Young Tim, who now owns the business with a new partner, managed to find a good new location on 44th Street between Third and Second avenues, only about a hundred yards from the old place. Once again the Thurber murals were carefully taken down and moved, along with the old bar and John O'Hara's broken blackthorn walking stick, and the new Costello's is thriving as a very pleasant place to meet with friends for a few drinks and a meal. But it isn't the same as it was when Tim and Joe were there.

2

BALENCIAGA, WHITE DOVES, AND THE LEGS OF BACALL

ONE EVENING IN 1955, WHEN I WAS TAKING A LONG look at Gable for *Look* magazine, I had dinner at his house with him and Kay Spreckels, who became his fifth and last wife a few weeks later. Gable was very proud of his handsome white brick house, with its sloping, low-hanging roof. "Looks like an eastern house, doesn't it?" he said. A Pennsylvania Dutchman, he hated California-style architecture and almost everything else in California, except the bird shooting in the northern part of state. He talked about the surrounding countryside in the San Fernando Valley and how it had changed in recent years. "When I bought this place from Raoul Walsh back in the thirties," Gable said, "I could saddle up my horse, Sunny, and ride across the hills from here to the ocean at Santa Monica without seeing another house. Now you can't ride around here without going through somebody's backyard. I gave up my horses, and the only animal on the place now is a little burro that Grace Kelly gave me as a birthday gift a few years back."

"And down there beyond the garage, Clark has a lot of doves," Kay Spreckels said. "Hundreds of them."

"Doves?" I said.

Gable said nothing. Obviously, he did not want to talk about the doves so we changed the subject.

I smelled a story behind the doves. A few days later, I managed to find out that there was one.

Gable's first formal date with Carole Lombard, the great love of his life, was on a night in 1935 when he escorted her to the White Ball of the Academy of Motion Picture Arts and Sciences. Ladies were asked to wear white at the ball. Carole Lombard decided to get really into the spirit of the thing. She arrived in a white ambulance, and was transported into the ballroom on a white stretcher carried by two white-uniformed attendants.

During the evening Carole and Clark quarreled, and she left him. He was living alone at the time in the Beverly Wilshire Hotel, having been separated from his second wife, Ria Langham Gable, a wealthy Houston socialite who was seventeen years older than he was. When Gable awoke on the morning after the ball, he found in his room two white doves, a peace offering from Carole. She had bribed a bellboy to sneak the birds into the room while he was asleep. Gable never gave away the doves. The flock of doves that he was keeping on his estate at Encino twenty years later were descendants of the two that he found in his room at the Beverly Wilshire that morning in 1935.

If Gable was reticent, there was nothing that Jack Kennedy did not want to talk about, but in an interview he was usually the one who asked most of the questions. When he met you, he wanted to know all about you and your family's history. Kennedy was unlike most important public figures I'd met, who tended to be wrapped up in themselves. When Harry Truman, for instance, cracked a joke and the listener did not laugh, Truman would bristle peevishly and say, "Didn't you hear what I just said?" But Kennedy was wrapped up in trying to find out about other people. He was the most curious man who ever walked the face of the earth.

A memorable story about Kennedy's curiosity, and about his kind concern for other people, came up when I was working with Kenny O'Donnell and Dave Powers on their book of memoirs, *Johnny, We Hardly Knew Ye.* But as often happens in the frustrating work of writing, I did not hear the full details of that story until after the book had gone to press. O'Donnell was recalling an overnight visit that Kennedy and he paid to the Lyndon Johnsons at the LBJ Ranch in Texas with two other Boston Irishmen, Torbert Macdonald and Bill Hartigan, shortly after the 1960 elections. Johnson insisted on dragging Kennedy out of bed at five o'clock in the morning to go on a deer hunt, much to Kennedy's disgust.

"That day happened to be the Johnsons' twenty-sixth wedding anniversary," O'Donnell said. "But Lady Bird and Lyndon never mentioned that to us, and none of us found out about it, except, of course, Mr. President. While we were getting ready to go deer hunting, he sent Bill Hartigan on a secret mission to Austin, to buy a gift and have it suitably engraved with a nice inscription. So he presented the gift, a piece of silver, to Lady Bird at dinner that night. She was completely surprised and astonished, and so was Lyndon."

"How did he find out it was their wedding anniversary?" I asked.

"I don't know," O'Donnell said. "He was always finding out about things like that."

A few months later, after the book was finished and printed, I was in Boston, having a drink with O'Donnell. Bill Hartigan appeared and sat down to join us. I reminded him of the anniversary gift–hunting expedition, which he remembered well. I asked him how Kennedy had learned that that particular day was the anniversary of the Johnsons' wedding day.

"You won't believe it," Hartigan said.

He recalled Kennedy being awakened that morning in the five-o'clock darkness, cursing Johnson and his deer hunt, and stumbling along the upstairs hallway to go down to breakfast. On the wall in the hallway, there was a framed sampler, a memento of the Johnsons' wedding day, with their names and the date, and wishes for a long and happy marriage.

"I didn't even notice it," Hartigan said. "But of course Kennedy not only saw it — as mad as he was, he had to stop and look it over and read every word on it. He pointed at the date, and he said to me, 'That's *today*! It says November 17, 1934. That's twenty-six years ago today.' He pulled out some money and handed it to me, and told me to sneak into town and get an anniversary gift. The town was Austin, and I didn't know where to get a gift, or what to buy. But Kennedy's luck was working for him. The first jewelry store I walked into turned out to be a place where Mrs. Johnson shopped regularly, and the jeweler showed me a piece of silver that she had been admiring for a couple of months. So I bought it and had it engraved with a few suitable words. That night at dinner, when Kennedy made a nice speech and handed it to Lady Bird, she was flabbergasted not only because he had discovered her wedding date, but also because he had come up with a silver dish that she had been eyeing for months."

Kennedy not only wanted to know everything about everybody; he also had to find out all the small details. When I was spending some time with him in 1959, doing a series of magazine articles on him and his family, I mentioned to him that I had seen his mother at La Guardia Airport in New York the day before. "She looked great," I said. "She was wearing a very snappy-looking suit,"

"What kind of a suit?" Jack asked. "What did it look like?"

I said it was a light gray tweed with a big and bold dark blue plaid design on the gray background.

"Oh, yes, I know that suit," he said. "She got it in Paris from Balenciaga."

Two weeks later we were at a dinner in Los Angeles. Jack, the main speaker, was seated, of course, at the center of the long head table. I was at a press table with some other reporters. Rose Kennedy was at another table with Pat and Peter Lawford. She was wearing the same plaid suit. During the meal, while everybody in the crowded room was quietly eating, a waiter said to me, "Senator Kennedy wants to speak with you." I stood up and walked up to the dais and along behind the table to where the senator was sitting, with everybody staring at me and wondering what important message I was carrying to him. He leaned back in his chair and said to me, "Do you see that fellow back there against the wall, reddish blond hair, light gray suit, and the woman with him is red-haired and she's wearing a bright green dress? That's Al Cluster. He was the commanding officer of the PT boat squadron I was in at Rendova during the war. Maybe, if you grab him when the dinner's over, he might be able to tell you some interesting stuff."

"Thanks," I said.

"And that suit my mother's wearing, isn't that the same one she had on when you saw her at La Guardia Airport?"

That night, after the dinner, Jack went to the Lawfords' house at Santa Monica to spend a few hours with his mother and his sister. I was sitting in his hotel suite, talking politics with Larry O'Brien, when he returned around one o'clock, carrying the morning newspapers under his arm. He said goodnight to us and headed for his bedroom. At the bedroom door, he paused, turned around, and said to me, "I told my mother that you liked her suit, and she was very pleased."

President Kennedy was by far the toughest of the Kennedys, even tougher than his father. "Compared to President Kennedy," Kenny O'Donnell said, "Bobby was as soft as a marshmallow." Writing about him when he was a senator, I found that Jack was disliked by older Irish politicians in Boston because he flatly refused to get federal jobs for their friends. One politician said to me, "He won't even get a decent job for his own uncle."

Something in the politician's indignant tone made me pause and ask, "Now what do you mean by that?"

"I mean just what I said!" the politician shouted. "Here he is, a United States senator, and his own uncle, his mother's brother, is working as a toll collector on the Mystic River Bridge! If you don't believe me, check it out!"

I checked it out; Tom Fitzgerald, Rose Kennedy's brother, was indeed working as a tollgate attendant on the Mystic River Bridge in Boston. Again, there was a punch line for that item that I did not hear until a few years later, after my magazine articles about the Kennedy family had been published and expanded into a book. Somebody who traveled with Jack when he was campaigning in Massachusetts told me that when his car approached the tollgate on the bridge, he would duck his head low under the dashboard as he sat beside the driver in the front seat to avoid being seen by his Uncle Tom. He was in no mood for small talk with a relative whose vote he already had.

The last time that I visited Richard Cardinal Cushing, the late archbishop of Boston who married Jackie and Jack Kennedy and celebrated President Kennedy's funeral mass, was in November 1968, a few weeks after the wedding of Jackie and Aristotle Onassis. Cardinal Cushing led me into his living room, saying, "I've got a couple of things to show you." There was a large wooden packing case in the room, with doors in the front of it that opened like a cabinet. The cardinal patted the sturdy packing case, and said to me with a smile, "It would make a nice bar, wouldn't it?" He opened the doors and revealed a replica of Michelangelo's famous *Pietà*, the statue of the crucified Jesus in the arms of his mother. The newly elected Pope Paul VI had presented the replica to President Kennedy during Kennedy's visit to the Vatican in the summer of 1963. The pope's predecessor, John XXIII, had died just before President Kennedy had left Washington to start that European tour. Pope John had been looking forward eagerly to meeting the first Catholic president of the United States. Before his death, anticipating the president's visit to Rome, Pope John had autographed a copy of his famous encyclical, "Pacem in Terris," which he planned to give to Kennedy.

"It's a shame John and Jack never met each other," Cardinal Cushing said. "The two of them would have hit it off great. Well, that day in Rome, after Pope Paul gave Jack this replica of the *Pietà*, Jack came around to see me at the North American College and I handed him that copy of 'Pacem in Terris' with Pope John's autograph on it, one of the only three signed copies in existence. Let me tell you, he was thrilled by it. And that brings me to the other thing I've got here to show you."

He showed me the autographed copy of "Pacem in Terris."

"So how did the *Pietà* and the signed encyclical end up in my house?" Cardinal Cushing said. "Jackel-line." (He never called her Jackie; she was always "Jackel-line" to him.)

"She came up here to Boston and talked to me before she married Onassis," the cardinal said. "I told her to go ahead and do it, if it would make her happy, and

I gave her my blessing. Let me tell you, when that news got out, I got a lot of abuse from a lot of people around here, but people like that don't bother me. The next thing I knew Jackel-line was on the telephone, calling the Federal Records Center here in Waltham, where the things from the Kennedy White House are being kept in storage until the Kennedy Library gets built. She told them to send the *Pietà* and the autographed copy of John's encyclical over here to me. And they did, that same day. Then, about a week later, I got this letter from the government."

He showed me the letter, which was from the federal archives. It informed the cardinal that the replica of the *Pietà* and the autographed copy of Pope John's encyclical, like all state gifts received by President Kennedy while he was in office, were the property of the United States government. The letter went on to explain that those two articles would have to be returned to Federal Records Center to be kept in storage until they could be displayed in the proposed John F. Kennedy Library.

"I called up Jackel-line and told her about the letter," Cardinal Cushing said. "She told me not to worry about it. She said the way things were going with the plans for the Kennedy Library it would probably never be built in my lifetime, or in her lifetime, either. So, for the time being, I'm hanging on to the *Pietà* and the encyclical, and when I look at them, I think of John and Jack and Jackel-line."

Two years later, after Cardinal Cushing's death, I asked an archivist on the staff of the then unbuilt Kennedy Library if the replica of the *Pietà* and the autographed copy of Pope John's encyclical had been returned.

"The *Pietà* came back, safe and sound," he said. "But nobody knows what happened to Pope John's encyclical. It's gone. Maybe Cardinal Cushing took it with him when he went to heaven."

Some of the most memorable well-known people whom I have met through my work as a writer are ones whom I never got to know well, because, for one reason or another, after the preliminary talks, plans were changed and I never heard their stories. One day in 1972, I found myself in New York having lunch at the Plaza with Gene Tierney, the movie star of the 1940s, and her husband, W. Howard Lee, a quiet and pleasant Texas millionaire who was previously married to Hedy Lamarr. Gene was then fifty-two years old. She looked marvelous, much more beautiful as a mature woman than I remembered her as the young star of *Leave Her to Heaven* in 1943 and *Laura* in 1944. Those black-and-white movies did not show the unusually pretty, deep-purple color of her eyes. When we walked through the lobby on our way to the restaurant, people turned around and stared at her.

Our meeting had been arranged because Gene was planning to write her memoirs, for which she needed professional help. A friend of hers in the publishing business had suggested me. After talking with her for five minutes, I decided that her book could be a good one. She is intelligent and witty, and she recalls her years in Hollywood with calm and clear realism. "They pushed me into one picture after another," she said, "and I did what they told me to do without complaining or asking any questions. There was nothing glamorous about being a movie actress. It was just a lot of damned hard work."

I asked her, as tactfully as I could, if she would be able to recall in her book the painful experience of giving birth to a retarded daughter, and the consequent periods of mental depression that forced her to give up her acting career.

"I know I'll have to go into all that," Gene said. "How can I write about myself and leave that out?"

"Could you tell me exactly how it happened?" I asked. "I've heard two or three different versions."

"I've heard four or five versions of it," she said. "Here's how it actually happened. I was a few months pregnant, and still working, because Twentieth Century–Fox would have you working up until the time came for you to go to the delivery room if you'd let them. They sent me on a personal appearance tour to plug one of my pictures. I came to this particular city in the Midwest, and there was the usual autograph-signing reception, with a crowd of people closing in on me to shake hands and tell me how much they liked *Laura*. A few days later I came down with German measles. I didn't need the doctor to tell me what that can do to a pregnant woman, and it did it. My little girl was severely retarded when I gave birth to her. I guess you know I was married then to Oleg Cassini, the designer. He was good to me through it all, and I managed to pull myself together and go back to work.

"Now it's about a year later, and I'm on another personal appearance tour, and I go back again to that same city for another autograph-signing session. A woman came to me with a big smile, and she grabbed my arm and said to me, 'When you were here last year did you happen to catch German measles?'

"I was stunned. I just stared at her.

"The woman said to me, 'You know, when you were here last year, I had German measles. My family told me I shouldn't come downtown to see you because somebody might catch the measles from me, but I just had to get a look at you because you're my favorite movie actress. You never did catch the measles from me, did you?'"

Gene was telling it calmly.

"Well, that did it," she said. "Then I really broke down and went into a severe mental depression. After that, I didn't want to be anybody's favorite movie actress, ever again. By the way, that little girl of mine is getting up into her late twenties. She lives in a nursing home in Massachusetts."

We agreed to give collaboration a try. "You'll have to come to Houston to work with me," she said. "Howard and I have a nice house there, and you'll like it. But there's one thing I must warn you about. I still get periods of depression. They come on me when I least expect it, and I can't talk to anybody or see anybody until I pull myself out of it, and sometimes that takes weeks. So before you get involved in this thing, you must realize that there may be interruptions, possibly long interruptions, before I'll be able to work with you again."

I said that I would take that risk. We finished our lunch and the Lees went off to do some shopping at

Altman's. I left the Plaza and walked down Fifth Avenue. At the corner of 52nd Street, I saw Bob Considine, the columnist and book author.

"Bob, guess who I just had lunch with," I said.

"Who?"

"Gene Tierney," I said.

Bob smiled and his eyes twinkled, which meant that he was remembering something pretty good. "Gene Tierney?" he said. "The night before Billy Conn fought Joe Louis the second time, after the war, he slept in Toots Shor's apartment. When Conn got into bed, Toots came in to tuck him in and turn off the light. He says to Billy, 'Now listen, you bum, there's no reason why you can't knock this guy out tomorrow night, and if you do, you'll be the champion of the world! You know what that means? It means anything you want in this whole world you can have.'

"Conn looks up at Toots and says, 'Gene Tierney?'"

The first editor I talked with about a Gene Tierney book was even more enthusiastic about the idea than I was. I made arrangements to go to Houston and then I telephoned Gene to set a date of arrival. Her voice sounded tense and depressed, with none of the cheerfulness she had had in New York.

"I've changed my mind," she said. "I've decided I don't want to write a book. I'm sorry."

She was obviously unable to talk and anxious to get off the telephone as quickly as possible, so I said goodbye and hung up without asking any questions. I never heard from her again. But in 1978, six years later, she wrote an autobiography, *Self-Portrait*, with Mickey Herskowitz as a collaborator, and it became a best-seller. The sad story of how she caught German measles from an autograph seeker in *Self-Portrait* is placed at the Hollywood Canteen instead of at a personal appearance tour in the Midwest, as she told it to me. But that's an unimportant detail, and, in mentioning it here, I am only being picky.

Gene Tierney would have appreciated a story about Louella Parsons that Marion Davies told to a friend of mine shortly after the death of William Randolph Hearst in 1951. Marion Davies was a pretty blonde chorus girl who became a movie star during the 1920s and 1930s under the sponsorship of Hearst, who financed her pictures, worshipped her and lived with her, and wanted to marry her, but his wife refused to give him a divorce.

Louella Parsons, who covered Hollywood for the Hearst newspapers, was a semiliterate woman who had trouble writing a declarative sentence and often got her facts wrong. She once wrote, "I don't know how many of my readers remember John Barrymore and Dolores Costello in *Trilby*, the George Du Maunier story, but my mind goes back to John just loving his part as Svengali." As Irving Hoffman pointed out in *Variety*, "There wasn't a thing wrong in the story except that the name of the picture was *Svengali*, not *Trilby*, the leading lady was Marion Marsh, not Dolores Costello, and the writer was du Maurier, not Du Maunier." But Louella was immensely powerful, deeply feared and respected in Hollywood because her column in the nationwide chain of Hearst newspapers had many millions of devoted movie-fan readers. When Louella heard that Clark Gable had married Carole Lombard, she refused to believe it because "They couldn't have done it without telling me about it first." Carole was so concerned about Louella's hurt feelings she installed a new bathroom in Louella's house to pacify her. James Cagney almost failed to get his first big role in *The Public Enemy* because Eddie Wood, an actor whom Cagney replaced as the leading gangster in the picture after three days of filming, happened to be engaged at the time to Harriet Parsons, Louella's daughter. Darryl Zanuck, the producer, said to director William Wellman, "We can't take Eddie out of the leading part. Louella will be furious." But Wellman insisted on Cagney. *The Public Enemy* made Cagney a star.

Louella owed everything that she had—her job as a columnist, and the money and prestige that went with it—to Marion Davies. It was Marion who talked Hearst into hiring Louella after Louella wrote an article in the *New York Telegram* praising Marion's performance in *When Knighthood Was in Flower*. Marion introduced Louella to the studio heads in Hollywood and to all of the big stars at weekend parties at Hearst's ranch, San Simeon. At times when Louella's job was in jeopardy, from faulty reporting or offending important film company advertisers, Marion came to her defense and saved her.

Marion's loyalty was not returned, however. When Hearst died at the age of eighty-eight it was in Marion's house at Beverly Hills, where he had been living in declining health for more than three years. During the last few days of his life, Marion was at his bedside around the clock. A few hours before Hearst died, his doctor gave Marion a sedative and urged her to go to her bedroom and get some rest. She slept for almost twenty-four hours. While she was asleep, Richard Berlin, the president of the Hearst Corporation, came to the house and took charge. When Marion woke up, she learned that Hearst had died, and that his body had been taken to San Francisco, where the funeral and burial would take place. Everything in Marion's house belonging to Hearst, including his pet dachsund dog, had been removed.

To spare the Hearst family from embarrassment, Marion agreed not to appear at the funeral. On the morning of that day, she asked Louella Parsons to stop at her house before going to San Francisco for the services. "I told her that I wanted her to do a little favor for me," Marion said to my friend later.

Louella came to Marion's house, pleading nervously that she was in a big hurry and that she could only stay for a moment. Now that Marion had lost her influence, Louella was leery of being chummy with her. "I handed her a small bunch of violets," Marion told my friend. "I showed her that there was no card, no name cn the violets, nothing to show where they came from. I asked her to put the violets on the casket." Louella squirmed and hesitated, but finally agreed to deliver the violets. Clutching the flowers, she hurried out of the room.

"About fifteen minutes later," Marion said, "I walked out into the front hallway of my house. On a chair beside the front door, there was the bunch of violets."

More frustrating than the memorable stories, anecdotes, and bits of dialogue that were never written for one reason or another are some of the things that I did write but never saw in print for reasons that I could not understand. I still writhe when I remember one sentence that was crossed out before an article that I wrote about Edward R. Murrow went to press. The missing sentence was Murrow's personal appraisal of four famous people whom he knew well: Eleanor and Franklin Roosevelt and Clementine and Winston Churchill. If it had been printed at the time that it was written, it might have raised a few eyebrows.

Murrow, who became Columbia Broadcasting System's star newscaster and commentator during the 1940s and 1950s, seemed rather stiff and formal when he was on the air, but actually, like Fred Allen, he was one of the most unpretentious and likable celebrities in the broadcasting business. He seemed to know all of the famous people in the world. When Murrow was in London, covering the Battle of Britain in 1940 and 1941, he and his wife, Janet, became well acquainted with Winston and Clementine Churchill. The two wives spent a lot of time together at 10 Downing Street, the prime minister's residence, because Janet Murrow was the American representative in London of the Bundles-for-Britain organization and Clementine Churchill headed the British end of that agency. Murrow often stopped at Downing Street to pick up Janet after her day of work. He told a story to illustrate the prime minister's precise use of the English language, even in his most casual remarks. "Churchill didn't just use the right word," Murrow said. "He always used precisely the right word." One day when Murrow was sitting in the front hallway at 10 Downing Street, waiting for

Janet to finish her work, a door opened and Churchill appeared. He saw Murrow and started in surprise. "Why, hello, Mr. Murrow!" Churchill said. "Have you time for *several* drinks?"

Murrow was a newsman who seldom called up a president or a prime minister to ask for an interview. Usually, the president or the prime minister called Murrow. In 1941 the Murrows returned from London to New York to spend Thanksgiving and Christmas at home. Mrs. Roosevelt invited them to have dinner at the White House on the Sunday evening of December 7; President Roosevelt wanted to hear from Murrow about how things were going in Britain. When the Murrows were checking into a hotel in Washington on that Sunday afternoon, they heard the news of the Japanese attack on Pearl Harbor. Mrs. Murrow telephoned Mrs. Roosevelt, expecting her to cancel the dinner invitation.

"Come anyway," Mrs. Roosevelt said. "We still have to eat."

The president was too busy to appear at the dinner table, but he sent word downstairs from his room that he wanted to talk with Murrow later in the evening. Murrow waited until after midnight. Then he was taken upstairs to see President Roosevelt. The president told Murrow the full details of the attack on Pearl Harbor, how many and which of our ships were lost, the casualties, all of the information that was not officially released to the public until several months later. Roosevelt also discussed his opinions on Japan and Germany, his plan to declare war, and the effect that the attack would have in Britain and Russia. He said nothing to Murrow about the conversation's being confidential or off the record.

The Murrows left the White House and went back to their hotel room, where Ed paced the floor until dawn, debating with himself over whether or not he should tell on a CBS news broadcast what Roosevelt had told him about the attack on Pearl Harbor. Finally he decided not to use the story.

"The worst of it is that I never made no notes on what Roosevelt told me that night," Murrow said to me twelve years later (he was a meticulous speaker on the air but he liked to sprinkle his private talk with "ain'ts" and double negatives). "If I ever get around to writing a book about my life, I ain't never going to remember the details of that historic conversation."

I asked Murrow if he considered Roosevelt and Churchill two of the greatest men he had ever met. His prompt reply was the line that never appeared in print when the article was published.

He shook his head and said, "Mrs. Roosevelt and Mrs. Churchill are both much bigger and better human beings than their husbands ever were."

Was that line crossed out because the editor of the magazine was a male chauvinist pig?

The big problem in trying to get Harry Truman to sit for a series of lengthy interviews, as *Holiday* magazine asked me to do in 1963, was that Truman did not care to talk at length with a writer unless he was going to be well paid for his time and trouble. Two years earlier, David Susskind's television production company, Talent Associates, made an attractive deal with Truman for a series of filmed reminiscences about his presidency. Merle Miller spent many months with Truman at his presidential library in Independence, Missouri, doing the interviews. Susskind assumed that he would have no trouble selling the Truman series to one of the three networks. As anybody in the television or advertising business could have told him, he could not have been more wrong. None of the big sponsors, especially the automobile manufacturers, wanted to glorify Harry Truman. They still hated him for keeping rigid price controls in effect until he left the White House. Dore Schary once told me about sitting in on a discussion about a proposed television show about the Civil War. The producers were trying to think of a well-known authority who might appear on the show to discuss the campaigns in the West. "Why not Harry Truman?" Schary suggested. "Nobody knows more about that phase of the Civil War than Truman does." A chill came over the conference table. Somebody explained to Schary why Truman was persona non grata to the big TV sponsors. "Oh, all right," Schary said wearily. "Maybe we can get Jackie Gleason to do it."

After the Susskind-Truman television project got the cold shoulder from the networks, Merle Miller fortunately held on to the tape recordings of the many long interviews that he had made with Harry. In 1973, after Truman's death, Miller used the conversations on the tapes to produce *Plain Speaking, an Oral Biography of Harry S. Truman*, a portrait of a bluntly outspoken president that was such a refreshing contrast to the Watergate disclosures that it zoomed to the top of the best-seller lists and stayed there for many months.

Looking down from the Hereafter at all the money that Miller's book of his words was earning, Truman must have been furious.

Tape recordings also enabled me to produce exactly the kind of Harry Truman talk piece that *Holiday* wanted without taking up so much of his time that I would have to cut him in financially, which I was in no position to do. The editors of the magazine had planned an article entitled "A Walk Through History with Harry Truman." The idea was to get Truman to spend a few days walking around the museum section of the Truman Library and talking with me about the various historic documents, presidential papers, and mementos of his White House days on display there. The exhibit included the famous early edition headline on the *Chicago Tribune* proclaiming Dewey's victory over Truman in 1948, the surrender agreement with Japan that ended World War II, fused silicates from the first nuclear explosions, pictures of Stalin and Truman at Potsdam, the typewritten first draft of President Roosevelt's message to Congress after the attack on Pearl Harbor with revisions in Roosevelt's own handwriting, and the sign saying "The Buck Stops Here" that Truman kept on his desk in the White House. The idea seemed fine until I learned, soon after my arrival at the library, that Truman was not about to give me that much time and talk without the well-known dough-re-mi. I consulted one of the federal archivists on the Truman Library's staff.

"No problem," the archivist told me. "Truman gives talks about the things in the library every day to groups of visiting schoolchildren, free of charge. You can trail along behind him and listen. Also, down in the basement, we have hundreds of tape recordings of similar talks that he has given here over the last few years. You can help yourself to all of them."

A half hour later, I found myself listening happily while Truman was saying to a group of high school students, "That big sword out there in the lobby with all those diamonds and rubies and emeralds on its scabbard was given to me by King Saud of Saudi Arabia. They say it's worth sixty or seventy thousand dollars. One diamond on it is as big as the end of my thumb. It must be ten or fifteen carats. When we were having our last reception in the White House, I told Mrs. Truman that if she'd trip up Senator Bricker — he was a Republican who gave me a lot of trouble — and make him slide across that Blue Room floor, I'd give her that diamond. And you know, she wouldn't do it?"

The tape recordings in the basement were full of Truman's salty and quotable remarks about Joseph Stalin, Douglas MacArthur, Dwight Eisenhower, and all of the past presidents of the United States. An avid student of American history, he seemed to know each of his predecessors personally. Truman became furious when he thought about Chester A. Arthur. He would recall, as vividly as if he had been there himself, that when Arthur became president, his first move was to sell all of the furniture in the White House at auction for nine thousand dollars. "They say he even sold an old pair of Abraham Lincoln's pants," Truman exclaimed.

When Truman learned that I was getting what I wanted at the Truman Library without causing him any bother, he became friendly and invited me into his private office for a couple of long talks. One day we talked about the Kennedys. "I wasn't against Kennedy before the convention in nineteen hundred and sixty because he was a Catholic, like a lot of people said," Truman said. (When he mentioned a year, he never said, "Nineteen sixty" or "Nineteen forty-eight," as most of us do. He always said, "Nineteen hundred and sixty" or "Nineteen hundred and forty-eight." After making a statement or voicing an opinion, he always added, as a conclusion, "That's all there was to it.") "I was against Kennedy in nineteen hundred and sixty because I had no use for his father," Truman said. "The Democratic Party needed money badly when I was running against Dewey in nineteen hundred and forty-eight. We were writing checks on Friday hoping that somehow or somewhere we might be able to raise enough money over the weekend to cover the checks before they got to the bank on Tuesday. Joe Kennedy was supposed to be a Democrat but he flatly refused to give us a nickel during that campaign, and I never forgot it. In nineteen hundred and sixty, he forced poor Mike DiSalle to switch the Ohio delegates from Stuart Symington to Kennedy by threatening to give Mike's Republican opponent for the governorship a million dollars. He bought the West Virginia primary, and that's where his son won the Democratic nomination, not at the convention in Los Angeles. I was never against the pope. I was against the Pop. That's all there was to it. Speaking of the pope, come into the next room. I want to show you a picture."

He led me into a research room in the archives section of the library where there was a large oil portrait of himself, painted when he was president. In the painting, he is wearing his Masonic robe and apron as a past Grand Master of the Missouri Masons. "They tell a joke about that picture," Truman said. "A Catholic priest was traveling through Mississippi on a very hot day. He stopped at a Baptist farmer's house and asked for a drink of water. The farmer looked at the priest's Roman collar and refused to give him the water. As the priest was turning away from the farmer's door, he looked inside the house and saw a big picture of Pope Pius hanging on the wall. He said to the farmer, 'How come you won't give me a drink of water because I'm a Catholic priest, but you have a picture of the pope in your house?'

"The farmer said, 'The pope? Why, the Jewish peddler who sold me that picture told me it was Harry Truman in his Masonic robes.'"

One of the most widely published pictures of Truman was not displayed in his library. It showed him playing an upright piano at an entertainment for disabled war veterans while Lauren Bacall sat smiling at the top of the piano, displaying her long and shapely legs. Truman had been painfully embarrassed when the picture appeared in newspapers all over the country. It was reported at the time that when Bess Truman saw the picture, she laughed and said, "Well, Harry, if it's come to this, maybe we'd better stop playing the piano."

Truman told me that the three wisest men he had ever known were two of his secretaries of state, George C. Marshall and Dean Acheson, and, rather surprisingly, Herbert Hoover. I gathered that he never had much of a personal relationship with Franklin Roosevelt. He recalled, with a smile of pride, a remark made by Strom Thurmond of South Carolina during the walkout of southern delegates from the 1948 Democratic convention because they objected to Truman's civil rights platform. A reporter pointed out to Thurmond that Truman's stand on civil rights was no stronger than Roosevelt's. "I agree," Thurmond said, "but Truman really *means* it."

I asked Truman how he had gotten to know Hoover. He said that one day, shortly after the end of World War II, he noticed an item in a newspaper about Hoover being in Washington at the Mayflower Hotel. "I recalled that President Hoover had done outstanding work during and after the First World War as our food administrator, supplying food to starving people in Europe and other parts of the world," he said. "We were having the same problem of postwar food shortages all over again. I decided that President Hoover would be just the right man to work on it, so I picked up a telephone and called him. I said to him, 'Mr. Hoover, this is Harry Truman. I wonder if you could spare a few minutes. I'd like to come over to your hotel and talk to you.' President Hoover said to me, 'But, Mr. President, you shouldn't come to my hotel room. I'll be glad to come over to the White House to see you.' I laughed and said, 'I knew you would say that, so I have already ordered a car to go to your hotel and pick you up. It should be there in a few minutes.' So President Hoover arrived shortly at my office with a friend of his, a doctor whose name I don't remember now. I talked with them for a few minutes about the problem of the food shortages in various parts of the world, and I asked President Hoover if he would take over a program to provide food for starving people with the full resources of the United States government behind him. He looked me straight in the eye for a moment, and then he said he would be glad to do what I asked and he got up abruptly and hurried out of my office. I said to his friend, who was still sitting there, 'Have I offended him? Did I say something wrong?' His friend said, 'No, Mr. President, I think Mr. Hoover had to leave the room because he was so emotionally moved. This is the first time since he left the White House in nineteen hundred and thirty-three that anybody in the government has ever requested his services.' President Hoover did a fine job for us planning a food program, and he and I became close friends. A few years after that I was down in Florida on a vacation, and I heard that President Hoover was staying at a fishing camp about twenty miles away. I drove over there to pay him a surprise visit. When the manager of the fishing club saw President Truman coming there to visit President Hoover, he was so surprised he almost fell over. He showed me to President Hoover's cottage and, when I opened the screen door and walked in, I saw President Hoover sitting at a table and writing with a pencil on a yellow pad of paper. I said to him, 'What the hell are you doing?' He jumped out of his chair smiling and said to me, 'Mr. President, I'm writing a book, and I'm saying some nice things about you in it that will probably hurt the sale of the book.'"

Truman told me, as he told practically everybody whom he talked with, how much he still despised Dwight

D. Eisenhower because Eisenhower failed to come to the defense of General Marshall, his mentor and friend, when Marshall was attacked as a pro-Communist "traitor" by Republican Senators Joe McCarthy and William Jenner during the 1952 presidential campaign. I told Truman something that Sherman Adams, Eisenhower's manager in that campaign and later his chief of staff in the White House, had told me a few years earlier when I was helping Adams write a book about Eisenhower's presidency. Adams said that Eisenhower wanted to say a few words of praise for Marshall during a campaign speech in Milwaukee, Wisconsin, where McCarthy was then running for reelection to the Senate. But the Republicans in Wisconsin felt it was wrong for Eisenhower to take even such an indirect slap at McCarthy in his home state, so Eisenhower had quickly agreed to remove the reference to Marshall from his speech.

"That sounds like Eisenhower sure enough," Truman said. "What was he planning to say about General Marshall in that speech?"

"Adams said Ike was going to praise Marshall and tell how dedicated he was to Marshall," I said.

"Dedicated?" Truman said. "If Eisenhower was really dedicated to General Marshall, he would have torn McCarthy to pieces in that speech. Eisenhower turned his back on General Marshall, the man who promoted him from lieutenant-colonel to general. That's all there was to it."

There were other Eisenhower stories that Sherman Adams did not want to mention in the book that he wrote about his six years as the chief of Eisenhower's

White House staff. Adams did not want to put anything into his book that Eisenhower might not like. After agreeing to write the book for Harper and Brothers and *Life* magazine, Adams produced several hundred typewritten pages that did not say much about Eisenhower and his administration that everybody did not already know. "There's nothing in this book," one of the editors at *Life* pointed out, "that wasn't in the Review of the Week section of the Sunday *New York Times* during the last eight years." Cass Canfield of Harper and Brothers and C. D. Jackson, who was then the publisher of *Life*, persuaded Adams to let me spend several months with him at his home in the White Mountains of New Hampshire trying to get him to pep up the script. I soon found out that the *Life* editor had been right: Adams had been drawing most of his material from a file of the *New York Times*'s Review of the Week that he kept in his cellar. He didn't want to write anything about Eisenhower that had not already been printed. One day I struggled to persuade Adams to put in writing some juicy stuff he had told me about Eisenhower's deep dislike for his vice-president, Richard Nixon, and about the efforts of John Foster Dulles, the powerful secretary of state in Eisenhower's cabinet, to keep Nixon safely away from any decision-making while Eisenhower was recovering from his first heart attack in a hospital at Denver. But Adams refused to knock Nixon. "I wasn't aware that I would be expected to discuss personalities in this book," he said.

One of the personalities Adams did not care to discuss was Bernard Goldfine, a New England textile manufacturer and an old friend of Adams. Rival Republican politicians and Democratic congressmen had forced Adams to resign from his position as Eisenhower's chief of staff after a congressional investigation of Goldfine's troubles with federal regulatory agencies revealed that Adams had made a few phone calls on Goldfine's behalf and had allowed Goldfine to pay a few of his hotel bills. Investigators also learned that Goldfine had given Adams a vicuña coat. A lot of politicians in New England at that time were wearing Goldfine's vicuña coats. But the vicuña coat in Adams's closet made headlines all over the nation and became a main factor in the chain of events that forced him to resign from the number-two position in the White House. Two years later, when I was working with Adams on his Eisenhower memoirs, he was still touchy about Goldfine. The first time I asked him a routine question about Goldfine, he walked out of the room and did not speak to me for the next two days. I learned that Adams had been planning to write the chapter in his book about his departure from the White House without mentioning Goldfine's name.

Then, on a Saturday evening, after I had been working with Adams for several months, he invited me to go out to dinner with him and his wife and two of their daughters and sons-in-law. We were to meet first at the Adams home and then we were to drive to an inn at Franconia Notch, a few miles away. When we were leaving the house, Adams went to the closet in his front hallway to put on his coat. It was the vicuña coat. I could hardly believe my eyes. After all the trouble that it had caused him — anybody else would have burned it — Adams, the thrifty New England Yankee, was still wearing Goldfine's vicuña coat.

Some of the things that Adams told me about Eisenhower and the Eisenhower Administration amazed me. Adams said that the British and French military attack on the Egyptians at the Suez Canal in 1956, which almost started a war between the Western European powers and Russia, came as a complete surprise to Eisenhower, and to everybody in the State Department and the Pentagon. "It really shocked the president," Adams said. "He had no warning that it was going to happen."

"Where was the C.I.A.?" I asked. "Do you mean to tell me that we didn't have anybody in the British foreign office, or anybody at the British air bases on Cyprus who could have tipped us off at least a couple of days before they started bombing Egypt?"

"Apparently not," Adams said.

I was working with Adams at his home in New Hampshire in the summer of 1960 when Nikita Khrushchev abruptly canceled his planned summit meeting with Eisenhower in Paris and called off a visit that Eisenhower was to make to the Soviet Union because Francis Gary Powers, an American U-2 reconnaissance pilot, had been shot down that week during a spying flight in Russia. The U-2 fiasco, disrupting the summit meeting, plunged the already chilly American-Soviet relationship to a new low, and caused great confusion in Washington.

"Why would we run a reconnaissance flight over Russia a few days before Eisenhower and Khrushchev were to hold a summit meeting?" I asked Adams. "Who okayed that flight? Didn't Eisenhower know about it?"

"He had to know about it," Adams said. "The president has to approve each one of those U-2 flights personally. Nobody else will take the responsibility."

"Didn't it cross his mind that the U-2 flight might mess up the summit conference?"

"I'm going to see him next week in Newport," Adams said. "I'll ask him about it."

Adams returned from a pleasant visit to the summer White House at Newport and reported that he had never seen Eisenhower looking better or more cheerful. Eisenhower had just been through a series of disappointments that might have crushed another president. On top of the U-2 debacle and the last-minute cancellation of the Paris summit conference and his trip to Russia, he had been forced to call off a planned visit to Japan because James Haggerty, making advance arrangements for Eisenhower in Tokyo, had a narrow escape from an angry mob of anti-American demonstrators. But, according to Adams, Eisenhower was in the best of spirits.

"He talked about the Japanese riots and his troubles with Khrushchev as if he was talking about something that happened in Korea back in 1953," Adams said. "He hates the thought of leaving the White House. The people on his staff say that he would run again against Kennedy for reelection if there wasn't a law against it."

"Did you ask him why he okayed that U-2 flight at the time of the summit meeting?" I said.

"I did," Adams said. "When I asked him that question, he seemed to be very surprised. He looked at me for a moment, and then he said, 'You know, that never occurred to me.' He said that the thought that they were scheduling the U-2 flight at the time of the summit meeting just never crossed his mind."

"If it didn't occur to Eisenhower," I said, "how come it didn't occur to some of the other people who were with him in his office when he signed the flight plan and approved the date?"

"That's a good question," Adams said. "Anyway, Eisenhower went on to say that he doesn't really think that Khrushchev canceled the summit meeting because of the U-2 flight. He thinks the real reason for the cancellation was that Khrushchev was jealous and angry because Eisenhower got a much bigger and warmer reception when he visited India last winter than the reception Khrushchev got there a while ago."

The Adams book about his years with Eisenhower was too reticent to be a best-seller. Even the title that Adams selected for his memoirs was hardly exciting enough to draw crowds to the bookstores; he called the book *First Hand Report*. The publisher of the French translation in Paris made a slightly stronger effort to make the book sound inviting, calling it *Les secrets de l'administration Eisenhower*, even though the secrets revealed by Adams were not hot ones.

Actually, one of the more memorable stories told to me by Adams did not concern his experiences in the White House. When we were talking one day about a news item which said that the Ivy League universities were turning down something like thirty-six thousand entrance applications every year, Adams recalled how he had gone about getting himself admitted to the freshman class at Dartmouth College in 1916. It is a tale that should make the parents of today's aspiring high school seniors grind their teeth in frustration and despair.

When Adams was graduated from Hope High School in Providence, Rhode Island, in June 1916, he was looking forward eagerly to spending a year roughing it as a lumberjack at a logging camp in Canada. He did not even think about the possibility of going to college until one day in August that summer when he learned, to his dismay, that a huge forest fire had leveled all of the timberland in Canada where he had been hired to work. His parents suggested college instead.

"I thought I might try Dartmouth," Adams told me. "The boys in my class at high school who were going to college had all applied at Brown. But Brown seemed to me too close to home, and too civilized. I had heard that the students at Dartmouth wore sweatshirts to classes. So I took a walk over to Hope High School and asked the principal to send my marks to Dartmouth. He said he would."

During the rest of that summer vacation period, Adams heard nothing from Dartmouth about whether his marks had been received or whether he was being considered. That was understandable because he himself had never bothered to write a letter to the admissions office at Dartmouth asking if he could enter the next freshman class. Nor did he talk to anybody at Dartmouth until he arrived on the campus at Hanover on the day in September that the college was opening.

"I just didn't get around to telling them that I was coming," Adams said. "I spent the rest of that summer with my grandfather, Cyrus Sherman, a Baptist minister, at his farm in East Dover, Vermont. On the day that

Dartmouth was opening for the college year, my grandfather was driving in his Model T Ford to a Baptist convention at Fairlee, Vermont, which isn't far from the Dartmouth campus in Hanover, New Hampshire. He offered to drop me off there."

After climbing out of the Model T in Hanover, Adams lifted his trunk from the back seat, left it on the sidewalk, waved goodbye to his grandfather, and walked to the dean's office in the nearby college administration building. He presented himself to the dean, Craven Leacock, brother of Stephen Leacock, the humor writer.

Dean Leacock said, "What can I do for you?"

Then, as now, a man of few words, Adams recalled saying to the dean, "I wish to enter Dartmouth College."

The dean asked if he had applied for admission. Adams allowed that he hadn't, but explained that his high school grades might have been mailed from Providence. A search of the files produced the grades and the dean found them satisfactory.

"I was then taken to the office of Ernest Martin Hopkins, who was starting that year his long tenure as president of Dartmouth," Adams told me. "President Hopkins signed my admission certificate. I picked out some courses. Dean Leacock assigned me to a room, number twelve College Hall. I went outside, picked up my trunk from the sidewalk where I had left it, and carried it upstairs to my room in College Hall, and there I was—a freshman in Dartmouth College."

And that, as Harry Truman would have said, was all there was to it—back in 1916.

To me, the most memorable of the people who will be recalled in this book are three comedians: Jackie Gleason, Jimmy Durante, and Fred Allen. Gleason insists that he is a comic actor, not a comedian. "There's nothing funny about me," he says. "I'm funny only when I'm playing the role of a comic character, like Ralph Kramden, the Brooklyn bus driver, or Reggie Van Gleason III, the society playboy." Actually, Gleason, a complex and moody man with an erudite knowledge of religions, spiritualism, philosophy, and psychology, talks and acts very much like Ralph Kramden. He is the opposite of Carroll O'Connor, the Archie Bunker of television, who acts and talks offstage like a college professor. When Gleason's mood, subject to change at any moment, becomes convivial, he is very funny, sprinkling his lively talk with witty images. Discussing the robust figure of his friend Toots Shor, Gleason once made a widely quoted remark: "When Toots runs upstairs, it looks like two small boys fighting under a blanket." Salvador Dali was showing Gleason a walking stick with a glass flask concealed in it when Jackie said, "The trouble with taking a drink out of a cane like that is that it makes you look like a medieval herald announcing the arrival of the king." At one time, several years ago, Gleason was considering co-starring with Orson Welles in a television version of Ben Jonson's *Volpone*. Somebody asked him if he had agreed to give Welles top billing.

"That's right," Gleason said. "I told Welles he could put his name first. Now I know how Fargo felt."

It was hard to picture Jimmy Durante confined to a

wheelchair, as he had been since suffering a stroke a few years ago. The last time I saw him, back in the 1960s, he was still pounding along in his wild and slam-bang nightclub act, delighting a packed audience at a place called the Beverly Hills, across the Ohio River from Cincinnati, as he had delighted such devoted admirers as Robert Benchley, Al Smith, George M. Cohan, and Jimmy Walker in a New York speakeasy called the Dover Club in 1925. Jimmy always preferred performing in the relaxed atmosphere of a nightclub to working in the movies or television because in a club he could scramble along doing whatever foolishness came into his head without watching a clock or following a script. ("Stop da music! Stop da music! Touch my nose again and I'll sue the joint for every penny!") In a nightclub, he was also free to sing his old songs which TV producers regarded as out of date – "The Strutaway," "What Will You Do When I'm Far Away, Far Away in Far Rockaway?," "So I Ups to Him" ("Exhausted and fatigued, I'm on my way to Nedick's for a yeast cake when he bumps into me and he demands an autopsy!"), and, of course, the number that he called "our national emblem," "Inka, Dinka, Doo." Jimmy told me that he first sang "Inka, Dinka, Doo" on the old Chase and Sanborn radio show in 1933. It grew out of an earlier comedy song, "Say It with Flowers," which Jimmy offered as advice to husbands away from home "attending conventions, Bar Mitzvahs, sales meetings and other extra-curricular excursions."

Jimmy behaved with the same loud and boisterous good humor when he was eating his morning cornflakes or making several bets on the same race at Santa Anita as he displayed in his nightclub act. Meeting a friend whom he had not seen in two days, he staged a big hello, going into a crouch with his legs wide apart, both arms extended, eyes popping, a big grin of delight spreading from ear to ear. Then he embraced the victim wildly, shouting, "God love ya!"

There is a memorable story about one of Jimmy's big hellos, which concerns Rosie, the elephant who played with him on the stage of the old Hippodrome in New York in 1935 in *Jumbo*, the mammoth circus show staged by Billy Rose with music by Richard Rodgers, lyrics by Lorenz Hart, and a book by Ben Hecht and Charles MacArthur. (In the show, Durante delivered what many critics still consider one of the funniest lines ever heard in a theater. Playing the role of Claudius P. Bowers, a harried press agent of a bankrupt circus, Jimmy tries to escape from the law with Rosie. As he is leading the large pachyderm along a street, he is stopped by a policeman who says to him, "Where are you going with that elephant?" Jimmy stares at the cop, indignant, and says, "What elephant?") Many years later, Jimmy and his friends Lou Cohen and Jack Roth, the drummer in his act, were visiting an animal farm in California where they watched an elephant performing tricks. Jimmy recognized the trainer as the same one who had taken care of Rosie during the run of *Jumbo*. After giving the trainer a big hello, Jimmy reminisced with him and said, "By the way, whatever happened to Rosie?" The trainer pointed at the elephant who was standing behind him, eyeing Durante with interest, and said, "You're looking at her."

Jimmy took a step backward in amazement, went into

his big hello crouch, and then he shouted, "Rosie! Well, God love ya!"

I reminded Jimmy of his reunion with Rosie when I visited him in his dressing room after the dinner show at the Beverly Hills. He was chewing on a lamb chop and watching an old movie on television. "That was a great line, that 'What elephant?'" he said. "Everybody gave me credit for it, but it was thought up by Charlie MacArthur. Who else but Charlie MacArthur could think up a line like that?"

He pointed his lamb chop at the movie on the TV screen. "They made that pitcha at Metro when I was first working there for Irving Thalberg, Norma Shearer's husband, that's how old it is," he said. "My dressing room on the Metro lot in those days was right next to Greta Garbo's, but, funny thing, in all the years I was there I never seen her once. I used to yell at her window every morning when I come to work, 'Hey, Greta! It's me, Jimmy! C'mon out!' One day her hairdresser come out and told me to be quiet, but I never saw Garbo. I don't know how she got in and outa that dressing room. She musta had a secret underground passageway."

We talked about the years of the 1930s when the Depression forced Jimmy to break up his comedy partnership with Lou Clayton and Eddie Jackson to work as a single in the movies for Thalberg at Metro. Clayton, who died in 1950, became Jimmy's manager. Jackson later rejoined the Durante nightclub act. One day while Durante was working at Metro, Clayton received a telephone call from Waxey Gordon, the New York gangster and racketeer. Gordon, an admirer of Durante in the speakeasy days, was backing a new

Broadway musical, *Strike Me Pink,* and he wanted Jimmy to play the lead in it. Clayton said that he would have to take the matter up with Thalberg.

"Thalberg?" Gordon said. "Who's Thalberg? You mean to tell me in Hollywood this guy Thalberg is a bigger guy than Durante?"

"Much bigger," Clayton said.

"Then to hell with Durante," Gordon said. "We'll get Thalberg to be in our show."

Jimmy chuckled and lit a cigar. "Clayton, God rest his soul," he said. "Did he ever tell you about the time he shanghaied me onto the *Normandie* and took me to England when I didn't want to go?"

Jimmy would never agree to booking a British tour because he hated ocean voyages. Nevertheless, one summer Clayton booked Durante without telling Jimmy about it. Secretly, Clayton arranged passage for himself and the Durante party on the *Normandie* and on the sailing day arranged to have Jimmy's luggage put aboard. Then he told Jimmy that Ray Goetz, the Broadway producer, who was also sailing that day on the *Normandie,* wanted Jimmy to play the piano and sing a few songs at a bon voyage party in his stateroom. Clayton figured that Durante would get so carried away at the piano that he would never notice that the ship was moving until it was well past Sandy Hook. All went according to plan until Durante, in the middle of a song, looked up from the keyboard and saw the Manhattan skyline gliding by a porthole.

"Lou!" he had shouted. "The ship's moving!"

"Don't worry, Jimmy," Clayton had said. "We'll get off at One Hundred and Twenty-fifth Street."

Jimmy pulled open a drawer in his dressing table and took out of it a photograph of himself, taken in 1933, with Lupe Velez and Hope Williams beside him. He gazed fondly at Hope Williams, the stylish stage comedienne of the twenties who preceded Katharine Hepburn as the leading lady in Philip Barry's plays.

"Nobody could walk across a stage like she could," Jimmy said. "Funny thing you just mentioned *Strike Me Pink*. This pitcha was taken backstage at a rehearsal of that show and somebody in New York just sent it to me. Hope Williams was with me in a show called *The New Yorkers*, too. For fifty dollars, I betcha can't tell me the name of a great song Cole Porter wrote for *that* show! It was 'Love for Sale.'"

Eddie Jackson and Jack Roth came into the dressing room and announced that it was time to get dressed for the midnight show. Jimmy started to take off his dressing gown. He paused to take another look at the picture of the youthful Durante with Hope Williams and Lupe Velez. Catching me watching him, he smiled.

"I got my memories," he said.

Back in the spring of 1949, when the broadcasting industry was going through a confusing transition from radio to television, Oliver Jensen, one of the editors of *Life*, asked me to write an interview on the situation with a top executive in one of the networks, David Sarnoff of NBC or William Paley of CBS.

"We'll end up with a lot of dull clichés," I said. "Why don't I talk to somebody who will have something interesting to say, like Fred Allen? Allen hates clichés so deeply he refuses to say 'Hello' or 'Goodbye.'"

Jensen agreed. I made a date to have lunch with Allen and our mutual friend, Al Durante, Jimmy's nephew, who handled Fred's publicity. "I'll bring along an empty salt shaker," said Allen, who was on a salt-free diet and hated it. I had gotten to know Allen a few months earlier when I spent a week with him, watching him prepare and rehearse one of his memorable Sunday night radio shows. He was one of the most intelligent and unpretentious stars in show business, and by far the wittiest talker I have ever heard. Even his casual remarks were often side-splitting. "Ray Bolger is getting awfully thin," Allen said after seeing Bolger in *Where's Charley?* "If he had an ulcer, he'd have to carry it in his hand." James Thurber's all-time favorite joke was Allen's line about the crows who were so badly frightened by a farmer's scarecrow that they brought back corn that they had stolen two years before. Another famous Allen line was one that he used in the opening scene of a Broadway revue, *The Little Show*, which had a corpse in it. Somebody else looked at the dead man and said, "But he looks good." Allen said, "Why shouldn't he? He just came back from Florida."

Allen arrived at our luncheon interview so filled with interesting and articulate opinions on what was wrong with the then new and struggling television medium that I did not need to ask him any questions. His remarks were so memorable that I did not bother to make any notes. When he sat down at the table, he said, "This insane modern civilization is getting to be too much for the Moses Model human body. Here we have an organism that was designed for biblical times. Yet we expect it to cope with artificial lighting, executive board meetings, the din of automobile horns and soap operas, carbon monoxide, cigar smoke, and bubble gum. No wonder we've all got ulcers and high blood pressure. Modern man should be equipped with a tin head and three eyes. The extra eye could be used for watching television so the other two won't get red. Everybody's cracking under the strain. I just saw that fellow with the lemons dangling all over his car. Have you seen him? He has hundreds of lemons dangling on the outside of his car and a big sign on it that says, 'This Hudson is a lemon.' I've seen him twice in the last week. A few minutes ago he was driving slowly down Sixth Avenue. I should think the manufacturer would have bought him off by now."

One of Allen's complaints about 1949 television was the small screen on most home receiving sets at that time, which made subtle comic pantomime difficult. "In order to express mild disapproval," he said, "you have to hit somebody on the head with a broom. The screen isn't the only small thing in television right now. It also has small minds, small talents, and small budgets. In fact, everything in television is so small that you can hide it in the navel of a flea and still have enough room beside it for Walter Winchell's heart."

Allen went on to mourn the decline of radio as an entertainment medium. The worst thing that happened to radio, he felt, was the introduction of an audience in the studio.

"Eddie Cantor brought in an audience because he couldn't work without a bunch of imbeciles laughing at his jokes," Allen said. "The sponsors thought it was a jim-dandy idea, so from then on everybody had to have a studio audience. The humor in the script had to be kept down to the level of the studio audience's intelligence, and that was a very low level. Would anybody with a brain and a sense of taste stand in line to watch a radio show, a half-dozen people in tortoiseshell glasses reading into microphones from sheets of paper? Some of the most successful comedy shows in radio had been done without audiences in the studio, the old original fifteen-minute 'Amos 'n' Andy' show, and Stoopnagle and Budd, who did a skit one week about two guys running a motorboat salesroom. There were only two boats on display in the place but they don't discover that one of the boats is missing until they take inventory at the end of the year. It was wonderful. Try stuff like that on a studio audience and you won't get a chuckle. You'd have to switch it around and give one of the guys a southern accent and have him say lines like, 'Do you-all wanna buy a yawl?'

"But can you convince the network moguls and the advertising agency rajahs that a few million unseen listeners have a sharper sense of humor than the two hundred morons who are sitting in the studio with their mouths open? Oh, no. Now television is starting under that same handicap. If radio had been handled with a little more imagination and common sense, it would be so solidly established today as an entertainment medium that television, or any other kind of vision, would be unable to disturb it. It's the poor average man who gets it in the end. He used to be able to listen to the radio and use his imagination. Radio could have him imagining a man walking up the side of a building like a spider. A few words in a radio script could create in the listener's imagination a fantastic setting that couldn't be constructed in a Hollywood studio for millions of dollars. Now they're even taking the listener's imagination away from him."

After they left me, Allen said to Al Durante, "How is he going to write a story? He didn't ask me any questions and he didn't take any notes." Not only did I have no trouble at all remembering what Allen had said and writing it; even more remarkable, the meticulous editors of *Life*, who were seldom completely satisfied with any piece of writing, published that interview without cutting or changing a word of it.

My work acquainted me, too, with many people who are not well known, some of them more vividly memorable than many of the well known. Covering the Miss America beauty contest in Atlantic City I found much more interesting than the beauty contest my several long talks with a talent scout, or beauty scout, who was covering the contest for Howard Hughes. The scout was not too impressed by any of the beauties in the contest. "If Rita Hayworth was here this week, looking as she did in her younger days," he said, "she'd turn this joint upside down." Because the scout was not doing any serious scouting, he was glad to pass the time telling me Howard Hughes stories. One evening he described Hughes's nationwide private espionage network. In every big city, the scout said, Hughes maintained connections with doormen, hotel desk clerks, telephone switchboard operators, newspaper editors, detectives, and chauffeurs of hired limousines who supplied him, at any hour of the day or night, with information that might interest him.

"A few years back," the scout said, "Hughes had a right-hand man in his Los Angeles office who was being worked into exhaustion. We'll call him Sam – that's not his real name – and Hughes was keeping Sam on the go around the clock. Sam felt that if he didn't get away from Hughes, just for a couple of days to get some sleep, he would have a breakdown. So he worked out a plan. He went to the airport in Los Angeles and bought a plane ticket to New York. The plane was scheduled to make a twenty-minute stop in Chicago on its way to New York. When the plane landed in Chicago, Sam got off and walked into the terminal and then kept on walking, out the door and into a taxicab. He went downtown to the Palmer House and rented a room there under a fictitious name. The bellboy showed him to the room. Sam took off his shoes and stretched out on the bed, alone at last and looking forward happily to a little peace and rest. Within five minutes, the telephone rang. It was Hughes. He said to Sam, 'What are you doing in Chicago when you're supposed to be at your desk here in Los Angeles?'"

Among the unforgettable characters I have interviewed is Emile Zola Berman. Berman, a New York trial lawyer specializing in negligence cases, was unknown outside of the legal profession when he began to make national headlines as the defense counsel in the highly publicized court-martial trial of Staff Sergeant Matthew C. McKeon, a Marine Corps drill instructor at Parris Island, in 1956. McKeon was accused of leading six Marine recruits to their deaths by drowning during a disciplinary night march. *Life* sent me to Parris Island during the trial to find out who Berman was. It was the first and only time that I was asked to write about a lawyer and it was a fascinating experience. Berman had dropped his highly lucrative negligence practice in the civil courts to defend McKeon free of charge because he was convinced that the McKeon case was a modern Dreyfus case, and, of course, Berman's parents had named him after Alfred Dreyfus's best-known supporter, Emile Zola. "Just as the French army turned its back on Dreyfus," Berman said, "the Marine Corps is using McKeon to cover its own responsibility for the deaths of those recruits. When he led the kids into the creek during a night march, McKeon was only following standard Marine Corps training procedure. Now the Marines are letting him take the rap. If you really want to know why I'm down here working for no pay in the summer heat of South Carolina, let me tell you about one of the great emotional experiences of my life."

Berman happened to be in Los Angeles on legal business in 1936 when Paul Muni's film *The Life of Emile Zola* was first shown at an elaborately formal premiere, attended by most of the important people in the movie industry. Berman managed to get two tickets to the premiere. He invited an elderly woman, who had been a close friend of his mother's in her girlhood in Brest-Litovsk, to go with him to see the movie.

"This old lady and my mother and my father were all red-hot socialist revolutionists back in the czarist regime," Berman said. "They went wild over Emile Zola when he defended Alfred Dreyfus against the French army. My parents not only named me after Zola, they named my brother, Alfred, after Dreyfus. So now this old lady is sitting with me in the theater, surrounded by Hollywood big shots, when the movie comes to the big dramatic scene in the courtroom where Zola is being denounced by the generals. She jumped to her feet and shook her fist at the screen in a rage, shouting in a loud, ringing voice, 'For shame! For shame!' All those Hollywood phonies were staring at her. Here, in that damned town of make-believe, was a real dramatic character in real life, probably the first one most of them had ever seen. Let me tell you, for me, it was a great moment. I was swept away by it. I never forgot it. The first thing I thought of when I read in the papers about this case against Sergeant McKeon was that old lady shaking her fist and yelling, 'For shame!' The next day a group of lawyers in New York asked me to join a committee to help McKeon's defense. I said to them, 'I'll not only join the committee – I'll plead the case.' "

Berman astonished the officers on the court-martial board by putting on the stand as witnesses for the defense the commandant of the Marine Corps himself, General Randolph Pate, and one of the most revered leatherneck heroes of World War II, Lieutenant General Lewis ("Chesty") Puller. McKeon was acquitted of two serious charges brought against him, oppression of troops and negligence leading to manslaughter, and found guilty of two lesser charges, simple negligence and drinking on duty. The appearance of General Pate as a witness for the defense caused great confusion in the Navy Department's offices at the Pentagon because it was the Marine commandant who had recommended the court-martial trial of McKeon in the first place. I asked Berman how he had manged to get the commandant to testify for McKeon. "I told the general it was the only way to get himself and the Marine Corps out of this jam," Berman said.

During the hot summer evenings at Parris Island, Berman sat in his underwear in his room in the bachelor officers' quarters, sipping Scotch and entertaining us with recollections of his experiences in courtrooms as a negligence trial lawyer. He recalled one case in which he won a judgment of $350,000 against the City of New York for a woman who was hit by a speeding police car. Berman demolished the police department's case by taking a dramatic gamble. The key witness, one of the patrolmen in the car, recited a detailed account of the accident that made it out to be the woman's fault. When he finished his story, Berman asked politely if he could see the patrolman's memorandum book. The patrolman obligingly pulled the book out of his hip pocket and handed it to Berman. Berman found the page in the book on which the patrolman had written a report on the accident at the time it happened. "Would you mind reading this to the judge and the jury?" Berman asked. The blushing cop, reading his own writing, completely contradicted all of his previous testimony.

In another jury trial, Berman represented an insurance company and the landlord of an apartment building in Harlem in a suit brought by a visitor to the building who claimed that he had fallen and broken his ankle because of a broken step on a staircase.

Berman's investigators found out that the visitor was a burglar, fleeing from the building after trying to break into one of its apartments. The intruder was being chased by the tenant of the apartment when he fell and suffered a fracture. When Berman revealed in the courtroom that the plaintiff was a crook who injured himself while attempting to commit a burglary, the jury was not impressed. They awarded the burglar several hundred dollars in damages. "The jurors felt that the burglar's reason for visiting the building had nothing to do with the case," Berman said. "Maybe they were right."

One of my companions at Parris Island was Jim Bishop, who covered the McKeon trial for the Hearst newspapers. When Berman was questioning us one evening about the domestic problems of a writer who does his work at home, Jim recalled the reaction of his wife, Elinor, when he decided to write a book entitled *The Day Lincoln Was Shot*. Elinor took a dim view of the project. While Jim was writing the book in a basement room of their house in Tenafly, New Jersey, he would hear Elinor upstairs complaining to her friends on the telephone. "You'll never guess what he's writing about," Elinor would say. "Lincoln. No, not the Lincoln Tunnel, Abraham Lincoln. There have only been about seven thousand books already written about Lincoln, but here is my husband knocking himself out writing another one. Can you imagine it?"

Jim was at his publisher's office in New York shortly before the publication of *The Day Lincoln Was Shot* when he heard the great news that it had been chosen by the Book-of-the-Month Club to be a main selection. Jim decided to make a triumphant return to Tenafly to lord it over Elinor. He hired a limousine and placed a bucket of ice containing a bottle of champagne on the front seat beside the chauffeur. Arriving at his house, he made a grand entrance, carrying the champagne, and made the big announcement.

"Guess what?" he said to Elinor. "My book about Lincoln has been taken by the Book-of-the-Month Club. You know what that means? It means about fifty thousand dollars."

Elinor was not too impressed. "Well," she said, "now maybe you'll be able to pay the Book-of-the-Month Club that seven dollars and fifty cents you've owed them for the last two years."

Being a writer may not be the most secure way to cope with the formality of earning a living, but a writer who doesn't confine himself to writing poetry or philosophy or insurance policies gets to meet a lot of interesting people.

3

A FEW LADIES

As a magazine editor and writer in the 1940s and 1950s I became acquainted with some of that era's well-known women, such as Eleanor Roosevelt, Grace Kelly, Mary Martin, and, very briefly, Clare Boothe Luce. When I was an editor at *Cosmopolitan*, long before it became the magazine for single girls that it is today, Carl Brandt, Mrs. Luce's literary agent, arranged for me to have lunch with her. Her recent conversion to Catholicism by Bishop Fulton Sheen had made newspaper headlines. She asked if she could write an article for me about Bishop Sheen. I could see the rapturous, but dull, praise of the bishop's deep religious faith that she had in mind. I explained that I felt she had been too personally involved with the bishop during her conversion to write about him objectively. A chill came over the luncheon table. Mrs. Luce did not like to hear "no"! Later I gave the assignment to another woman writer, an atheist who had never met Bishop Sheen. During her first interview with him, the bishop converted her. The article about him was never written.

Eleanor Roosevelt had a very different reaction when I had to say no to a request she made. During World War II, when I was the managing editor of *Yank*, Mrs. Roosevelt invited my wife and me to have dinner with her at her New York apartment. Her close friend and protégé, Joseph Lash, who later wrote her biography, was then a sergeant in the army, stationed on an island in the South Pacific. Mrs. Roosevelt asked me if I could arrange to have Lash transferred to *Yank*'s editorial staff. "I couldn't do it," I told her. "Can you imagine what the *Chicago Tribune* and all the other Republican newspapers would have to say about that? They'd say that the White House is controlling *Yank*." Mrs. Roosevelt looked at me for a moment. Then she nodded and said, "You are absolutely right. That never occurred to me." We all relaxed and had a pleasant evening. Later, at the time of her husband's death, Mrs. Roosevelt personally ordered the White House press aides to include a *Yank* reporter in the strictly limited number of correspondents allowed on the funeral train during its ride to the burial at Hyde Park. After the war, she gave me interviews and invited us, along with other guests, to her Hyde Park home. I think the differences are interesting to note.

One afternoon in the winter of 1955, my wife, Mary, was kneeling on the floor of the bathroom in our house on Long Island, scrubbing its linoleum covering, when I rushed in and said to her, "I've got to drive to the city right away. I just found out that I have a date to meet

Grace Kelly at five o'clock in her apartment on East 66th Street." In later years, when friends asked Mary what it was like to be married to a writer, she often recalled that scene in the bathroom. "There I was, on my hands and knees, scrubbing the bathroom floor," she would say, "and there he was, hurrying off to New York to visit Grace Kelly in her apartment. That's what it's like to be married to a writer."

Grace Kelly, at that time a twenty-five-year-old film star not yet married to Prince Rainier of Monaco, was the most aloof and difficult person I have ever tried to interview. Compared to Princess Grace, Jacqueline Kennedy Onassis, who talked with me freely and often a few years later, seemed like Gabby Hayes. I heard later from the publicity people at Metro-Goldwyn-Mayer, who arranged our meeting, that she had kicked like a steer against it. While we talked, or while I tried to get her to talk, she kept her secretary and chaperone, an older woman with the appropriate name of Prudence Wise, seated closely beside her.

"I can't offer you anything to drink," she said to me after I introduced myself, "because I don't have anything for you to drink. Let us also understand one thing – I won't answer any questions about my personal life. I'll talk about my work, but my private life is my own business, and nobody else's."

I decided not to ask Grace about a story that a national weekly scandal sheet had published a few months earlier – a lurid and obviously fictitious account of Grace Kelly's alleged love affairs in Hollywood, studded with such names as Clark Gable, Bing Crosby, Cary Grant, and Ray Milland. There were other stories making the rounds that might have made interesting copy but were not verifiable, so it seemed the article was going to be pretty flat, for Grace Kelly was not noted for her candor. Yet she did reveal to me one bit of news about herself that had not been printed previously. She said that unlike such other movie stars as Ava Gardner, Elizabeth Taylor, and Lana Turner, she was never recognized by cab drivers or department store sales clerks when she was shopping in New York. "Nobody ever says to me, 'You're Grace Kelly,'" she said. "They always say to me, 'Did anybody ever tell you that you look a lot like Grace Kelly?' Today, on Fifth Avenue, I got into a cab, and the driver said to me, 'When I saw you wave to me, I said to myself, I'm going to have Grace Kelly in my cab. You look just like her.' I said to him, 'I'm awfully sorry I'm not Grace Kelly.' He said to me, 'So am I.'" As today's youngsters would say, big deal.

Mary Martin, when she was at the height of her long career as one of the biggest stars in show business during the 1950s, was entirely something else again—cheerfully willing to talk at length about everything that had ever happened to her. The only trouble with Miss Martin's talk, from a writer's viewpoint, is that it is a little too sunny. She seldom has a sharp word to say about anybody. Her philosophy of life is summed up in an old Chinese proverb which she inscribed in needlepoint on a rug, a task that she worked on for three and a half years. It says: "If there is righteousness in the heart, there will be beauty in the character. If there is beauty in the character, there will be harmony in the family home. If there is harmony in the home, there will be order in the nation. When there is order in the nation, there will be peace in the world."

Mary displayed the proverb when she was interviewed in her Connecticut home on television by Ed Murrow during one of his *Person to Person* shows. Murrow received more than two thousand requests from listeners for copies of the proverb. He borrowed the rug, photographed it, and sent out pictures of it. To her astonishment, Mary's appearance on *Person to Person* brought her more personal fan mail than she received during the entire three-year run of her biggest stage hit, *South Pacific*.

One of the producers of *South Pacific* was Leland Hayward, the dynamic and persuasive show-business promoter. Turning James Michener's book of World War II stories, *Tales of the South Pacific*, into a Rodgers and Hammerstein musical show, co-starring Mary Martin and Ezio Pinza, was Hayward's idea. Mary told me later that she did not realize, when she signed up to appear in *South Pacific* as Nellie Forbush, the navy nurse, that the role would require her to shampoo her hair three times a day (and six times on days of matinee performances) while she was singing one of the show's hit songs, "I'm Gonna Wash That Man Right Outa My Hair." She washed her hair before each show to bring out its curls, again during the shampooing scene, and once more after the show to get out the soap that she did not have time to rinse out onstage. "When Oscar Hammerstein and Dick Rodgers first offered me the part," she told me, "I had doubts about a musical comedy voice like mine competing in a duet, like 'Some Enchanted

Evening,' with a heavy operatic basso like Ezio Pinza. Dick said to me, 'You'll just have to take my word on it. I've figured it out and I know it can be done.' Of course, Dick was absolutely right."

Because of Leland Hayward's close association with Mary Martin in *South Pacific*, the Ford Motor Company gave him the job of producing its gala fiftieth anniversary television show in 1953. Given a free hand financially, Hayward planned a lavish musical revue which was to be shown live on both of the major television networks, NBC and CBS, simultaneously, something never done before or since. Hayward assured the Ford company that he would have no trouble whatsoever persuading Miss Martin to co-star with Ethel Merman in the show, even though she had never appeared previously on TV and had turned down several attractive offers from other television producers. He reached Mary on the telephone in London, where was ending a run in *South Pacific*, and he was astonished when she turned him down flatly. To escape from the persistent Hayward, Mary and her husband and manager, Richard Halliday, went on a long cruise to South America on a freighter, keeping the name of the ship and its destinations a secret.

Hayward refused to give up. He sent a radio message all over the Atlantic, addressed "To All Ships at Sea." The message begged the Hallidays to send him a wire immediately, telling him where he could see them. Reluctantly they arranged to see Hayward a few days later in Cuba. "There he was, standing on the dock when our ship arrived," Mary said, recalling their meeting. "He claimed that his visit to us was purely social.

He had simply been overcome by a warm desire to spend a few days with us. As a matter of fact, I think Leland waited almost five hours before he brought up the Ford anniversary show."

The two-hour Ford show on two networks turned out to be a much bigger popular success than Hayward or the networks expected it to be. The highlight of the program was a long and snappy duet medley sung by Miss Martin and Miss Merman. Show-business people could not recall Ethel Merman ever sharing a spotlight with another woman singer at any previous appearance in her career. Evidently she felt that Mary Martin could be trusted not to grab more than her share of the spotlight. Despite all of Hayward's careful planning, the show ran short and ended with a big gap. The masters of ceremony, Oscar Hammerstein and Ed Murrow, found themselves standing on an empty stage with no more acts to introduce and ten more minutes to fill before the final curtain would fall. They tried to plug the hole with casual ad-libbed conversation. When the show finally went off the air, Hammerstein and Murrow were astonished when Hayward accosted them in a roaring rage, blaming them for the time lapse. "You've ruined the whole show!" he shouted. To escape the criticism that he was expecting from newspapers and from the Ford company and network officials, Hayward hurried to the airport and caught the next plane to London. There he learned to his complete astonishment that the Ford show had scored a big critical and popular success. Nobody minded the time lapse at the ending because the previous 110 minutes had been filled with spectacular entertainment. Murrow told me later that he and Hammerstein soon received long wireless messages from Hayward praising them for their fine work in the show with no mention of his enraged outburst.

Mary Martin's story of her life in show business was an interesting one to write because, after almost ten years of frustrating struggle and obscurity, she suddenly became a big star on the opening night of her first appearance on Broadway while she was singing one song, "My Heart Belongs to Daddy," in Vinton Freedley's 1938 production of Cole Porter's musical comedy *Leave It to Me.*

"I've never seen anything like it, before or since," a Broadway producer told me later. "She was a hick from Texas. She didn't know much about how to dress and she had a lot to learn about makeup and fixing hair. She wasn't especially good-looking. But she certainly knew how to handle herself on a stage. After she sang that one song, everybody in town seemed to be talking about her. From then on, she was all set."

Mary told me that she was not interested in anything but singing and dancing from the age of five, when she appeared in a show at her hometown, Weatherford, Texas, singing "The Lilac Tree," a popular song about a little girl who tells a little boy that she will give him a kiss when apples grow on a lilac tree. Her father, a lawyer and a judge, tried to get some book-learning into her head by sending her to a boarding school in Tennessee. She escaped from the school at the age of seventeen by marrying Benjamin Hagman, a boy from Fort Worth. They had one son, Larry Hagman, who became a film and television actor. The marriage lasted for five years. After it broke up, while Mary was operating a dancing school in Weatherford, she talked her father into financing a trip to Hollywood, where she spent three years trying to get a job in a movie studio.

"Everybody told me to remodel my nose, which was too big," Mary told me. "I managed to support myself, not too well, by singing in nightclubs. Now let me tell you an interesting story about myself and Bing Crosby. At least, I think it's interesting. One night Bing heard me singing 'Shoe-Shine Boy' at a small place called The Casanova. He kept me at the piano, singing that same song over and over again, until three o'clock in the morning. He said he loved my singing and he promised to help me get a job in the movies. But weeks and weeks went by and I never heard from him."

While she was waiting to hear from Crosby, Mary had her first big lucky break. At a Sunday-night "opportunity show" in the old Trocadero nightclub, she performed before an audience of important show-business people an old classic aria, "Il Bacio" ("The Kiss"). First she sang the song conventionally straight. The audience seemed bored. Then she did the song again with a hot swinging rhythm. When she finished her number, everybody in the room stood up and cheered. The next day she received telephone calls from several movie studios and an invitation from Laurence Schwab to appear in a New York musical, which she accepted. Schwab's project never materialized but he arranged for her to get the "My Heart Belongs to Daddy" role in *Leave It to Me*.

"Now comes the rest of the Bing Crosby story," Mary said. "After the run of *Leave It to Me*, I landed a nice movie contract at Paramount. There I met Dick Halliday, a story editor at the studio who became my second and last husband and the father of my second and last child, our daughter Heller. Her name is really Mary, but ever since she was a baby we've called her Heller because she's always been a heller. I had to pass up a chance to play in *Holiday Inn* with Bing Crosby and Fred Astaire while I was at Paramount because I was in the hospital at that time, getting Heller born. I worked with Bing on a few other pictures, but I never mentioned to him that night at The Casanova when he kept me at the piano singing 'Shoe-Shine Boy' until three in the morning. Finally, one day on the set when we were together, I walked over to a piano and started to tap out 'Shoe-Shine Boy.' Bing said to me, 'Don't play that song, Mary. It hurts me. One night I sat up until all hours listening to a girl sing that number. The next day I went to a lot of trouble arranging a screen test for her. Then I went back to the joint where she was working to tell her the big news. She was gone and nobody there could tell me how to get in touch with her. I often wonder what happened to her.' I said to Bing, 'You're looking at her right now.' Isn't that something?"

One of the brightest and most imaginative editors that I have worked with was Herbert Mayes, who enjoyed every minute of his long and successful career at *Good Housekeeping* magazine before moving on to even bigger success at *McCall's*. Most editors get ideas for magazine articles and books from writers or from literary agents or publicity directors. Herb Mayes thought up his own ideas. One day in 1954, when Richard Rodgers and Oscar Hammerstein were at the peak of their success as musical comedy creators, Herb called me on the telephone and said, "How about writing a piece for me on *Mrs.* Rodgers and *Mrs.* Hammerstein? I've talked to them, and they both say it's okay with them. They're both good talkers, bright and unpretentious. Nothing phony about them."

As a matter of fact, Dorothy Rodgers and Dorothy Hammerstein, and both of their famous husbands, who often joined me when I talked with their wives, turned out to be four of the brightest and least phony people I have ever met. Rodgers told me that both of the Dorothys were much more involved in their husbands' creative work than they would admit to me. "When I write a song," he said, "I try it out first on Dorothy. When Oscar writes a lyric or a part of the story, he shows it to his Dorothy. If my girl nods, and says, 'Very good,' I know it's not so good. If she says nothing, but I see her eyes filling up with tears, I know it's all right. When Oscar is hard up for a lyric line, he often gets one from his Dorothy." I asked the Hammersteins one day what their all-time favorite lyric was. They both answered immediately and simultaneously: "Irving Berlin's 'All alone by the telephone.'"

"Those five words tell a whole heartbreaking story," Hammerstein said. "No lyric writer could ever do better."

Among the various unforgettable characters whom I have known over many years in the winding course of my work, Dorothy Rodgers stands out as the one with the most incredible array of talents, business and artistic interests, and time-consuming hobbies. In her youth, Mrs. Rodgers was a promising sculptor. "I gave it up when I married Dick," she said. "I figured one creative artist in the family was enough." She once spent three and a half years crocheting a white bedspread with a Swedish popcorn design and she has often spent nine straight hours making up a double crostic puzzle for a friend. She is also an inventor.

One of the best-known Rodgers inventions is the Jonny Mop, a device for cleaning toilet bowls with a disposable pad that can be flushed down the drain. "My friends used to call me 'The Queen of the Bathroom,'" she told me, "but they stopped laughing when I showed them some of the Jonny Mop royalty checks." When I met her, she was working on a small air-conditioning unit to be worn under clothing on hot days and she was getting a patent on a device that would allow a child who locked himself inside a refrigerator to open its door. There had been recent reports about children locking themselves inside refrigerators and dying from suffocation. Dorothy had designed a panel for the inside of the door that unlatched the lock when even the slightest pressure from a child's hand was applied to it.

Mrs. Rodgers had gotten into inventing, and also into interior decorating, after operating for many years in New York a service for restoring broken glassware, furniture, and various knickknacks, which she called Repairs, Incorporated. She fixed everything from Helen Hayes's cuckoo clock to the murals in the Sert Room at the Waldorf Astoria after they were slashed one night by a moody drunk. One of her customers asked her to find a Lucite ornament stand on which to display his late grandfather's jawbone. "I was dying to ask what happened to the rest of his grandfather, but I didn't have the nerve," she said. Another one brought in a dead white dog named Minnie, stuffed and mounted inside a glass bell jar, clutching a bunch of white roses between her paws. Minnie's owner wanted to have her dry-cleaned. Repairs, Incorporated had Minnie cleaned and returned her to her owner as quickly as possible.

Richard Rodgers's favorites among his songs were "My Heart Stood Still" and "With a Song in My Heart," both written with his earlier lyricist, Larry Hart, and "Oh, What a Beautiful Mornin'," the first song that he wrote in collaboration with Oscar Hammerstein for the first musical show that they wrote together, *Oklahoma!* "I remember how happy Dick was with those lyrics when Oscar handed them to him," Dorothy Rodgers said. "He said, 'How can we miss with lines like, "The corn is as high as an elephant's eye"?'" Unlike some other composers, Rodgers wrote music to fit lyrics written previously and carefully polished before he saw them. "I spent a week trying to decide whether or not to put the 'Oh' before 'what a beautiful mornin','" Hammerstein told me. "Then Dick sits down and knocks off the music in a couple of minutes." Actually, Rodgers did write the music for "Bali H'ai" in five minutes and knocked off "Happy Talk" in twenty minutes.

"But there's a big but in there," Rodgers said when I asked him about his speedy composing. "Before I sit down at the piano to tap out the tune, I spend months thinking about the script of the show as a whole, studying situations in it that seem to call for a song, and deciding whether the situation requires a ballad or a love song, a fast dance number or a comic duet." Hammerstein died in 1960 at the age of sixty-five. After his partner's death, Rodgers wrote one musical show, *No Strings*, alone and four others with different collaborators; the last, *I Remember Mama*, only months before his death.

Herbert Mayes introduced me to another memorable woman in 1949 when he asked me to go to Boston and write an article for him about the twelfth edition of *Bartlett's Familiar Quotations*, which had recently been published by Little, Brown and Company. The assignment perplexed me. I wondered what I could write about that famous book of quotations that could possibly interest the women readers of *Good Housekeeping*. Louella D. Everett, then the associate editor of *Bartlett's* who had been digging up and assorting all of its newer quotations during the previous thirty years, provided me with an unexpected ray of sunshine that made the article readable.

For more than forty years, between 1918 and 1960, Miss Everett was well known to readers of the *New York Times Book Review*'s Queries and Answers column, now sadly a memory of the past. Back in 1902, when she was eighteen, Miss Everett began collecting verses and filing them according to subject matter, some of them dating back to 1840. She soon accumulated more than a hundred thousand poetic items from old newspapers and magazines, filed and cross-indexed alphabetically. When Queries and Answers published a request for the title or the author of an obscure line of verse, she would supply the correct answer, and she never missed. To pick one sample at random, a reader once asked, "Where do these lines comes from? 'My fathers sleep on the sunrise plains, and each one sleeps alone. . . .'" Miss Everett's prompt reply: "Those are the opening lines of a poem entitled 'The Westerner' by Badger Clark."

As Miss Everett's fame as a verse detective grew in the 1920s, poetry lovers all over North America began to write to her directly, at her home address in Boston, instead of hoping to contact her through the Queries and Answers column. She received hundreds of letters every month, which she answered in her spare time, never receiving a dollar for her time and work. A doctor, grateful for some sleuthing, once sent her ten pounds of sausages, two pounds of pancake flour, and a jar of raspberry jam as a thank-you note. Another man, grateful for an answer that she dug up for him, proposed marriage. She turned him down tactfully, not revealing that she was already married to a Bostonian named Charles H. Young, whose name she never used in her work as an editor. The rejected proposer wrote back to her, urging her to accept, instead of matrimony, a grave and a monument in his family's cemetery plot.

Miss Everett once spent three years tracking down the identity of an obscure bit of verse. When she passed on her findings to the woman who asked for it, the woman informed her that she was no longer interested in poetry. In 1927 Carolyn Wells wrote a verse about her for the Queries and Answers column, which began:

Louella D. Everett of Boston, Mass.,
Must be an industrious, painstaking lass.
I'm sure she neglects all the diners and dancers
To spend her whole time on Queries and Answers. . . .

Actually, Miss Everett devoted only a small fraction of her long and busy working hours to answering queries. When I visited her in 1949 in her small Back Bay apartment, which was crowded with books and filing cabinets, she told me that when she was not selecting and checking quotations for *Bartlett's*, she worked as a public stenographer, typing medical papers, with elaborate footnotes, from nine-fifteen in the morning until seven at night, without pausing for lunch. She was an exceptionally witty and bright woman. "I like books and indoors," she said. "I never leave this apartment, except to go to Boston Symphony concerts. I hate fresh air, trees, grass, clothes, cooking, and potted plants. Several years ago, somebody gave me a Jerusalem cherry tree. The noise of those cherries dropping on the floor kept me awake all night."

After talking with Miss Everett, I had a drink at the Ritz Carlton with Gordon Bassett, a cheerful, elderly Bostonian who handled the back-breaking job of compiling the index to that edition of *Bartlett's Familiar Quotations*. It took Bassett more than a year to write the 123,042 entries in the index. Each quotation, and every allusion to other quotations in each footnote, was not only indexed but cross-indexed from every possible angle.

"I wrote the last entry one morning between two and three o'clock," Bassett said. "I must confess that I experienced a certain sensation of satisfaction and relief. In fact, I felt like going out and getting a drink. Then came the work of arranging the entries in alphabetical order and having them typed and checked. At one time, we had twenty-three people working on that phase of the job. Then the galley proofs had to be checked and corrected by Miss Everett and myself. I talked with her often on the telephone, but I never met her personally until after all of the work was finally finished. Then I decided one day to take a walk to Miss Everett's apartment to exchange reminiscences with her about the long ordeal that we had shared. I had a nice visit with her. When I was leaving, we shook hands and she said to me, '*Bartlett's Familiar Quotations* is a bond that we shall always have between us.'"

Miss Everett died in 1967 at the age of eighty-three, not quite as old as John Bartlett, who edited nine editions of *Familiar Quotations* before he died at eighty-five in 1905. Some recent editions of *Familiar Quotations* have been edited under the direction of Emily Morison Beck, daughter of Boston's famous historian Samuel Eliot Morison. Appropriately, the offices of its publisher, Little, Brown and Company, are located on Beacon Hill, one of the most book-loving and book-loaded neighborhoods in the world. It was there that one of the residents, Mrs. James T. Field, once remarked thoughtfully to her friend Willa Cather, "You know, my dear, I think we sometimes forget how much we owe to Dryden's prefaces," while one of Mrs. Field's Beacon Hill neighbors, Sarah Palfrey, great-aunt of the champion tennis player of the same name, took up the study of Hebrew during her final illness at the age of eighty-eight so that she would be able to greet her Creator in his native tongue.

4

MEMORABLE M's

DURING THE INCREDIBLE PERIOD IN THE EARLY 1950s when Senator Joe McCarthy of Wisconsin was riding high in national prominence as a reckless and irresponsible Red hunter, a friend of mine named Hyman Goldberg asked me why I didn't change my name for business reasons. It was a good question. Trying to work as a writer named Joe McCarthy during those jittery times was often a problem.

Actor Robert Montgomery was startled by a telephone message that I left at his office, asking for an appointment with him. I had been asked to write a magazine article about his daughter, Elizabeth Montgomery, who was then starting her successful career as a television actress. Her father had left Hollywood to work as a television producer in New York. He was also directing President Eisenhower's TV appearances. One day while he was having a meeting with Eisenhower in the

White House, Montgomery was handed a message that said Joe McCarthy wanted to talk with him about his daughter. "I almost fainted," Montgomery told me later. "I said to myself, 'My God, what kind of un-American activities has Elizabeth gotten herself into?'"

But if I had been working under another name, I might never have gotten to know Edward R. Murrow, the only news commentator in the cautious television and radio broadcasting business of that time with the courage to attack and expose Senator McCarthy on the air.

As strange as it seems today, Murrow's calm and factual exposure of Senator McCarthy's reckless and false charges that the State Department and the army's high offices were crowded with Communists and pro-Communists made Murrow himself a controversial figure in the nervous cold-war climate of 1954. The mention of Murrow's name started hot arguments in bars and on commuting trains. One night after watching a baseball game at Ebbetts Field in Brooklyn, Murrow was invited into the clubhouse. A sportswriter who was there indignantly demanded to know why the Dodgers were entertaining a Communist.

My first meeting with Murrow came as a result of somebody at *Look* magazine having a bright idea. Dan Mich, the editorial director, asked me to come to his office and said to me, with a straight face, "We'd like you to do a profile-type piece on Ed Murrow. You know, not just what he's been doing lately, but the whole works—his background as a lumberjack in the State of Washington, his war reporting in London, the whole works."

At first, I thought he was joking. "What's the matter?" Mich said. "Don't you want to do it?"

"Sure, I'd like to do it," I said. "But don't you think it might be a little misleading for the readers?"

"Misleading?" Mich said innocently. "Oh, you mean the by-line? I spoke to Mike Cowles about that." (Cowles was then the owner and editor of *Look*.) "Mike and I agreed, of course, that it would be necessary to run an editor's note on the article, explaining that you're not a senator from Wisconsin."

I could see the editor's note in small type, tucked into a lower corner of the page where most readers would be unlikely to see it.

"Let me think about it," I said. "I'll call you this afternoon."

I went downstairs to a telephone booth in the lobby of the Look Building and called my wife, Mary, who always has the right answer for a difficult question.

"Do you want to write about Murrow?" Mary asked.

"Of course I want to write about him. It will be an interesting piece to write. Besides, we need the money."

"Then what's your problem?" Mary said. "Go back and tell Mich that you'll be glad to write it under another name."

By offering to write about Murrow under a pseudonym, I was putting Mich on a spot. If he turned me down, he would be admitting that his magazine had been plotting to capitalize on my name. He had to give in and let me write the article under the name of Joseph Doyle, my mother's family name.

Murrow and his bright and attractive wife, Janet, were both amused by my story of how I got the assignment. The Murrows turned out to be two of the loveliest people whom I have met in the course of my work. Now that I stop to think about it, many of those most memorable people have names beginning with an *M* – Audrey Meadows, Robert Moses, and Bernard Patrick McDonough, to pick three of them at random. As everybody knows, Audrey Meadows plays Jackie Gleason's wife Alice in *The Honeymooners*, which has been rerunning steadily all over the world for more than twenty years. Robert Moses, snappy conversationalist and a builder of parks and parkways, created New York's last World's Fair. Bernard McDonough, a self-made millionaire industrialist from Parkersburg, West Virginia, bought a huge seventy-room castle in Ireland five minutes after taking his first look at it. More about Meadows, Moses, and McDonough a little later in this recollection of memorable M's.

As I have mentioned earlier, Edward R. Murrow, the TV and radio news commentator, and Ed Murrow, the former lumberjack who loved to clear away brush with a tractor on his country estate, were two entirely different people. On the air, Murrow was a stiffly formal, stilted and rather pontifical-mannered speaker. "On television," a woman at a party once said to him, "you sound like God's older brother." Off the air, he was modest and unassuming, one of the most unaffected and trusting people I have ever known. Five minutes after I first met Murrow, I was astonished to hear him telling me, with no word about his remarks being off the record, that William S. Paley, the chairman and chief executive at CBS, and Murrow's close friend and admirer up until that time, had been angrily opposed to his attack on Senator McCarthy.

"I went to see Paley the other day," Murrow told me. "I told him that we had a problem. I just found out that one of the writers on my news staff had been a member of the Communist Party for a few months back in the thirties, when he was a student at Columbia. I told Paley I was worried about what might happen if McCarthy found out about it. Paley glared at me. All he said was, 'If McCarthy finds out about it, you're on your own. Don't expect any help from me, or from anybody else around here.'"

Actually, Murrow's condemnation of McCarthy's reckless Red hunting, which created a sensation on television in 1954, would seem like rather mild stuff today. Instead of spending much time on his weekly *See It Now* news commentary show voicing his own strong disapproval of McCarthy, Murrow devoted most of the half hour to filmed excerpts of the senator's own speeches that made McCarthy seem ridiculous. The show also displayed a film of McCarthy grilling a former State Department employee named Reed Harris, who had written an almost unknown pink book back in 1932.

Murrow invited McCarthy to reply on *See It Now* at a later date. In his rather sloppy rebuttal, the senator claimed that Murrow had been a Soviet propagandist twenty years earlier. He also displayed an issue of the *Daily Worker*, which, he said, contained an article by William Z. Foster, a Communist Party leader, praising Murrow.

Replying to McCarthy's rebuttal, Murrow pointed

out that the only mention of his name in Foster's *Daily Worker* article was in a paragraph that read: "During the past 10 days, Senator McCarthy has received a number of resounding belts on the jaw. These came from Adlai Stevenson, E. R. Murrow, Senator Flanders, the Army leadership and some broadcasting studios. Even President Eisenhower himself had to give McCarthy a slap on the wrist."

Talking with me privately about why he had decided to come out against McCarthy on the CBS network, Murrow was much more articulate and indignant than he had been on the air. "I was fed up with McCarthy asking us to make up our minds about certain people without showing us evidence," he said. "I was outraged by his questioning people about their political opinions. No congressional committee has the right to question anybody about what he thinks. About what he does, or has done, yes, but not about his thoughts. The thing about McCarthy that kills me is his disrespect for due process of law."

He puffed for a moment thoughtfully on the cigarette that was hanging from a corner of his mouth. He was never seen, on or off the air, without a cigarette. Comedians at that time, doing an imitation of Murrow, usually smoked four or five cigarettes simultaneously.

"Let me put it another way," he said. "When I was leaving London after the war, I was asked to give a talk on BBC about things in England that had impressed me. Two things stuck out in my mind. During the worst part of the Blitz in London, when the R.A.F. had only one squadron of planes that wasn't in combat against the Germans, the House of Commons spent two days debating about the treatment of enemy aliens on the Isle of Man. If England was going to fall, they didn't want it to fall with concentration camps on English soil. The other thing was a case of an Italian sailor who knifed a Britisher in a waterfront brawl. He came up for appeal before a high court on the day that England declared war on Italy, and the court freed him. The people I talked with in the pubs were all glad that the court had done the right thing without being swayed by patriotic emotion. That's due process of law. Mention due process of law to Joe McCarthy and he won't know what you're talking about."

At the same time that he attacked McCarthy on *See It Now*, Murrow was producing and acting as the master of ceremonies in *Person to Person*, which could have been, but wasn't, one of the most memorable live interview shows in the history of television. *Person to Person* was a weekly series of visits to the homes of various celebrities who carried on informal and unrehearsed conversations with their guest, Murrow, sitting at a microphone in the CBS studio at the Grand Central Building in New York while his hosts or hostesses introduced him to members of their families and showed him various rooms in their houses or apartments. If such a two-way conversational show, shown from two distant and separate locations simultaneously, had been filmed in advance, it would have presented no big technical problems, but Murrow insisted that it had to be done live. That meant beaming the television signals from the home to the nearest transcontinental coaxial cable in distant parts of the country, or, if the home was in the New York area, beaming the TV signal directly from the host's living room to a CBS receiver on top of the Empire State Building, and by wire from there to the Grand Central studio where Murrow was sitting.

When the *Person to Person* technicians were setting up an interview with Richard Simon, the book publisher, they found a big tree standing smack in the middle of the sightline between Simon's house in Riverdale and the Empire State Building's tower. That meant that the signal had to be aimed around the tree, in two hops, like a billiard shot. It was directed from Simon's house to a reflecting disc on the roof of a nearby apartment house, off to one side of the tree, and then bounced from the disc to the Empire State tower. Then the owner of the apartment house refused to allow the reflector on his roof unless Murrow promised to let his daughter, who had aspirations to be a singer and dancer, put on a performance on *Person to Person* at a later date. The technicians manged to find another rooftop.

Murrow's office was constantly flooded with requests from various unknown and not particularly interesting people who wanted to appear on *Person to Person*. One of them was a contractor who offered to install air-conditioning equipment free of charge in the homes of Murrow and his assistant producers if he and his family were displayed on the show. When the proposition was turned down, the contractor said, "All right, but maybe this summer, when the weather starts to get hot and sticky, you'll change your mind."

The various hosts and hostesses on *Person to Person* included such persons as heavyweight boxing champions Jersey Joe Wolcott and Rocky Marciano, Eleanor Roosevelt, Groucho and Harpo Marx, Cardinal Richard

J. Cushing, Tallulah Bankhead, Eva Gabor, Roy Campanella, and Richard and Dorothy Rodgers. Tallulah, finding herself in front of a camera with no script to follow, was speechless. "For the first time in my life," she said later, "I had no playwright or scriptwriter telling me what to say, so I couldn't say anything." Groucho Marx wanted to appear on the show saying to Murrow, "Good evening, Senator McCarthy." Murrow talked him out of using the gag, which would have been the only funny line in the show, because Murrow felt it was too personal. As a matter of fact, Murrow's refusal to allow personal and probing dialogue on *Person to Person*, because he felt that he had to behave like a polite guest in the homes that he visited, was the big obstacle that kept his interview show from becoming one of the great television productions that it could have been. The reruns of *Person to Person*, shown recently on public television, included Murrow's visit with Jacqueline and then Senator John F. Kennedy at the small and seedy three-room apartment on Bowdoin Street in Boston that Kennedy had lived in occasionally as a bachelor, and had kept in later years as a legal voting address. Jackie's appearance there on *Person to Person* amused everybody who knew the Kennedys because it was probably her first and only visit to that flat, which was much too crummy for her comfort; on her visits to Boston with her husband, they always stayed at the nearby luxurious Ritz Carlton Hotel. If Murrow had brought this up in the Bowdoin Street interview, his talk with the Kennedys might have been more interesting but, of course, he never mentioned it during their dull and aimless conversation.

A few months after Murrow's attacks on Senator McCarthy, the senator's waning credibility was demolished during the memorable televised hearings of the Senate's investigation of the Army-McCarthy controversy, which involved flimsy charges by the senator and his counsel, Roy Cohn, that the Pentagon was hiding Reds in high offices, and countercharges from the army that the senator and Cohn were trying to get preferential treatment for their recently drafted friend, Private G. David Schine. The Senate later censured McCarthy, charging him with misconduct. He died a few years after his fall from power.

Murrow's relationship with Paley never regained its previous warm respect. The chill between them that broke out during their disagreement over Murrow's stand on the McCarthy issue grew colder and deeper during the next few years. In 1961 Murrow left CBS to become the director of the U.S. Information Service under the new Kennedy Administration, but by that time his increasing lung cancer was making his work difficult. During the top-secret "Ex Comm," or National Security Council executive committee, discussions on the Cuban missile crisis in 1962, Murrow was too ill to attend the meetings. His agency's deputy director, Don Wilson, had to sit in his place at the conference table. Murrow managed to hang on as the Information Service's director for two more years. He died of throat cancer shortly after he was forced by failing health to retire.

Fourteen years later, on a bright spring morning in 1979, a group of Ed Murrow's friends and admirers gathered at a park in Washington, on Pennsylvania

Avenue across from the U.S. Information Agency, to watch his widow unveil a bronze plaque dedicated in his memory. It was the first memorial honoring a news reporter ever erected by the federal government in the District of Columbia. Secretary of the Interior Cecil Andrus, like Murrow a native of the State of Washington, remarked to a correspondent, "We've begun with one of the best."

One of the speakers was Eric Sevareid, Ed's colleague at CBS for many years. "He was so American in his toughness and tenderness," Sevareid said. "He was in the front rank of those who slew the dragons of evil in his day, Hitlerism and McCarthyism, but he was not a chronic crusader, not a zealot. He knew that next to power without honor the most dangerous thing was power without humor. He would not approve of everything being done in television news coverage today. He knew that in a mass medium the news must be simplified so that as many as possible may understand it. But he would not have approved of today's trivialization of the news and he would have abhorred its vulgarization."

Bob Considine often recalled the unique respect and admiration that Murrow won as a news commentator in England during World War II. "Only two men were ever applauded and cheered whenever they walked into the Savoy Grill in London," Bob said. "One was Winston Churchill. The other one was Ed Murrow."

Audrey Meadows retired from television back in 1961 when she married Robert Six, the wealthy chief executive of Continental Airlines, but Audrey is still being seen constantly in various parts of the world, playing the role of Alice Kramden, the bus driver's wife, in reruns of Jackie Gleason's enduring TV comedy, *The Honeymooners*. The long life of *The Honeymooners* in that 1955–1956 thirty-minute weekly version, with Art Carney and Joyce Randolph as Ed and Trixie Norton, the couple upstairs, is astonishing because it consists of only thirty-nine half-hour shows. Gleason, who directed and produced the show in addition to starring in it as Alice's blustering husband, Ralph Kramden, stopped it after that one season, breaking a three-year, eleven-million-dollar contract with Buick, his sponsor, because he felt that its sources of comedy material were going dry. A later attempt to produce a one-hour musical version without Meadows and Randolph as the wives was not especially successful. The limited repertoire of the one-season half-hour version has made it, of course, very much more repetitious than other old comedy reruns, such as Lucille Ball's *I Love Lucy*, which has hundreds of half-hour segments. Devoted fans of *The Honeymooners*, who have been watching it constantly over the years, know each show by heart, but familiarity only seems to enhance the attraction of this enduring television classic, which has been seen and reseen not only all over North and South America but in such countries as Australia, Iran, Nigeria, and Saudi Arabia.

When I first met Audrey in 1952 she was playing the Alice role in the original fifteen-minute version of *The Honeymooners*, one of the comedy skits on Gleason's earlier and highly successful Saturday-night one-hour variety show. She gave me an entertaining report on how she had managed to land the part. At the time that she applied for it, she was appearing on Broadway in the musical comedy *Top Banana,* which starred Phil Silvers, and also on television five nights a week in the fifteen-minute ad-libbed comedy *The Bob and Ray Show,* with Bob Elliott and Ray Goulding. Nobody on *The Bob and Ray Show,* including Bob and Ray, knew exactly what would happen next during one of their performances. One night Audrey found herself standing on her head during the whole quarter hour of the show while Bob and Ray ignored her and did other things. When she applied for *The Honeymooners,* Gleason told her that she was too chic and stylish for a role as a bus driver's weary wife.

"When I was leaving Jackie's apartment after that interview," Audrey told me, "I remembered that I had once played a role as a frowsy housewife in a skit with Bob and Ray that they called 'The Bad Housekeeping Seal of Disapproval.' I said to my agent, Val Irving, who was with me, 'I wish I had a picture of myself in the costume and makeup I used in that Bad Housekeeping bit.' Val snapped his fingers and said he would send a photographer to my apartment the next morning. A few days later Val showed Jackie the picture of me in my cook-and-bottle-washer outfit. Jackie took one look at the picture and signed me up immediately for the Alice Kramdem part. Can you imagine that? No audition, no script reading. He just gave me the part after taking one look at that picture."

Audrey paused for a moment, thoughtfully, and then she smiled.

"So I went to work with Jackie," she said. "I got along fine with him, and with Art Carney and Joyce Randolph.

All of them are real pros. As you know, Jackie hates to rehearse. Sometimes, when we are doing the skit live, on the air, he finds out that he's running five minutes too long. He cuts lines of dialogue while we're doing the skit but we have no problem improvising with him. Well, about six months went by and Jackie never said a word to me about why or how he had picked me for the part. Then one day he asked me, out of the blue, if I knew how to fry chicken. I told him how I did it, what spices I used and so on. He said, 'Sounds good. Can you come over to my place tonight and fry some chicken?' I thought he might be having four or five people coming to dinner. When I got there, his place was jammed. In the kitchen, he had twenty chickens waiting for me. I cooked them. After everybody had eaten up the chickens, Jackie came out to the kitchen and said to me, 'Have you ever wondered why I hired you for the show last fall so quickly? Now I'll tell you why I picked you. I *knew*, the minute I looked at that picture of you, that you were a girl who could cook twenty chickens without getting excited.'"

I later wrote a magazine article about Audrey and her older sister, Jayne, another memorable M, entitled "The Meadows Sisters and How They Grew." It was an easy assignment; Audrey and Jayne were both entertaining talkers with many stories about their adventures as actresses on Broadway and in Hollywood before they both got into television. Jayne was then a panelist on the popular quiz show *I've Got a Secret*, and playing in various TV dramas and thrillers. She was later married to Steve Allen and appears with him often on television.

At the time that I interviewed them, the Meadows sisters were sharing an apartment in midtown Manhattan.

Both Jayne and Audrey were born in a town on the Yangtze River in China where their father, an Episcopal minister, was then serving as a missionary. When Jayne was seven years old and Audrey was five, their family moved to the small town of Sharon, Connecticut, where their father, the Reverend Francis Cotter, became the pastor of the local Episcopalian church. "We only knew a few words of English when we came to Connecticut," Audrey said. "In China, we talked nothing but Chinese. But in Connecticut we soon learned English, and neither of us have stopped talking English ever since. As teenagers, we started looking for acting jobs. I had been planning to go to Smith College, but Jayne was determined to be an actress. She said it was the only way to get out of Connecticut. She talked me into going on trips to New York with her when she was looking for stage work. We commuted with two women neighbors who had a flower business in New York and did missionary work with alcoholic bums on the Bowery. On the way to the city in the morning, their station wagon was loaded with manure for their flower shop, and on the trip home at night the car was loaded with a freshly picked collection of bleary-eyed stew bums. Jayne would describe to them in detail her interviews at Brock Pemberton's office or Chamberlain Brown's office, but they didn't seem to understand what she was talking about."

Audrey tells endless stories about Jayne. They range from the one about Jayne paying a woman fifteen dollars to teach her how to relax to the one about

Jayne traveling from New York to Hollywood on a train during World War II wearing a silver ring attached to her nose. The ring was supposed to protect her from allergies. She told a group of soldiers on the train that it was latest chic fashion in costume jewelry. Actually, it was designed by her doctor's butler.

"I was allergic to everything at that time," Jayne said. "I stopped being allergic when I signed a movie contract with Metro-Goldwyn-Mayer. They told me to change my name because Jayne Cotter didn't sound glamorous enough, so I changed it to Meadows, my grandmother's name. Audrey was then touring the South Pacific in a U.S.O. version of Mike Todd's musical *Mexican Hayride*. She caught malaria and stayed with me in California for almost two years while she was recovering. She changed her name to Meadows, too, because she is my sister. Then she landed a role in *High Button Shoes*, which led to *Top Banana* and *The Bob and Ray Show* and *The Honeymooners.*"

"Only a few weeks ago," Audrey said, "I was telling some stories about Jayne on a midnight disc jockey radio show in a nightclub. Two men sent a note to the disc jockey, Bill Williams. The note said, 'Get her to tell the one about her sister in the Turkish bath.' I didn't even know the men. I found out that at another restaurant, on another night, they heard me telling about Jayne at the Turkish bath while I was sitting with some friends at a nearby table. I told Bill Williams that I couldn't tell the one about the Turkish bath because it would take a half hour. I said, 'Instead, I'll tell you the one about Jayne and the man who claimed to be a radionic specialist.'"

After the broadcast, Audrey was approached by Phil Foster, the nightclub comedian. "Who wrote that stuff for you about your sister?" Foster asked. "I'd like to get him to do some material for me."

"Nobody wrote it," Audrey said. "I really have a sister named Jayne who does those things. If you don't believe me, come and visit us next Sunday afternoon and see for yourself."

The following Sunday, when Foster was sitting in the living room at the Meadows apartment, Jayne arrived, breathless, from a rehearsal. In the foyer, she dropped a suitcase of clothes that she had been wearing at the TV studio. During an hour of polite conversation, Jayne said little that was interesting. Foster stared at her impatiently. Then she leaped from her chair, screaming, "The blood is running all over my clothes!" She ran to her suitcase and threw it open. Later, when she calmed down, Jayne explained that she had carried home a large steak in the suitcase with her television costumes and she suddenly wondered if it had leaked.

Foster turned to Audrey and said, "I see what you mean."

When I was finishing my interviews with the Meadows sisters, I said to them, "Have you girls ever considered writing a book about yourselves?"

Jayne said, "A few years ago, when I wasn't busy, I actually did start to write a book about my life. I showed the script to a woman I know. She read a few pages of it. Then she looked at me, rather curiously, and she said, 'Have you ever been to a psychiatrist?'"

I was astonished when I learned that *The Power Broker*,

Robert Caro's lengthy and critical 1976 book about Robert Moses, had won a Pulitzer Prize. I first met Moses when he was organizing and bossing the 1964–1965 New York World's Fair. I found him to be one of the brightest, wittiest, and most sharply articulate talkers I have ever interviewed. When Caro's big book on Moses came out, I read it eagerly, expecting it to be filled with entertaining dialogues, but I could not find a laugh anywhere in its many pages. Later I read in a news story that Caro had signed a contract to write another long book about Lyndon Johnson. I don't know how anybody could possibly write a book about Lyndon Johnson without a few smiles in it, but if anybody could achieve that feat, it would be Caro.

Moses's casual conversation was full of entertaining, highly original wisecracks and anecdotes. He referred to red tape and bureaucratic doubletalk as chow mein or dry ice. Talking with me about the four years that he spent putting together the World's Fair, he said, "In my daily bouts with vainglorious foreign governments, giant corporations, and U.S. senators and big-talking promoters with shady credentials, I was often reminded of a state assemblyman from Brooklyn who wanted to put up a monument honoring John Ericsson, the builder of the Civil War ironclad *Monitor*, in that neighborhood. I was the city's park commissioner so I hired a sculptor to design a model and submitted it to the assemblyman for his approval. He sent the model back to me with its inscription revised. Ericsson's name had been removed to make room for the name of the assemblyman."

When Moses took over the management of plans for the fair, he was astounded to learn that it was originally designed as a single building, circular in shape, with all of its various exhibits and shows under one roof. He denounced the doughnut-shaped structure as "constipating and stultifying" and immediately began to plan a variety of exhibits housed in separate buildings. Moses, in turn, was then denounced by architects and art critics who charged that he was turning the fair into an unsightly hodgepodge.

"Needless to say, we survived that tempest in a martini," he said to me. "But for a while, we were held up as ignorant bums, shills, and dull-witted Boeotians because we failed to heed this advice from Olympus. In a fair like this, you've got to have plenty of variety. Five people, coming here from five different parts of the country, are looking for five different types of things. It's like the story Oliver Gogarty used to tell about George Moore taking his first trip to Palestine and meeting Thomas Cook on the ship. Cook invited Moore to be his guest on a sightseeing tour in the Holy Land, and asked him what sight there he would like to see first. 'I should think it would be the Church of the Holy Sepulchre,' Cook said.

"Moore shook his head firmly. 'No,' he said. 'First, I want to have one of your camels carry me to the place where the woman in the Bible was taken in adultery.'"

Moses was at his conversational best when he talked about Alfred E. Smith and other Tammany Hall political leaders whom he worked under as a public works builder. "Al Smith was a great witty talker," he said. "I still use one of his dismissal remarks when I am faced with a politician's self-seeking petition. Al would say, when he dismissed such a proposition, 'That's too much corned beef and cabbage to sell for a nickel.' Al Smith was the greatest man I ever knew. I'm a Republican, but I always got along fine with Tammany politicians, much better than I got along with Republican reformers. When Jimmy Walker was the mayor of New York, I tore down a house in Queens where he was keeping a lady friend, to make way for the Grand Central Parkway. Jimmy obligingly moved his love nest to another building, and a few years later, I tore down *that* building for the Cross Island Parkway, but Jimmy didn't take it personal. Do you remember Jimmy's favorite nightclub, the old Central Park Casino? Its prices were much too high and the place was too exclusive and swanky for a public-park concession, but the fellow who operated it refused to cut his prices. When I became the city's park commissioner, I closed the place. One night, very late, about two o'clock in the morning, the watchman at the Casino called me on the phone at my home and told me that Walker's men had a truck backed up to the Casino's door. I said to the watchman, 'Don't let anybody take any stuff out of there.' The watchman said to me, 'They're not taking stuff out. They're putting stuff back in!'"

One New York Democratic leader who never had a friendly relationship with Moses was Franklin D. Roosevelt. Back in the late 1920s, when Roosevelt was running for the governorship, he wanted his political aide and adviser, Louis McHenry Howe, to be appointed as secretary of the Taconic State Park Commission at five thousand dollars a year. Howe told Moses, who was then chairman of all the state parks, that he had no intention of working at the job; the salary was to help him financially while he devoted his full time to Roosevelt's political campaign. Moses went to Roosevelt and demanded Howe's removal from the park job. "I told him," Moses told me, "that if he wanted a valet, he had to pay him himself, not out of park funds."

Roosevelt never forgot the slight. During the Depression, when Roosevelt was in the White House, Moses was directing the construction of the Triborough Bridge for New York's Mayor Fiorello La Guardia, who was counting on a thirty-five-million-dollar grant from Roosevelt's federal PWA funds to finance the project. Roosevelt told La Guardia that he could not get the federal grant unless Moses was dropped from the job. A committee of prominent New York Democrats sent a spokesman to the White House to protest Moses's removal. Roosevelt threw up his hands and exclaimed, "Isn't the president of the United States entitled to at least one personal grudge?" Moses stayed in charge of the bridge building project.

"The Triborough Bridge was built all wrong," Moses told me. "In public works, you have to compromise now and then to get what you want. The bridge should have crossed the East River from Queens to Manhattan by way of Ward's Island at East 103rd Street. But an influential newspaper publisher with a lot of pull in Washington happened to own a lot of property around 125th Street and he wanted the bridge there. If we didn't do it his way, we wouldn't get the bridge. So the righteous Fiorello gave in. The Little Flower knew when he shouldn't try to push his piety too far. Better to go to Manhattan by way of 125th Street than not to go at all."

Moses recalled with a smile the opening-day ceremony at the bridge on July 11, 1936, with Roosevelt and his secretary of the interior and director of public works, Harold Ickes, as the guests of honor and main speakers. Moses acted as the master of ceremonies but, at Roosevelt's request, he was asked not to introduce the president or Ickes. During their speeches, Roosevelt and Ickes never mentioned Moses, who was sitting a few feet from them on the platform while they talked, and neither of them spoke to him at any time during the festivities.

"Naturally, the reporters asked me later about the silent treatment," Moses said. "I recalled and quoted Samuel Johnson's famous letter to Lord Chesterfield, who was supposed to be Johnson's patron and financial supporter while Sam was writing his famous dictionary. His Lordship, of course, never gave Johnson a shilling but he was taking bows as his sponsor. I said that the letter was one of the finest pieces of polite vituperation in English literature. In it, as you'll recall, Johnson points out that he wrote the dictionary 'without one act of assistance, one word of encouragement or one smile of favor' from Chesterfield. I felt the same way about Roosevelt while we were building the bridge, but, after all, the important thing was the completion of the bridge, not how I felt about Roosevelt while it was being completed."

Moses's greatest achievement as a public works commissioner was his direction of the building of the Verrazano-Narrows Bridge across the narrow stretch of New York Harbor between Brooklyn and Staten Island. It is the highest and longest suspension bridge in the world, with towers as tall as a seventy-story skyscraper and a clear span of 4,260 feet, sixty feet longer than San Francisco's Golden Gate Bridge. Because of its great length, the engineers had to allow for the curvature of the earth's surface when they located the bridge's two towers. Both of the towers at their base are exactly perpendicular to the surface of the earth but at the top they are 1 5/8 inches farther apart than at the base.

Moses told me that he liked everything about the bridge except its name. "It's too fancy sounding and too Italian," he said. "This is America, not Italy. I wanted to call it simply the Staten Island Bridge because that's where it goes. But the Italian Historical Society in Brooklyn insisted on calling it after Verrazano and the state legislators backed them up. Who was Verrazano anyway? He was a Florentine explorer and mapmaker who wasn't even working for Italy when he claimed the discovery of New York Harbor in 1524. He claimed it for the king of France, who paid for his trip. The people who named the bridge after him didn't even know for sure how to spell his name. They didn't know if it had one z or two, and they finally had to send somebody to Italy to find out that it was usually spelled with one z, although sometimes it had two z's."

Robert Caro's book, charging him with impatient disregard for government red tape and with arrogance, left him undisturbed. "You can't make an omelette without breaking a few eggshells," he said.

Bernard McDonough is one of America's most unusual big business executives, a man of plain tastes who always answers the telephone in his office himself and insists that all of the top bosses in his vast industrial complex must do likewise. He feels that the common business office practice of having a secretary ask a telephone caller to identify himself is the height of rudeness. "Answer the phone yourself, no matter who may be calling," he tells his executives. "Never give anybody the impression that he may be too unimportant for you to talk with him." He also frowns on plush executive office suites, company-owned cars, and other tax-gimmick corporate expense-account luxuries. When he checks into a hotel, he waves aside the bellboy and carries his bag to his room, unlocking the door himself. "I don't need anybody to show me where my room is, or how to open its window," he says.

McDonough owns and operates an industrial corporation which includes sand, gravel, cement and concrete companies, the Endicott Johnson shoe manufacturing company, and a shovel factory in his hometown, Parkersburg, West Virginia, where he worked on his first job in 1918 at the age of fifteen for $10.50 a week. Later he moved to Washington where he worked his way through Georgetown University and its law school driving a taxicab. Then he decided not to practice law. Instead, he became involved in construction work, earned several million dollars, and bought the shovel factory from Boston's Ames family for two million dollars. Under McDonough's direction, it became the largest shovel factory in the world, with sawmills in six states turning out its wooden shovel handles.

In 1962, McDonough traveled in the western part of Ireland, where his grandparents were born. He had read about the serious unemployment there which had forced more than four hundred thousand young people to emigrate during the previous ten years and he was planning to start some kind of an industrial business in Ireland to create jobs. For various reasons, mainly Ireland's lack of iron ore, he gave up the idea. While he was at Shannon Airport waiting for a plane to New York, Brendan O'Regan, the airport's manager, mentioned to him that the nearby Dromoland Castle, one of Ireland's biggest palatial private residences, was for sale.

As a youngster in West Virginia, McDonough had often heard his grandfather, Patrick McDonough, talk about Dromoland Castle. Pat McDonough had walked past Dromoland on his hike from his family's home in Galway to the ship at Queenstown that took him to New York in 1862. He had stopped to admire the castle. O'Regan mentioned that it was still the ancestral home of Sir Donough O'Brien, the sixteenth baron of Inchiquin, whose family were given their British title and most of the land in County Clare when they pledged allegiance to King Henry VIII and his Church of England in 1543. As wealthy landlords, the barons of Inchiquin had lived in splendor on the rents of tenant farmers until Ireland won its independence from Great Britain in 1922. Then they were forced to sell their tenant farms and lost their income.

"So now Lord Inchiquin has finally decided that he can't afford the castle and he's trying to sell it," O'Regan said to McDonough. "Why not take a look at it? It's only ten minutes from here, and you've got more than an hour before your plane leaves. I'll drive you over there."

McDonough told me later that he knew he was going

to buy the castle when he took his first look at it. "I had no idea what I was going to do with it," he said. "But I said to myself, nobody could build a building like this today for any amount of money. I *had* to buy it."

The main structure of the castle, a huge and stately Gothic-styled gray stone building with more than seventy rooms and with four high turreted towers on its roof, stands on a hillside above walled gardens, rolling green meadows, and a blue lake. Completed in 1826, after fifteen years of construction work, it is the third castle built on the site by the Inchiquin lords. Behind it is an older quadrangular wing, built in 1736, with twenty-nine more rooms, called Queen Anne's Court. In the old luxurious years of the Inchiquin lords and ladies, Queen Anne's Court was the castle's servants' quarters. One of its rooms had a ceiling two stories high. McDonough learned later that it had been used exclusively for drying laundry.

Lord Inchiquin was waiting on the front steps of the castle to welcome McDonough and O'Regan when they arrived. McDonough asked the landlord how long his family had lived at Dromoland. "About a thousand years," the lord said. He explained that his ancestral namesake, Donough O'Brien, son of King Brian Boru, had ruled that part of Ireland in the eleventh century but the first of the three Dromoland castles was not built until 1686.

"Donough?" McDonough remarked with interest. "That's *my* name."

A few minutes later, when Lord Inchiquin was show-ing the visitors the castle's front hallway, McDonough asked how much he was asking for the castle's two buildings and its gardens. The lord named a price. McDonough said, "I'll take it."

Brendan O'Regan said to me later, "Lord Inchiquin was so surprised I thought he was about to faint. In Ireland, the selling of a small house usually takes at least six months of talk and haggling. Here was a famous castle being sold for the first time in its history, and it was all over in a flash."

The price finally agreed upon, when three hundred acres of surrounding land and fishing and hunting rights to the rest of the fifteen-hundred-acre estate were added later to the transaction, was around $600,000.

"But that was only for starters," McDonough says. "Now that I had bought the castle, I wondered what I was going to do with it. Then I remembered why I had made that trip to Ireland—to make jobs for young people. It dawned on me that turning the castle and Queen Anne's Court into a hotel for tourists with about one hundred rooms in it would certainly create a lot of jobs. So at the age of fifty-nine, I found myself getting into the hotel business for the first time in my life."

He also found himself spending more than a million dollars turning the castle into a hotel with a central heating system and sixty-seven bathrooms for sixty-seven new guest rooms. In Dromoland's grand old days, when the Inchiquin lords and ladies often entertained crowds of British nobility at pheasant-shooting parties, the castle had only two bathrooms and no heat except from fireplaces. During the winter and spring of 1963, McDonough had four hundred and eighty-five skilled laborers at work inside the building—carpenters, electricians, painters, plumbers, masons, and steam fitters.

At one time, there were sixty-five painters on the pay-roll. Another crew of a hundred gardeners and foresters worked outside on the grounds, pruning trees, land-scaping, and laying out the castle's new nine-hole golf course. Queen Anne's Court was gutted inside and rebuilt with twenty-nine new guest rooms.

McDonough was astonished to learn that the castle had no architectural plan or blueprint showing how it was built. This meant that he had to direct the work himself, instead of hiring a contractor to do it, because there was no way of knowing what work had to be done in order to install the electric wiring, heating, and plumbing for the new guest rooms.

"We had to feel our way along," he said, "guessing how thick the walls were and wondering what was be-hind them. Some of the walls turned out to be five feet thick, and so solid that we had to run plumbing pipes outside the building. We were always finding fireplace chimneys where we least expected them. Instead of running straight up to the roof, like American chim-neys, the fireplace chimneys in an old Irish castle curve and twist and slant every which-way before they get to the roof—and there were hundreds of chimneys in the walls at Dromoland."

American construction men, brought to Ireland by McDonough to supervise the renovation work, were fascinated by the design of Dromoland's water-supply system, big enough to provide water for a whole town. Water was pumped uphill to a reservoir from deep wells in a valley three miles away. Power for the pumping was supplied by a water wheel, turned by water diverted from a nearby river. Then water flowed downhill from the reservoir to the castle propelled only by the force of gravity, so strong in the downhill-sloping pipes that Lord Inchiquin had used it to provide power for a sawmill. The original water system worked so well that it was left unchanged for Dromoland Castle's first year as a hotel. Then it was replaced by a modern electric pump.

During the reconstruction work, McDonough was on the telephone constantly, ordering or tracing a shipment of plumbing fixtures from New York and trying to keep in touch with his company's business in West Virginia. He became so irritated by Ireland's slow and lackadaisical government-owned telephone service that he offered to buy the telephone system so that he could put it into efficient operation. "Then the thing that really got me mad," he said later, "was that the government took six months before it decided to turn down my offer."

Making the renovation work more complicated was McDonough's determination to get the whole job completed within six months, between January and June 1963, so that Dromoland would be ready to receive guests at the start of that summer's tourist season. "Six months?" one of the Irish workers said to him. "Are you forgetting that when we built this castle, without all these new bathrooms and no electric wiring and no heating pipes, it took us fifteen years?"

But McDonough met his self-imposed deadline. Toward the end of the work, painters, plumbers, and carpenters were often working together in one room. As soon as the carpeting was put down, new furniture was rushed in on top of it. Before the work started, during the previous December, Carlton Varney of the

Dorothy Draper interior decorating firm made photographs and then sketches of each room, showing how it would look. When the reconstruction work was finished, the specified furnishings, bought in nearby Limerick, were put into it. Nothing had to be changed.

When McDonough was hiring a staff of eighty employees to manage and operate the new hotel, he learned that Ireland had no training school for young people interested in the hotel business. He built the 126-room Shannon International Hotel at Shannon Airport for that purpose. Young men and women who were trained in on-the-job management and accounting at the airport hotel are now employed in hotels all over Ireland. McDonough also built the attractive American-style motel-type Clare Inn on the Dromoland estate's grounds, overlooking its golf course, and another resort hotel near Limerick, which he later sold.

Discussing his hotel business adventure recently, Bernard McDonough said, "I went to Ireland to see if I could give Ireland a little help, and Ireland helped me. I'm getting up into my late seventies, an age when other men collect paintings or play golf. I've tried golf, but after two or three holes I think about something connected with my work and I walk off the course, looking for a telephone. I like to work. At a time in my life when my industrial companies were more or less running themselves, I found in Ireland a completely new and interesting kind of worthwhile work, just what I needed. Working at something new and different is an experience that I highly recommend to everybody."

Besides, there is a certain satisfaction in owning a famous castle that your own Irish grandfather admired from outside its gate when he was making his way to America as a penniless emigrant more than a hundred years ago.

5

THE KENNEDYS

In 1928 SINCLAIR LEWIS WROTE A QUICKLY FOR-
gotten novel entitled *The Man Who Knew Coolidge.*
Some people in Blue Point, Long Island, where I live,
think of me as the man who knew Kennedy because I
have written two books and several magazine articles
about President John F. Kennedy and other members
of his family. "You knew President Kennedy," the local
vacuum-cleaner repair man said to me a while ago.
"Was there really anything going on between him and
Marilyn Monroe?"

"Who knows?" I said. "A newspaper in Dublin says
that so far three hundred and seventy-five Irish women
have confessed that they had intimate relations with
President Kennedy during the four days that he spent
in Ireland in 1963."

The vacuum-cleaner man said, "But I saw a picture
of Marilyn Monroe dancing at one of Kennedy's birthday parties. It was in *Time* magazine."

I pointed out that the editors of *Time* had neglected to mention in the caption that the birthday party, where the picture of Marilyn was snapped, was a charitable fund-raising event in Madison Square Garden. Along with Kennedy, there was a crowd of fifteen thousand other people in the hall while she was doing the dance. A few months after that party, in 1962, I went to Boston to write an article about Edward M. Kennedy's political baptism, his first campaign for the United States Senate. Steve Smith, the Kennedys' brother-in-law, was managing Teddy's campaign. I said to Steve, "Everybody in New York is saying that Jack is friendly with Marilyn Monroe."

Smith seemed surprised. "Jack?" he said. "I thought Bobby was the one who was friendly with Marilyn Monroe."

While Marilyn had not been his companion, it was true that President Kennedy hated to be alone. During the summer nights when he was in the White House and when Jackie and the children were at Hyannis Port, he asked Dave Powers, his close friend and staff aide, to sit with him in the executive mansion's upstairs living quarters while he worked and listened to old recordings of dance tunes from the thirties and forties — "The Very Thought of You," "Beyond the Blue Horizon," "Stardust," and "Body and Soul." Dave would stay around, yawning and drinking the president's Heineken, until after the president undressed and tucked himself into bed and said, "Good night, pal." Then Dave would turn off the lights and return to his own home and family in McLean, Virginia.

"I used to call myself 'John's other wife,'" Dave recalled recently. "Those nights when Jackie was at the Cape, I sat with the president every night from Monday to Thursday, and, despite what you've been reading lately, I never saw anybody else in the house except the agent from the Secret Service who was on duty in the downstairs hall."

You might ask how about Dave's wife and children, alone in Virginia all those nights, and that would be a good question. Kennedy had a conspicuous disregard for the domestic lives of his associates. A check on the number of his staff members whose marriages broke up during his 1960 campaign, or while he was in the White House, such as Ted Sorensen and Pierre Salinger, might be surprising. Shortly before the start of that campaign, in August, Dave Powers was allowed a week off to visit his wife, Jo, and their newly born daughter, Diane. The next time Dave saw Diane, when he came home to vote in Massachusetts on Election Day in November, she was three months old. However, as busy as he was after the election, Kennedy did spend a Saturday night having dinner alone with Jo and Dave at his father's home in Palm Beach and apologized to Jo for Dave's long absence.

"When he put his hand on my shoulder," Jo said later, "and said to me, 'You know I couldn't have done it without Dave,' I was actually so happy and thrilled that I almost forgot about those three months I had gone through alone with a new baby on my hands."

Jack Kennedy, of course, was powerfully attractive to women, even long before he became a glamorous public figure. A friend of Clark Gable's once said that when he walked along Fifth Avenue in New York with

Gable, women of all ages, recognizing the film star, would stop dead in their tracks and gasp. It was the same with Kennedy. I remember him creating a stir on a plane, in 1959, that seems hard to believe when I recall it.

It was a late-night flight from New York to Los Angeles. Most of the passengers, other than Kennedy and myself, were the airline's stewardesses, who were returning to California after taking a course of training in the East on the new big jets, which were then beginning to go into service. Kennedy and I sat down together and began to talk; I had arranged to travel with him to Los Angeles because I was writing a series of magazine articles about him and I had found that the only time he could carry on a long conversation was on a long plane trip when he had nothing else to do. While we talked, I noticed that a large group of the stewardesses, about twenty of them, were quietly gathering around us, all of them staring at Kennedy. Some of them were sitting or kneeling on nearby seats and others were leaning on the backs of seats but all of them were watching Kennedy intently. None of them spoke or appeared to be listening to Kennedy. They sat and stared at him for more than an hour without moving or making a sound. Now and then, Kennedy glanced at the pretty girls, smiled, and went on talking to me calmly, as if we were alone. The audience of enraptured, silent stewardesses did not bother him in the least. Finally, somewhere over the Midwest, a few of the girls began to drift away to find a place to sleep and then others left, after taking a long last look. When Kennedy decided to turn in and get some rest—

the slower prop planes had berths in those days—a couple of the stewardesses were still staring at him, sorry to see him go.

In his younger days as a bachelor congressman, Jack Kennedy had no trouble making dates with some of the most famous beauties of those years and many of the less famous ones. Gene Tierney says that she had a romance with him on Cape Cod in the summer of 1947 after she was separated from her first husband, Oleg Cassini. "I think maybe we had about ten dates," Gene recalled recently. "He was very attractive, more so as a young man than he was later on. He had the most beautiful eyes."

Rumors that Kennedy was involved romantically during the early 1950s with Grace Kelly, long before she became Princess Grace of Monaco, are doubtful. Ray O'Connell, a close friend of the Kennedys, says that Jack met Miss Kelly only once before he became president. That was on a night in the winter of 1957 when he was recovering from serious spinal surgery in a hospital in New York.

"We were trying to cheer Jack up," O'Connell said later. "Grace Kelly was a good friend of mine. I talked her into getting dressed up in a nurse's uniform and we sneaked her one night into Jack's hospital room, where no visitors were allowed. When Jack opened his eyes and saw Grace Kelly sitting beside his bed, he thought he was dreaming. But he was hardly strong enough to shake hands with her. He couldn't even talk."

The next time Kennedy saw Grace Kelly was in the White House when she was a princess, paying him a formal visit. Pictures taken at the reception show that

Princess Grace seemed to be having a hard time trying to take her eyes off the president, but their conversation consisted of a discussion of women's clothes.

"I see that you're wearing a Givenchy dress," the president said.

"Yes," said the princess. "How did you know it was a Givenchy?"

"I ought to know a Givenchy when I see one," the president said. "I've paid for enough of them."

Jack Kennedy's reputation as a Lothario, quite obscure during his lifetime, never seemed to give him or his family much concern. His father, usually a fierce protector of the Kennedy public image, took such gossip lightly. The first time that I talked alone with Joseph P. Kennedy about his son, he said, "You'll hear all kinds of things about this fellow. You'll hear that he has Addison's disease and you'll hear that he's been mixed up with a lot of girls. Why wouldn't he be mixed up with girls, the way they throw themselves at him? As I was saying only the other day to Clare Boothe Luce, I said to her, 'Clare, I wish I had his leavings.'"

People who worked closely with Jack Kennedy on Capitol Hill and in his political campaigns and in the White House agree that he was too busy pursuing his career during those years to have time for the extracurricular activities now credited to him. "If he had been that busy with girls," one of his campaign managers says, "he never would have made it to the White House. He got there by working at politics eighteen hours a day, almost every day, for fourteen years, and, after he got there, he worked around the clock. That left him little time for anything else. Or certainly not as much time for anything else as they now claim he gave to something else."

Even in his bachelor days as a young congressman, Kennedy spent his weekends making political speeches. His friend John Galvin recalled seeing him alone in Boston at that time on a pleasant autumn Saturday afternoon when the Harvard-Princeton football game was being played at Princeton.

"I knew how much Jack wanted to be at that football game," Galvin said. "There were any number of gorgeous girls who would have dropped everything to go to Princeton with him that day, and he knew it. I asked him what the hell he was doing hanging around in Boston on a beautiful Saturday when he could have been living it up at the game with a nice number hanging on his arm, and driving into New York afterward for a dinner at '21.' You know what he said? He said he had to make a speech at a plumbers union dinner in the South End that night."

If Jack Kennedy had a widespread interest in girls, it probably stemmed from his curiosity, which seemed to be his outstanding characteristic. He always wanted to find out everything about anybody he met. The first time I met him, at a Clover Club dinner in Boston in 1953, he quizzed me at length about how much money I was able to earn as a freelance writer — not just round figures, but specifically how much did I get for each piece of writing that I had done recently. Six years later, on a campaign trip, I was sitting with him and Mary McGrory, the *Washington Star* columnist, in a small plane flying from Sacramento to Los Angeles. Kennedy, an avid comic strip reader, was hidden behind the comics section of a Sunday newspaper, engrossed in Captain Midnight. Mary asked me about my wife, who had gone to college with her in Boston. Kennedy's head came out from behind the comics section. He wanted to know how Mary happened to know my wife. What college did they go to? What was my wife's maiden name? Mary Dunn? Was that the same Dunn family who operated a furniture moving and storage warehouse business in the Jamaica Plain section of Boston? The next evening we were at a Democratic cocktail party at a seaside place near Monterey. Kennedy, talking with some local dignitaries, saw me out of the corner of his eye laughing with two middle-aged women who were recalling their student days at Wellesley College. In a flash, he was standing beside me, smiling at the ladies.

"What's so funny?" he asked. "What are you people talking about?"

He was afraid that he might be missing something interesting.

A writer who approached the Kennedys to do a magazine article or a book about them was checked out carefully, especially if he was working for a Republican publisher like Gardner Cowles of *Look* magazine. When Jack Kennedy was becoming a prominent presidential candidate in 1958, the editors of *Look* asked me to write a series of articles about him and his family. At that time, Bobby and Jack Kennedy were both involved in warfare with Jimmy Hoffa and his Republican-allied Teamsters Union. Bobby, as the chief counsel of Senator John L. McClellan's Senate Rackets Committee, and Jack, as a prominent member of that committee, were both starring in the widely televised hearings on Hoffa's union activities, which Hoffa referred to sarcastically as "McClellan's Playhouse 90." A close friend of mine, who was also a friend of Hoffa's and a public relations counselor of the Teamsters Union, asked me to have lunch with him.

"I hear you're writing some pieces for *Look* about Jack Kennedy," Hoffa's man said. "Is it going to be a hatchet job?"

"Who wants to know?" I asked. "Jimmy Hoffa?"

"No, not Jimmy," he said. "Jack Kennedy wants to know. Jack asked me to find out from you whether *Look* is planning to do a hatchet job on him."

I was so astonished that I almost swallowed the rocks in my Scotch. Jimmy Hoffa and the Kennedys were supposed to be bitter enemies. Of all the people in New York and Boston whom Jack could have selected as an emissary to sound me out about how I was going to write about him, he had picked one from Hoffa's own payroll. Later on, when Kennedy was reassured that I had not been assigned to belittle him and he and I became frank-speaking friends, I questioned him about his odd choice of an intermediary. He laughed, and said, "I figured you'd give him a straighter answer than you might give to Peter Lawford."

Lawford was then married to Jack's sister Pat. They lived in a palatial beach home at Santa Monica built by Louis B. Mayer. The master bedroom had walls, floor, and ceiling all made from solid marble. When Jack was campaigning in Wisconsin during the 1960 primaries, he was dismayed to learn that Lawford was much better known in that state than he was. Local Democrat leaders were introducing him to voters as "Peter Lawford's brother-in-law." Most of the Kennedys liked Lawford, but Joe Kennedy, the patriarch of the family, was not thrilled to have one of his daughters married to a Hollywood star whose close friends were Frank Sinatra, Dean Martin, and Sammy Davis, Jr. Jack told me that when Lawford asked Joe's permission to marry Pat, the ambassador, as everyone called Joe, stared at Peter and said to him, "If there's anyone I think I'd hate as a son-in-law, it's an actor, and if there's anyone I think I'd hate worse than an actor as a son-in-law, it's a British actor."

The ambassador was the most colorful personality in the Kennedy family, a blunt, outspoken, and vigorous man who went horseback riding every morning and played golf every afternoon until he was crippled by a stroke in 1961 at the age of seventy-three. He seemed to know everybody. One day when Dave Powers was eating lunch with him at Hyannis Port, the butler came into the dining room and said, "Mr. Kennedy, the cardinal is on the telephone." Joe said, "Which one?" Among his close friends were Herbert Hoover, Henry Luce, Westbrook Pegler, Richard Cardinal Cushing, and Arthur Krock, the longtime chief of the Washington bureau of the *New York Times*. His long list of bitter enemies included Eleanor Roosevelt and Harry Truman. I spent a memorable day talking with the ambassador on his cabin cruiser off Cape Cod in the spring of 1959 while I was working on the series of *Look* articles about Jack and the Kennedy family. He asked me if I had yet talked with many of Jack's friends.

"Yes," I said, "and to some of his enemies, too."

"Jack's enemies wouldn't have much to tell you," Joe said. "Now if you talked to some of *my* enemies, that would be something else again. They could tell you plenty."

I was very much surprised to learn that Joe Kennedy still had a high regard for Franklin D. Roosevelt, who had a bitter disagreement with Kennedy in 1941 when Joe, as the American ambassador in London, was strongly opposed to Roosevelt's plan to give military aid to Britain. "We'll only be left holding the bag," Kennedy said at that time, prompting Roosevelt to remove him from his post at the Court of Saint James. Up to that time, Roosevelt and Kennedy had been close friends and frequent dinner companions. Kennedy had been a prominent administrator in the New Deal, first as the organizer of the Securities Exchange Commission and later as chairman of the Maritime Commission when he settled $73,000,000 in shipping claims against the government for $750,000 and threw a punch at Harry Bridges, the maritime union leader, during a heated argument in a hotel room. Before Roosevelt decided to run for a third term in 1940, Kennedy had been widely mentioned as a possible Democratic candidate for president in that year's election.

"I didn't care too much for some of the people around him, but Roosevelt was a good man," the ambassador said while he was mixing gin rickeys on his cruiser anchored off Craigville Beach. "He and I had a lot of laughs. You know, he appointed me as his ambassador in London in 1938 without bothering to mention it to Cordell Hull, who only happened to be the secretary of state at that time. Then Roosevelt arranged a meeting in the White House so that Hull could get a look at me."

Kennedy poured the gin rickeys and gave me an entertaining account of the meeting. When he sat down with Roosevelt and Hull, Joe mentioned a luncheon conversation that he had had a few days earlier with Arthur Krock. Roosevelt had recently appointed Hugo Black to the Supreme Court. The appointment had been followed by the sensational disclosure that Black, in his younger days in Alabama, had been a member of the Ku Klux Klan. Discussing that news with Kennedy, Krock remarked that he was shocked that Black had accepted a seat on the Supreme Court without letting Roosevelt know about his Klan membership.

Roosevelt said to Kennedy, with Cordell Hull listening, "Joe, when Krock said that to you, what did you say to Krock?"

"I said to him," Kennedy said, "'If Marlene Dietrich asked you to go to bed with her, would you tell her you weren't much good in bed?'"

Recalling the scene on his boat off Cape Cod twenty years later, the ambassador said, "Roosevelt collapsed laughing. Hull sat there staring at me with his mouth open. He must have been saying to himself, 'My God, is this the kind of a guy we're going to send to the Court of Saint James?'"

While the ambassador and I had been talking at the stern of the boat, Jack and Jackie Kennedy and Rose Kennedy's niece, Ann Gargan, had been sunning themselves on the front deck. They came back and joined us for a clam chowder lunch. I told the Kennedys about a discussion of the duties of the presidency that I had

had with Senator Eugene McCarthy a few days earlier in Washington. To my astonishment, McCarthy had said that the president's work is not too demanding. The government more or less runs itself, he argued, and all that is needed in the White House is a leader who can rally the people in a time of crisis, inspiring and encouraging them and holding them together.

"You must be kidding," Jack said. "In other words, all we need is a reassuring speechmaker? Was he serious?"

"Baloney!" the ambassador said. "I've seen the president's job from the inside, and I know what it requires. In the presidency, you need a man with both the wide factual knowledge and the courage to make the right decisions and to make them stick. The biggest part of the president's job is stepping into fights between the secretary of state and the secretary of defense, between the secretary of the treasury and the Federal Reserve System, between the secretary of the army and the secretary of the navy, and putting his fist down and deciding what is going to be done—calmly and objectively, basing his decision on his own careful study of the issues, without taking anybody's word for it, and without being influenced by his own personal feelings. The labor people raised a stink when I was chairman of the Maritime Commission and I ordered a bunch of seamen on an American ship in South America to be put in irons because they pulled a strike on their captain. I did it because the strike had nothing to do with the way the ship was being run. They were striking in sympathy with a South American longshoremen's fight that had nothing to do with us. I asked Roosevelt what he would do if I was in the wrong. He said, 'If you're wrong, you'll have to swing for it.' He was absolutely right, of course. Jack has that calm and objective judgment. If he didn't have that in him, I wouldn't vote for him."

Our talk turned to a subject that the Kennedys loved to discuss: the shenanigans of the old Boston Irish politicians, such as John F. ("Honey Fitz") Fitzgerald, James Michael Curley, and Mike Ward, Curley's henchman, who became a close friend of Jack's during his first campaign for Congress in Boston in 1946. We exchanged stories about the nonstop talking of Honey Fitz, Rose Kennedy's father and onetime mayor of Boston who almost defeated the first Henry Cabot Lodge in a race for the United States Senate in 1916. Honey Fitz did not live quite long enough to see his grandson Jack beat Lodge's grandson and namesake in a fight for the same Senate seat in 1952. Honey Fitz talked endlessly to anybody he happened to meet about a wide variety of subjects—the great Boston fire of 1872; his boyhood experiences of listening to literary conversations of Ralph Waldo Emerson, Henry Wadsworth Longfellow, and James Russell Lowell at the Old Corner Bookstore; flying with Claude Graham-White, the British aviator, in 1911. I told the Kennedys about how Edwin O'Connor, author of the Boston political novel *The Last Hurrah*, happened to encounter Honey Fitz one night while walking in the North End of Boston. Fitzgerald had never seen O'Connor before but he grabbed the surprised writer by the arm, pointed at the nearby Faneuil Hall and recited its history. "Now come with me, young man," Honey Fitz said, "and I'll show you the house where I was born." Still chatting, he led O'Connor upstairs in a tenement house on Hanover Street and opened the door of an apartment where the mother of an Italian family was preparing dinner. "Good evening, Mrs. Genaro," Honey Fitz said to the housewife, who seemed accustomed to such visits. "I am showing this young man the home where I was born. Pay no attention to us." Then he led O'Connor through the apartment, and into each of its bedrooms, pointing out where he slept as a child and where his parents slept, and where he did his studying while attending Boston Latin School.

We talked about some of the Fitzgerald stories recalled by his political adversary, the colorful James Michael Curley, in Curley's autobiography, *I'd Do It Again!* Curley was teaching Irish immigrants civics, to prepare them for citizenship tests, when Fitzgerald was riding high in politics as the mayor of Boston and a candidate for the Senate. Curley asked one of his students who made the laws of the nation.

"John F. Fitzgerald," the Irishman said.

"Who makes the laws in Massachusetts?" Curley asked.

"John F. Fitzgerald."

"Who is the president of the United States?"

"John F. Fitzgerald."

Curley added, "And if I hadn't stopped the man there, I'm sure he would have gone on to tell me that John F. drove the snakes out of Ireland and discovered America."

Joe Kennedy laughed and said, "After I got to be a big shot in Washington and the ambassador in London, the Boston papers were still referring to me as John F. Fitzgerald's son-in-law."

"Curley was really a character," Jack said. "One day Grandpa and my brother Teddy were waiting for me outside the apartment building on Bowdoin Street where I was living after I got elected to Congress. We were going to drive to the Cape together for the weekend. Teddy was going to Milton Academy and he was carrying his schoolbooks in a green flannel bag. I was late showing up as usual, and Teddy asked Grandpa to hold his bag of books while he went into the drugstore in the building and got himself an ice-cream soda. While Grandpa is standing there with the bag of books, Curley comes marching along the street. He took one look at the bag, nodded to Grandpa, and said to him, 'Still carrying your burglar's tools.' Grandpa was furious."

I turned to Joe Kennedy and said to him, "Your father-in-law and Curley weren't always enemies. I just found a story that was in the *New York Times* two months before the Democratic convention in 1932 which said that you and Honey Fitz brought Curley down to Warm Springs for a meeting with Roosevelt."

"We had a lot of laughs with Roosevelt and Curley that day," the ambassador said. "Fitz and Curley were the only Democrats in Massachusetts who were for Roosevelt before the convention in thirty-two. Everybody else in the state was still for Al Smith, as they had been in twenty-eight. One day at a political meeting in Boston, Fred Mansfield blasted Curley for being disloyal to Smith. Curley roared at him, 'And where were you, Freddy, when I was campaigning for Al Smith in

1928? You were sitting at home, with your little red slippers on, reading *The Ladies' Home Journal*!' Curley couldn't go to the convention as a delegate from Massachusetts that year because the delegation was solidly committed to Smith. So Curley showed up on the floor at Chicago as the chairman of the delegation from Puerto Rico and made a big speech when he announced that he was casting Puerto Rico's six votes for Roosevelt. After Roosevelt was elected, Curley told everybody that he was going to be the secretary of the navy. But the only job Roosevelt offered him was the ambassadorship to Poland. Curley went berserk and turned it down. He went to Jim Farley to complain about it, and he got into Fairley's office by telling Farley's secretary that he was Senator Pat Harrison. You know, there was a lot of talk in those days about the Polish Corridor, meaning that Poland was a corridor of freedom between Germany and Russia. Farley said to Curley, 'Why don't you take the job, Jim? Think of the money you could make putting a pavement on the Polish Corridor!'"

A recently shown rerun of the 1960 television debates between Kennedy and Richard Nixon reminded me of the amused contempt that Kennedy had for Nixon when we talked about him on the ambassador's boat that day in 1959. Kennedy's dislike for Nixon had nothing to do with the differences in their political views. He admired, and enjoyed talking with, such conservative Republicans as Barry Goldwater and General Douglas MacArthur. Nixon was simply too dull and too coy for Kennedy's taste. "When you compare Nixon and Goldwater," he said, "Goldwater seems like Abraham Lincoln." Kennedy went on to make a memorable comment about Nelson Rockefeller, who was then the new, popular, and not yet divorced governor of New York. Kennedy said that if he was able to get the Democratic nomination, he could be beaten by the combination of anti-Catholic prejudice in the Bible Belt of the South and the Midwest and an attractive Republican like Rockefeller.

"But the Republicans haven't got sense enough to nominate Rockefeller," Kennedy added. "They'll nominate Nixon. Against Nixon, I might even get a few votes from the Ku Klux Klan."

While the ambassador and Jack talked politics with me, Jackie Kennedy listened and said little. An avid reader of history, Jackie gave her husband many of the historical anecdotes and quotations that he used in his speeches. But she had no interest in current party politics and political gossip. A prominent Democrat once asked her where the party should hold its 1960 convention. "Acapulco," Jackie said with a straight face. She flatly refused to play the role of a politician's carefully tactful wife or to be charming, for political reasons, to people she found dull or irritating. A Washingon lawyer recalls listening to a sharp exchange between Jack and Jackie at a party when she wasn't putting herself out to be nice to some of the important people in the room.

"The trouble with you, Jackie," he said, "is that you don't care enough about what people think of you."

"The trouble with you, Jack," she said, "is that you care too much about what people think of you."

After the 1960 election, Jackie remarked to a friend that she dreaded moving into the White House. "I've hardly seen Jack in the last five years," she said. "Caroline and I have said so many goodbyes to him at airports that her first word, when she started to talk, was 'plane.' Now that he's president, I suppose we won't see him at all."

But their short stay in the White House brought the Kennedys together in a closer intimacy than they had ever enjoyed in their previous seven years of married life. For the first time, he found himself living and working under the same roof, eating lunch and often dinner alone with his wife, entertaining his children in his office. It was a whole new experience for both him and his wife and they loved it.

Jackie also found the White House an exciting and fascinating place to live. She discovered long-forgotten pieces of valuable furniture stored in the basement, pulled them out and had them refinished to replace cheap reproductions upstairs. One of her finds was a magnificent desk that Queen Victoria presented to President Rutherford B. Hayes in 1878. It was made from timbers of a famous British warship, the H.M.S. *Resolute*. Jackie had it moved into the president's oval office, much to his delight. She also opened up the chimneys of the first-floor fireplaces, which had been closed and unused for many years, and built log fires in them.

When the *New York Times* reported that fires were burning in the White House's fireplaces, I was visiting Rachel and Sherman Adams at their home in New Hampshire, helping him with the writing of his memoirs of the Eisenhower White House. Mrs. Adams beamed with pleasure when she saw the story. "I'm a Republican," she said, "but let me tell you I'm certainly glad that *somebody* finally got some fires lit in those fireplaces!"

At everything she did, whether it was arranging with André Malraux the first American exhibit of the *Mona Lisa*, or converting President Eisenhower's solarium on the top floor of the White House into a pre-kindergarten classroom for Caroline and her friends, Jackie was a First Lady with a sharp eye for small details. When President Kennedy visited Ireland in 1963, he was presented with an antique silver goblet by the people of New Ross, the port town in County Wexford where his great-grandfather boarded the ship that took him to America in 1850. Seeing how pleased her husband was with the goblet, Jackie sent it to the White House's Flower Room, another of her innovations, with a note of instructions:

> This antique silver goblet is to be kept on the table to the left of the fireplace in the President's office. Would you have the Flower Room keep it filled? I would like it to have, always, three or four fat roses — red or white, the kind you find in a garden, not the florist type ones. Or when this becomes impossible, a couple of big red geraniums, or a red peony, dahlia, or, even in winter, just red carnations. The thing I want to avoid is a dainty bouquet which would look too feminine for a man's office, so I think it's best if we stick to one kind of flower only in the goblet. Thank you.
>
> JBK

The day of President Kennedy's funeral, November 25, 1963, was also the third birthday of his son, John F. Kennedy, Jr. After the funeral, and after a buffet reception for visiting dignitaries, Jackie staged a small birthday party for John in the family's living quarters upstairs in the White House. Dave Powers, John's close friend, was the only guest at the party who was not a member of the Kennedy family. Seeing how much John was enjoying Dave's jovial company at the party, Jackie telephoned Jo Powers, Dave's wife, and asked for her permission to invite Dave to spend the following Thanksgiving weekend at Hyannis Port with the Kennedy children.

On his way to Cape Cod on Thanksgiving Day, Dave picked up a copy of that week's *Life* magazine, which featured the famous pictures of the Kennedy assassination filmed at the scene in Dallas by one of the spectators, Abraham Zapruder, a local garment manufacturer. Zapruder's strip of motion picture film showed Jackie, in a daze after the shooting, climbing out of the back seat of the moving presidential open limousine and then crawling on the rear deck of the car, apparently trying to escape from the bloodshed. The film also showed Clint Hill, one of the Secret Service guards, jumping from the running board of the escort car behind her and running forward to keep her from falling into the street, where she would have been hit by the closely following Secret Service car.

The next pictures on the film strip showed Hill throwing himself onto the rear deck of the presidential car, and reaching for Jackie, who grasped his hands. Then the driver of the car, realizing what was going on, stepped on the accelerator and the car lurched forward. It is hard to tell from the pictures at that point whether Jackie was pulling Hill aboard or if he was pushing her back to safety. As the car picked up speed, Jackie slid back into the rear seat area beside her dying husband and the wounded governor of Texas, John B. Connally, and his wife, Nellie, and Hill was spreading his body above them as a protecting cover against any further gunfire.

When Dave showed Zapruder's pictures to Jackie at Hyannis Port, she was astounded. She had no recollection of leaving the back seat of the car and crawling out on the rear deck after her husband and Connally were hit by the assassin's bullets. "Dave, what do you think I was trying to do?" she asked. Powers could only suggest, lamely, that maybe she was trying to get help from the president's doctor, Rear Admiral George C. Burkley, who was riding in a bus at the rear of the motorcade procession.

Then Dave showed Jackie a newspaper story that said President Lyndon Johnson had announced that he would award a special Treasury Department medal for distinguished service to Rufus Youngblood, the Secret Service agent who protected him during the gunfire in Dallas. During the parade, the then Vice-President Johnson and his wife, Ladybird, were riding in an open convertible with Senator Ralph Yarborough of Texas, behind the Secret Service backup car, or two cars behind the presidential limousine. Youngblood, Johnson's guard, was beside the driver in the front seat. When the first shot was heard, Youngblood pushed the Johnsons and Yarborough to the floor of the car and spread his body over them as protection while the driver quickly followed the president's car to Parkland Memorial Hospital.

"If anybody in the Secret Service deserves a medal for bravery in Dallas," Dave said to Jackie, "it's Clint Hill. He almost killed himself trying to keep you from falling off the rear deck of your car."

Jackie agreed, and asked Dave to call James Rowley, the chief of the Secret Service who had been appointed to that position by President Kennedy. She asked Dave to make arrangements with Rowley to have Clint Hill decorated with the same medal during the following week so that she could attend the ceremony before she and her family moved out of the White House. Dave found Rowley hesitant and apprehensive about offending Johnson. He suggested arranging an award to Hill at a later date.

Jackie was furious. She said to Dave, "Call Douglas Dillon." Dillon, the secretary of the treasury, was Rowley's superior officer.

Dillon agreed to arrange the award to Hill immediately. The following Monday when Jackie returned to the White House, Rowley came there to show her the citation that would be given to Hill when his medal was awarded. Jackie sat down and went over the citation with a pen in her hand, changing a few words and adding a sentence here and there. Rowley explained to her that the citation was an official form and could not be revised.

Jackie looked at the Secret Service chief and said to him, "Have you forgotten who appointed you to your job?"

The next day the medal was presented to Clint Hill in Secretary Dillon's office with Jackie present. The citation had all of the changes that she had suggested.

Friends and admirers of President Kennedy are certain that he would have been one of our greatest presidents if he had lived to complete a second term in office. They also contend that he never would have allowed our military involvement in Vietnam to expand into a full-scale war as it did during Lyndon Johnson's administration.

When I was writing *Johnny, We Hardly Knew Ye*, the Kennedy memoirs of Kenneth P. O'Donnell and David F. Powers, they told me that he was planning to withdraw American troops from Vietnam at the time of his death in 1963. Our role in supporting South Vietnam was then limited to providing Green Beret "advisers" to the native combat units; there were no American combat units or draftees then stationed in the Indochina area. The American forces in South Vietnam, which later grew to more than five hundred thousand during the Johnson Administration, then numbered only around sixteen thousand, most of them involved in supply work.

During 1963, Mike Mansfield, the Democratic leader in the Senate, had been urging Kennedy to make a complete withdrawal from the Vietnam war. O'Donnell told me that at a private meeting with Mansfield, the president agreed to pull all of our forces out of Vietnam — but not until after his reelection in 1964. "If I do it now," Kennedy said, "I'll be damned as a Communist appeaser and I won't get reelected. I can't do it until 1965 — after I'm reelected." While I was writing the Kennedy book, I checked O'Donnell's recollection of that conversation with Mansfield, who assured me that it was correct.

As a matter of fact, Kennedy did issue an order in October 1963, shortly before his trip to Dallas, which called for the return of one thousand American troops from Vietnam before the end of that year. But a few days after his death, that order was quietly rescinded.

6

CLARK GABLE

IN 1954, STILL HANDSOME AT THE AGE OF FIFTY-
three after a reign of almost twenty-five years as the
biggest male star in the movies, Clark Gable seemed to
have reached the twilight of his career. He had not
had a big box-office success since *Gone with the Wind*
back in 1940. Metro-Goldwyn-Mayer, feeling the first
pressure of competition from television, decided not
to renew his $7,500-a-week contract. Gable's personal
life had been sour since the death of his beloved Carole
Lombard in a World War II plane crash; his recent
impulsive marriage with Lady Sylvia Ashley, the chic
blonde widow of the senior Douglas Fairbanks, who
looked like Carole Lombard, had been a mistake. When
Gable packed up his belongings and moved out of the
dressing room on the Metro lot, where he scored his
first impressive hit as a gangster in *A Free Soul* with
Norma Shearer and Leslie Howard back in 1931, his
future seemed dismal.

Then, as seldom happens in Hollywood or anywhere else, Gable suddenly found himself back in the limelight, hot stuff again. One of the last films that he appeared in under his Metro contract, *Mogambo*, with Ava Gardner and Grace Kelly, a remake of an African hunting movie called *Red Dust* that he had starred in with Jean Harlow back in 1934, turned out to be a highly popular moneymaker. At the same time, *Gone with the Wind* was shown in theaters again and a whole new generation of teenage girls and young married women swooned over Gable's portrayal of Rhett Butler. His fan mail tripled. A girl in Fort Thomas, Kentucky, wrote to him, "I'm 16, but when I see you I feel as though I'm 24." Gable made the biggest financial deal of his career with Twentieth Century–Fox, two pictures for ten percent of their gross receipts, which would bring him close to a million dollars even if the two movies were only moderately successful.

Look magazine published a picture of Gable on its front cover. To the astonishment of the editors and the circulation managers, that issue sold out on newsstands all over the United States, making the biggest sale of any issue of *Look* in many years. Naturally, the circulation managers wanted more Gable, right away. Dan Mich, the editor of *Look*, called me. Could I do a long series of pieces on Gable? Not just an article about what he had been doing lately, but his whole life story, how he worked in the oil fields as a kid and how he got started in Hollywood as an extra in silent pictures.

"He's down in Mexico, in a small country town called Durango, making a Western movie for Fox," Mich said. "He says if you go down there, he'll be glad to spend a lot of time talking with you, but with one stipulation. He doesn't want to answer a lot of personal questions about his love life. That shouldn't be any problem. Plenty of people in Hollywood will tell you about his love life. Did you see the article in *Confidential* about his first wife, Josephine Dillon?"

Confidential was the *National Enquirer* of the 1950s. It had recently reported that the first Mrs. Gable, seventeen years older than Clark, was living in poverty in a ramshackle barn in the San Fernando Valley.

"Go and see Josephine Dillon," Mich said. "Talk to some of the people who knew Carole Lombard. Spend plenty of time with Gable's secretary, Jean Garceau. She used to be Lombard's secretary. They say he's keeping steady company now with Kay Spreckels and they may get married soon. By all means get to meet this Kay Spreckels. In other words, we don't expect you to get this piece written by the end of next week. Spend a lot of time on it."

I called a friend of mine in Hollywood, an executive at Twentieth Century–Fox who knew Gable well. I asked him if Gable, at the age of fifty-four, seemed to have as much sex appeal as he displayed back in the early 1930s in *It Happened One Night.*

"Why do you think Darryl Zanuck just made this two-picture deal that practically gives Gable half interest in our studio?" the Fox man said. "Let me put it this way. Guys like Brando and William Holden appeal big to certain types and age brackets of women. But nobody else in the last thirty years makes all women glassy-eyed like Gable does. Only a couple of months ago I took my wife to a cocktail party. My wife is a well-balanced matronly woman, no kid, she's got a son in college. At one point during the party, I looked around for her and saw her in a corner, talking to Gable. Something seemed to be wrong with her. I took a closer look at her. While she was trying to carry on this casual conversation with Gable, her whole body, from her head to her feet, was shaking with excitement. She was really shaking all over."

A few days later I landed in a small Air Mexico plane at the small airport near Durango, in the plains below the Sierra Madre mountains, where Gable was filming *The Tall Men*, a picture about a cattle drive from Texas to Montana back in the Old West of the early 1890s. The outdoor scenes were being filmed around Durango because that section of Mexico looked more like the Old West of the United States than our western states look today. Also, the large herd of longhorn cattle needed for the picture was available at Durango's big cattle ranches. Johnny Campbell, the Fox publicity man assigned to *The Tall Men*, was sitting in a jeep at the airport, waiting for me. Johnny told me that Earl Theisen, a *Look* staff photographer in Hollywood, was already on the location, taking pictures of Gable to illustrate my article.

"That's a break for you," Campbell said. "Clark and Earl are old friends and Clark thinks the world of Earl. Earl told him you're all right, so that should save you about a week in getting acquainted with Clark. Don't press with a lot of questions during the first ten minutes that you're talking with him. We had a writer down here from a Sunday newspaper magazine a week ago. He came on strong with a lot of personal questions, and Clark clammed up and told him nothing. If you spend a couple of days letting him look you over and get acquainted, then he'll relax and talk freely. He's a real good guy, down to earth and no airs about him, not at all like most of the stars in this phony business."

Johnny drove me into the town of Durango to check me into the room reserved for me in the nicest small hotel in the town. In those days, when Hollywood was still Hollywood, the living quarters in a location town were assigned according to protocol and rank, like the quarters in a division headquarters town in France or Italy during World War II. The big star, in this case Gable, had the nicest private house that could be rented. He lived there alone with a couple of servants and his own cook. The leading lady in *The Tall Men*, Jane Russell, had another house, which she shared with her stand-in and makeup woman. Two leading supporting actors, Robert Ryan and Cameron Mitchell, had their own houses, as did the director, Raoul Walsh. People in the next lower salary and professional-status echelon—the head cameraman, the assistant director, the less important supporting actors, Gable's longtime stand-in, Lew Smith (who posed in his place on the set while the cameras were being adjusted and the color checked), the makeup men, the wardrobe mistress, and the script girl—stayed in the higher-priced local hotel where Johnny Campbell, Earl Theisen, and I were staying. Other actors and technicians in the company, such as the assistant cameramen and sound technicians, prop men and electricians, were quartered in another, less expensive hotel down the street.

Gable usually ate his dinner alone every night in

his rented house, stayed there in the evening studying the next day's script, and, from Monday to Saturday, went to bed early. But on Sundays, when the company was not working, he would spend the whole day at our hotel's veranda balcony, drinking and exchanging small talk and reminiscences with Lew Smith and Don Rogerson, his makeup man for many years, Layne ("Shotgun") Britton, the old Hardin Simmons football star who was then working as Jane Russell's makeup man and bodyguard, and me. I was told that such fraternizing with friends in the lower ranks was most unusual behavior for a big star on location.

After lunch, Johnny Campbell drove me to the location in the countryside near Durango where *The Tall Men* company was filming that day's scenes. Johnny introduced me to Gable and to Raoul Walsh and Robert Ryan, who were discussing the next scene with him. I shook hands with Jane Russell, still beautiful ten years after her celebrated bosom had been glorified by Howard Hughes in *The Outlaw*. A few days earlier in New York, I had met Fred Allen on the street and he had shown me a clipping from Leonard Lyons's column about Miss Russell's recent religious conversion which he had been carrying in his wallet. It quoted her as saying, "I love God, and when you get to know Him, you find He's a Living Doll." I decided not to mention this to Miss Russell because she did not seem to be in a mood for conversation. She was seldom seen speaking to anybody during the several weeks that I spent with *The Tall Men* company. After Gable had played several love scenes with her and had sat with her eating lunch every day, I asked him what he thought of her.

"I don't know," Clark said. "I really don't know her."

Earl Theisen appeared, carrying three cameras, and sat down to talk with Gable and me while the set-ups were arranged for the next scene. Gable discussed with Theisen a recent hunting trip in Africa that Ernest Hemingway had made on an assignment for *Look*. Theisen had traveled on the safari with Hemingway to photograph it.

"I got along fine with Hemingway, but he did strange things at times," Earl said. "Every morning, when he woke up, he would come out of his tent, carrying a bucket of soap and water. He would take off his pants and stand there, with everybody in the camp watching him, and proceed to wash his crotch and his balls with the soap and water. In full view of everybody in the camp."

Gable said, "Well, you've got to admit that he was being very sanitary. Did you do any bird shooting when you were in Africa?"

"No," Theisen said. "All I shot was pictures."

"The bird shooting in Africa is just great," Gable said. "I did a lot of it a couple of years ago when I was over there with Grace Kelly and Ava Gardner, making *Mogambo*. On days when we weren't working, Kelly would get up at dawn and go out shooting with me. Bird shooting is the only kind of shooting I care about. When there was big game nearby, Kelly and I would go out with a sixteen-millimeter movie camera and take pictures of them. Make no mistake about it, Kelly is quite a girl. One day she crawled beside me into the middle of a herd of big elephants while I took pictures. At one point, the big old bull elephant was only about fifty yards away from us. He lifted his head and started looking around. The professional white hunter who was with us almost died. He wanted to get out of there fast. But not Kelly. She was enjoying every minute of it. Yessir, quite a girl."

Gable turned to me and grinned. "If I was fifteen years younger, I would have made a real play for her," he said. "When the picture was finished, I had a hard time saying goodbye to her."

Raoul Walsh sat down and joined in the conversation. Walsh had been an actor and then a director since the early days of the movies. I mentioned to him that I well remembered his performance as the young Marine sergeant in the silent film version of W. Somerset Maugham's *Rain*, with Gloria Swanson as Sadie Thompson and Lionel Barrymore as the Reverend Davidson, the stern missionary who tries to convert her and then commits suicide when he falls in love with her and tries to attack her sexually.

"That was a great movie," Walsh said. "You know something awful about it that I just heard a while ago? There isn't a single print of that film to be found anywhere. Nobody knows what happened to it. It's completely disappeared."

Gable said, "I wish to God most of the pictures I made at Metro these last fifteen years would disappear."

I asked him to name the worst picture that he ever appeared in.

"That's easy," he said. He called his stand-in, Lew Smith, who was sitting nearby. "Lew, tell this fellow about the death scene in *Parnell*. Irving Thalberg, who was the production chief at Metro in those days, got all steamed up about making a picture about Charles Stewart Parnell, the great Irish patriot who loused himself up by falling in love with a married woman. Somebody asked me afterwards who Parnell was. I said to him, 'To tell you the truth, I never heard of him and I still don't know much about him.' The picture was so bad that even in Ireland people hated it."

"The death scene in *Parnell* took three weeks to shoot," Lew Smith said. "The director was a guy named John Stahl who was very fussy about the small details. He had Clark dying for a week in a chair. Then he died for a week in a bed. Then he died for another week lying on a chaise lounge. When Stahl started one of the death scenes, he would ask for absolute silence and then he'd give a signal to start some sad music on a phonograph to set a proper mood. Finally Clark and I put our heads together, and I switched the record on the phonograph. That day when Stahl gave the signal to start the music, out it came, loud and noisy – 'I'll Be Glad When You're Dead, You Rascal, You!'"

Gable smiled, and said, "On the great day when we finally finished *Parnell*, my friend, Miss Lombard, hired a plane to fly over the Metro studio dropping thousands of congratulation messages all over the lot."

A few days later, I asked Gable which of his many pictures was his all-time favorite.

"The one I like best is *Mutiny on the Bounty*," he said. "It's the only one I keep at home and I run it occasionally and enjoy watching it. During the thirties and forties when I was at Metro, I made about sixty or more pictures, some pretty good and a lot of them trash. You've got to remember we couldn't pick our pictures the way these independent operators like Brando and Burt Lancaster and Frank Sinatra can pick theirs today. They're not under a long-term contract to a studio like we were. A producer has to show them a finished script, and, if they like it, maybe they'll do it. Back in the old days, the actors like me and Spencer Tracy and Cagney and Bogart, we were under a contract, we got paid every week and we did what the studio told us to do. We just hoped that the picture might turn out to be a good one, but good or bad, we did it anyway, without asking too many questions. It was the same with the girls—Joan Crawford, Norma Shearer, Jean Harlow, Claudette Colbert, Lana Turner, Carole Lombard, and even Garbo. Garbo was under contract like the rest of us and she had to play in anything that was assigned to her whether she liked it or not. I made one picture with Garbo called *Susan Lennox: Her Rise and Fall.* I found her nice to work with, very pleasant and considerate, nothing temperamental about her. But she had one strict rule—every afternoon, on the dot of five o'clock, she would quit work for the day and walk off the set, even if she was in the middle of a big scene. When it got near five o'clock, she would keep her eye on her maid, who had a wristwatch. When five o'clock came, the maid would get up from her chair and start walking off the set. Garbo would stop whatever she was doing and start walking after the maid."

Gable recalled playing the role of a Barbary Coast gambler named Blackie Norton in *San Francisco*, which also featured Spencer Tracy, Jeanette MacDonald, and a terrifying reproduction of the San Francisco earthquake.

"Everybody who saw the picture remembers the earthquake, but nobody remembers the rest of the picture," Gable said. "It was pretty good and it made a lot of money. It was written by Bob Hopkins and Anita Loos, and my Blackie Norton character was modeled after Wilson Mizner, the great wit and con man who had been one of Anita's boy friends. Mizner started the Brown Derby restaurant in Hollywood. Hanging out there and listening to him talk was one of the greatest experiences I ever had. Mizner was the one who said, when somebody told him Calvin Coolidge had died, 'How can they tell?' Everybody gave Dorothy Parker credit for that line, but Mizner was the one who said it. One time in the Brown Derby, Mizner said to a stupid movie producer, 'A demitasse cup would fit over your head like a sun bonnet.' He was describing a cardsharp another time and said, 'He could do more with fifty-two soda crackers than any other hustler could with a new deck of cards.' One time he was talking about a friend of his in the Klondike who froze to death while he was tying a shoelace, and he said, 'We had to bury him in a drum.' Lew Lipton, a screenwriter out here, asked Mizner if he didn't think that a certain actress we knew was a little mannish. 'Not at all,' Mizner said. 'I understand it took her all winter to color a meerschaum pipe.' Even when he was dying, he got off a pretty good wisecrack. A priest told him he ought to make peace with God because he might die any minute. Mizner said, 'No two weeks' notice?'"

I asked Gable if he didn't consider *Gone with the Wind* an exceptionally good movie.

"Oh, sure, it was a *great* movie," he said. "I've made

three great movies, *It Happened One Night, Mutiny on the Bounty*, and *Gone with the Wind*. And you know something? I had to be dragged into all three of them. I thought each of them was a lousy idea before I got involved in them. That shows you how much I know about movies."

Gable's own employers at the time, Metro-Goldwyn-Mayer, owned the screen rights for several years to the short story by Samuel Hopkins Adams on which *It Happened One Night* was based. Metro finally decided that the idea was a dud and sold it to Columbia. Metro owed Columbia the loan of a male star in return for a previous favor. Columbia wanted to borrow Robert Montgomery for *It Happened One Night* but Montgomery was not available. Metro loaned them Gable instead. Several well-known actresses turned down the leading female role before Claudette Colbert reluctantly accepted it.

"I kicked like a steer against going into that picture right up until the day we started to shoot it," Gable said. "I had never acted a leading role in a light comedy before. Up to then I had been strictly a leading man for women like Crawford, Shearer, Harlow, and Marion Davies. I didn't think I could handle a funny leading part. Frank Capra, the director, told me to try it for a few days. After about four days, I asked him how I was doing. He said, 'I'm not complaining.' So I decided to stay."

It Happened One Night became the most popular movie of 1934. The picture showed Gable, as a newspaper reporter, and Colbert, as a missing heiress, traveling by bus and hitchhiking from Florida to New York.

The film was said to have increased bus travel forty-three percent that year. Gable is seen in the picture getting dressed without putting on an undershirt and wearing an unusual sport jacket with a sewn-in belt in the back and a row of pleats across the widely padded shoulders. The underwear industry complained that its sales of undershirts had dropped. The belted and pleated jacket became known as the Clark Gable Jacket and sold big in men's stores. *It Happened One Night* won Gable his one and only Academy Award for acting and established him as a star in his own right, rather than a leading man for star actresses.

"I was afraid to play Fletcher Christian in *Mutiny on the Bounty*," Gable said. "I thought I'd look like a mug going up against Charles Laughton and Franchot Tone and all those British accents that were in the picture. Also, they seemed like a stuffy bunch to be stranded with on Catalina Island, where Irving Thalberg was planning to shoot most of the picture. But Thalberg took me to the Trocadero one afternoon and talked me into it over several drinks. As it turned out, we all enjoyed ourselves on Catalina. Laughton and Tone weren't stuffy at all. One morning, when we were boarding the ship to make some scenes at sea, Laughton showed up on the dock on a firetruck, a hand-drawn one pulled by four firemen. He had some trouble starting his car, and thinking that he might miss the boat, he ran to a fire alarm box and pulled the alarm. When the firemen came, Laughton talked them into pulling him to the dock, all decked out in his Captain Bligh costume. It was quite a scene."

Gable looked back on the filming of *Gone with the*

Wind, his most famous picture and one of the most successful and popular moving pictures of all time, as an unhappy and frustrating experience. David O. Selznick, the producer of the Civil War epic, had originally planned to cast a less expensive actor in the leading role of Rhett Butler. Gable told me that he had no desire to play the part because he thought that the millions of readers of the best-selling book by Margaret Mitchell would be dissatisfied to see him in the Butler role. "You know how little I knew about the book when they asked me to play the Butler part?" he said one day in Mexico when we were discussing the picture. "I told them I couldn't do it because I would look terrible with my hair and my mustache dyed red. Somebody in the room told me that the Butler character's name was Rhett, not Red. When I finally looked at the book, I thought it would be a nice part for Ronald Colman."

Selznick received so many letters from *Gone with the Wind* fans demanding Gable in the Butler role that he went to Metro-Goldwyn-Mayer's studio boss, Louis B. Mayer, and asked for a loan of Gable. To get Gable, Selznick had to give Metro a one-million-dollar interest in *Gone with the Wind* and its valuable distribution rights. Subsequently, Metro bought out Selznick's interest in the picture and now owns it almost completely.

"So thanks to me, Metro ended up owning *Gone with the Wind*," Gable said with understandable bitterness seventeen years later. "What did I get out of that picture? No percentage of the profits, no bonus, nothing except my usual weekly salary while I worked on it."

Actually, in return for his agreement to play Rhett Butler, Metro gave Gable a loan of $300,000 which was repaid out of his salary a few years later. But that transaction was forced upon the studio by Will Hays, the moving picture industry's self-appointed guardian of its moral reputation. The movie fan magazine *Photoplay* published at that time an article entitled "Hollywood's Unmarried Husbands and Wives." The exposé named Gable and Carole Lombard, along with Barbara Stanwyck and Robert Taylor, Charles Chaplin and Paulette Goddard, Constance Bennett and Gilbert Roland, and George Raft and Virginia Pine, as couples who were living together without matrimonial licenses. Gable at that time had been separated for more than three years from his second wife, Maria Langham Gable, a divorcée from Houston who was seventeen years older than Clark. Ria refused to give him a divorce without a settlement of $300,000, which Gable refused to pay. When the *Photoplay* article stirred up the Hays office, Metro offered to advance Gable the $300,000 in return for his promise to marry Carole Lombard and to play in *Gone with the Wind*.

"The day I was to start work on the picture," Gable said, "Selznick sent a messenger to my house around six o'clock in the morning with a ninety-page memo about how he wanted me to play the Rhett Butler part. Selznick was always writing long memos about something that just occurred to him. And he changed his mind about how the picture should be written or filmed every ten minutes. It took him a hell of a long time to decide what girl he wanted in the Scarlett O'Hara part. Every woman in Hollywood was after it. So was almost every girl in the United States. A couple of weeks before we started — this was on Christmas morning in

1938 – a girl had herself delivered to Selznick's house inside a big wooden box that was painted to look like a copy of *Gone with the Wind*. She stepped out of the box wearing a Scarlett O'Hara costume. We were well into the picture and the scene showing the burning of Atlanta had already been shot before Selznick finally decided to give the part to Vivien Leigh. At one time we had four units working under four different directors. I never saw a finished script of that picture. The script was changed every day and God knows how many writers worked on it."

Gable recalled with a laugh a story about one of *Gone with the Wind*'s script problems. Selznick hired a new writer and asked him to rewrite a romantic scene between Rhett Butler and Scarlett O'Hara. "But I haven't read the book," the writer said.

"That makes no difference," Selznick said. "All you have to do is to take this scene that we've already written and make it a little more interesting."

In a few days, the writer returned with a new version of the scene. Selznick looked it over, groaned, and shook his head.

"You've got it all wrong," he said. "You've got Scarlett being courted by Rhett. At this point in the story, she's supposed to be engaged to Ashley Wilkes."

The writer stared at Selznick in surprise and said, "Who is Ashley Wilkes?"

Gable said that he was so confused by the Rhett Butler role that he almost walked out of the picture during the first two weeks of filming. "Nobody was telling me anything," he said. "George Cukor was the director and all he did was criticize my Southern accent.

Then Selznick decided to fire Cukor and I talked him into hiring Victor Fleming, a good friend of mine who could tell me what to do. But Vic was a practical joker. You remember the big scene where I grab Vivien Leigh and run up a long flight of stairs carrying her in my arms? Vic had me doing that scene over and over again. He'd say, 'Try it again, a little faster this time.' I got exhausted and yelled at him, 'This dame is getting as heavy as lead!' Fleming, the bastard, broke up laughing and said, 'We got it the first time you did it. I just wanted to see how long you could keep it up.' I could have killed him."

Fleming collapsed from nervous exhaustion while directing *Gone with the Wind* and had to be replaced for a while by Sam Wood, the director of the recent hit *Goodbye, Mr. Chips.* During the filming of the scene showing the evacuation of Atlanta, Vivien Leigh was knocked down and nearly trampled by a team of runaway horses. "We had to work nights," Gable said. "Everybody was in a bad mood. Let me tell you, that picture was an experience that I would never want to go through again. How it ever turned out so well, I'll never know. It must have been the cutting and editing job that Selznick did on it. He certainly knew how to put pieces of film together."

Some of the more memorable conversations that I had with Gable in Durango, and later at the Fox studio in Beverly Hills and at his home in Encino in the San Fernando Valley, were recollections of his youthful experiences working in the Oklahoma oil fields and struggling to become an actor, first as an extra in the

Hollywood silent pictures of the late 1920s and later on the stage in Houston, New York, and Los Angeles. Gable told me that he looked back on his early years as a stage and screen actor, when he was never secure financially, with much more pleasure than he found in recalling his career as a big star in the thirties and forties. "After I got to be a big box-office name in the movie business, I found out it wasn't fun anymore," he said. "Everybody was trying to use me and hustle me. Being a star, frankly, never impressed me much. Except for the money, which was good to have, the rest of the hoopla left me cold. I was always happier when I was away from the studio."

Gable's calm view of Hollywood stardom was revealed one day when I asked him about the Oscar he had received for his performance in *It Happened One Night* in 1934. I had noticed that the Oscar was not on display in his home at Encino and inquired about its where-abouts, wondering if he kept it in a safe deposit vault. Gable smiled and said, "Maybe I shouldn't mention it, because the people out here take those Academy Awards pretty seriously. I gave my Oscar away a long time ago to a six-year-old kid, Richard Lang, the son of Walter and Fieldsie Lang. Fieldsie was Carole's closest girl friend. Her boy enjoyed playing with the Oscar, so I told him to take it home and keep it."

When I visited Gable's house, his secretary, Jean Garceau, showed me a scrapbook with a picture of Gable's birthplace, a drab-looking frame house in Cadiz, Ohio, and a birth certificate, which said that he was born there on February 1, 1901, and named William

Clark Gable. His parents, William and Adeline Hershel-man Gable, were Pennsylvania Dutch.

"My grandfather, my old man's father, ran a hotel in Meadsville, Pennsylvania," Gable said one day while we were talking on *The Tall Men* set. "But my father wouldn't have any part of the hotel business. He got hooked on oil prospecting when the oil boom started in Pennsylvania, and never wanted to do anything else. My mother died when I was a baby. My father got married again to a wonderful woman who was very kind to me, a well-educated and cultured person. We moved then to Hopewell, Ohio, but my father was never home much. He was always away, digging for oil, looking for the big strike that never came. When I was about seven years old, my stepmother took sick. The doctor told my father to stay home and take care of her. So he gave up prospecting for oil and bought a farm near Ravenna, Ohio, and settled down there. But it just about killed him. He hated to give up drilling for oil."

When Clark was a teenager, he left high school and took a job at the Firestone rubber plant in Akron, molding treads on automobile tires. One night, for the first time in his life, he went to a theater and saw a play. It was *Bird of Paradise*, Richard Walton Tully's popular romance about an American who falls in love with a native princess on one of the Hawaiian islands. The young Gable was carried away by it. He became acquainted with the actors in the theater's stock company by hanging around every night in the restaurant where they ate supper after the show. Soon he was happily working for nothing backstage in the theater as a call boy and playing occasional walk-on parts as a policeman or as a butler. Stage fever infected him in Akron as oil fever had conquered his father during the boom at Oil City in Pennsylvania.

"Then my stepmother died," Gable said. "My father didn't stay long on that farm after her funeral. He packed up and headed for the oil fields in Oklahoma. He ordered me to come with him. I hated leaving that theater in Akron, but I was only eighteen and he was still my boss."

Gable found himself working twelve hours a day as a gang laborer at an oil refinery in Oklahoma, cleaning the insides of stills with a pick and shovel. Then he worked with his father as a tool dresser, shaping hot metal with a sixteen-pound sledgehammer. The work developed Gable's broad shoulders, but he hated it.

"I couldn't get that theater in Akron out of my mind," he said. "I counted the months until I would reach my twenty-first birthday. I figured my father wouldn't have any hold on me after I got to be twenty-one. That day, I told him I was leaving. He told me I was crazy, wanting to be an actor, but I went."

Gable paused in his reminiscences and smiled. There he was, sitting in the star's folding leather chair on *The Tall Men* set, waiting to do a scene with Jane Russell. His cowboy costume had just been carefully soiled with dust by a wardrobe man so that he would look as if he had been riding herd on a trail. But he was thinking of his father.

"You know, I didn't see my father again after that for fifteen years," Gable said. "When I was out here in Hollywood, making five thousand dollars a week in the movies, he was still moving around in the oil fields in Oklahoma and Texas, still working by himself. We kept in touch with each other by mail. There were no hard feelings between us. But I never saw him for fifteen years. He was just independent, wanted to live his own life. Then he wrote and told me that he was thinking of quitting the oil drilling. He was planning to buy a farm in North Dakota. I told him then to cut out the foolishness and to come out here and live with me, and he did. I had a house in Brentwood then. Well, he had a brother in Los Angeles who was a stockbroker. His brother died. My old man came to me one day and told me he was planning to marry his brother's widow. He said, 'I've known Edna since she was a girl, and she's alone now, and so am I. I think I'll marry her.' He was sixty-five years old. He went ahead and married Edna, and, you know, he was happier with her than he ever was before in his whole life. In 1948, she died, and my old man died less than two weeks later."

When Gable left his father in Oklahoma, he went to Kansas City and talked himself into a job with the Jewell Players, a down-at-the-heel troupe of touring actors. They did tent shows in the summer and hired school halls and opera houses in the cold weather.

"I'll never forget the leading lady," Gable said. "She was a tall, stately old dame with a wonderful deep voice. She had only one eye. Lost the other eye in a fencing scene on the stage. She had worked in London with Sir Beerbohm Tree, and she was a terrific actress. The company did melodramas like *Her False Step* and

Are You a Mason? When we came to a college town, we did Shakespeare. I took care of the horses—we had horse-drawn wagons—drove in tent stakes, set up seats, played a cornet in the band, and played small parts. I played colored mammy parts, character parts wearing whiskers, and offstage voices. I was too tall and too big to play a juvenile leading role. In those days, the leading men had to be short and slim. Some weeks I was paid ten dollars and other weeks I wasn't paid at all."

The traveling stock company collapsed on a cold day in 1922 at Butte, Montana. Gable found himself stranded with twenty-two cents in his pocket. He went to the local telegraph office and wrote a message that he planned to send collect to his father, asking for train fare back to Oklahoma. After writing the message, Gable realized that he was confronted by a fork in the road. If he sent the wire, he would have to go back to working in the oil fields with his father and probably would never be able to act on a stage again. He tore up the message and dropped it into a wastebasket.

In Butte, Gable found a job in a mine. Then he pawned his suitcase, bought overalls to keep his one suit clean, and hopped a freight train that was headed toward the Pacific coast. He dropped off the train in Bend, Oregon, where he found a job at a mill, piling logs of green lumber. "It was the hardest work I ever did," Gable said. "Those logs were rough-barked and heavy and I didn't have any money coming to me until payday, so I couldn't buy a pair of gloves. To toughen up my hands, I soaked them at night in salt water, vinegar, and alum. By the time payday came, my hands were so hard I didn't need to buy gloves."

Gable worked in the lumber camps until he had enough money to go to Portland and look for a theatrical job. When his money ran out, he would go back to the woods and find work at a mill or as a lumberjack or pathfinder. During his stays in Portland, Gable had a romance with a young local actress named Franz Dorfler. Fifteen years later, in 1937, when Gable was a star at Metro-Goldwyn-Mayer, a British woman named Violet Norton turned up in Hollywood charging that he was the father of her daughter Gwendoline, who was born in Essex, England, in 1923. Mrs. Norton said that Gable had made love to her using the name Frank Billings. On the witness stand, she recalled that Gable had hummed "I'm Forever Blowing Bubbles" while he was seducing her. Metro's lawyers pressed Gable to remember some witnesses who could testify that he had spent the autumn months of 1922 in Oregon, and not in England as Mrs. Norton claimed. Gable remembered Franz Dorfler. Miss Dorfler was found working as a kitchen maid in a restaurant. Louis B. Mayer quickly gave her a job as an actress at Metro and provided her with a new hair-do and an expensive wardrobe so that she would make a more favorable impression on the jury. Miss Dorfler testified firmly for Gable, who kissed her cheek as he led her from the witness stand back to her seat in the courtroom. The jury found Mrs. Norton guilty of using the mails to defraud. She shouted, "I still think Clark Gable is the dad of me kid!"

In 1923, around the time that Mrs. Norton was giving birth to her child in England, Gable gave up working in the woods and found a job in Portland as a repairman with the local telephone company. Still yearning to be an actor, he became closely acquainted with Josephine Dillon, a former actress in the New York theater and later a dramatic coach in Hollywood. Rudolph Valentino had been one of her pupils. She had recently moved to Portland to direct a local theatrical stock company. Miss Dillon, a judge's daughter and a graduate of Leland Stanford University, was a woman of culture, charm, and warm kindness, seventeen years older than Gable. He probably found her to be a replacement for his beloved stepmother, Jennie Dunlap Gable. She also had the knowledge of the theater, acting skill, and the techniques of diction and dramatic expression that the twenty-two-year-old Gable desperately wanted to learn. She taught him how to lower his then rather high-pitched voice, how to walk across a stage, how to make an impressive entrance, and she gave him minor roles in her stock company's plays. When Miss Dillon returned to Los Angeles a year later, Gable followed her there. They were married and lived together for a few years in a small cottage on the outskirts of Hollywood. Still being tutored by his wife in stage techniques, Clark earned a little money now and then as an extra in moving pictures and in stage productions.

When I was visiting Gable in the summer of 1955, I asked him if he had seen the article about Josephine Dillon in the current issue of *Confidential* magazine. "I saw it," he said. "My lawyer says I ought to sue them. I wouldn't dignify them with a suit. The way I figure it, if you sue, ten million people who never saw or heard about the article will find out about it and read it." Then he abruptly changed the subject.

The *Confidential* article depicted Miss Dillon as a poverty-stricken old lady, living in a dilapidated old barn on a back street in North Hollywood while a few blocks away, on Ventura Boulevard, Gable roared past in the evenings "in the back seat of a sleek, chauffeur-driven limousine – bound for one of his new and youthful conquests." The article said that Miss Dillon had asked Gable for money a few years earlier when she was ill in a hospital and penniless, but that Gable had ignored her plea.

I visited Miss Dillon at her home and found her more embarrassed by the article than Gable was. She was a pleasant and highly intelligent woman, with quiet pride and dignity. "I have no idea who could have written that article," she said. "Maybe it was somebody who came here, snooping around and posing as a relative of one of my dramatic pupils. I give acting lessons to several youngsters."

The barnlike structure that *Confidential* described as Miss Dillon's home was a studio in which she gave dramatic lessons. She lived in a comfortable adjoining house. The studio was an old building but hardly dilapidated. It was attractively furnished with valuable antiques and lined with books about the theater.

"Whoever wrote that story doesn't know much about furniture," Miss Dillon said. "This rug on the floor is a genuine Oriental. That desk came to California around Cape Horn. It belonged to my grandfather. That piece in the corner is an original George Washington music cabinet. It's true that I don't have any money. What teacher does? But I've never asked Clark Gable for anything. When I divorced him, I refused to accept alimony. My people don't believe in alimony. I've been in a hospital once in my life. It was an army hospital during the war. I went there to entertain the soldiers."

Miss Dillon talked freely and without bitterness about her marriage with Gable, and about Gable himself.

"Don't let anybody tell you that he isn't a great actor," she said. "The Clark Gable you see on the screen, the playful rogue with the happy-go-lucky mischievous glint in his eye, that's not the real Gable. The real Gable is moody and thoughtful and gloomy. He is a complex man who keeps his troubles to himself and broods about them. He got to be a big star in Hollywood through determination and hard work. When we were living together in a twenty-dollar-a-month cottage, we tried to save twenty-five cents a week so he could go to a movie and study the acting of the leading man. Some weeks, when we managed to save fifty cents, I went with him. He would sit for hours at the piano, trying to lower the tone of his voice. When I first met him, his voice was too high and hard and nervous, as it is in many big men, like Jack Dempsey and General Patton. He had the straight-lipped, set mouth of a do-or-die character and the narrow eyes of a man who has had to fight through things alone. That had to be changed. As we worked on his speech, lowering his voice and developing the easy firmness and remarkable resonance that it had when he became a star, the muscles in his face relaxed. His eyes opened. His forehead smoothed. His lips became flexible and his now-famous smile was born."

A few days later I mentioned to Gable that I had talked with his first wife. He seemed startled.

"How is she?" he asked.

"She's looking fine," I said. "We had a nice talk. She told me about the old jalopy you used to drive to the studios when you were looking for work, and how you used to give Janet Gaynor a ride home when you saw her at the employment office trying to get a job as an extra. She said that on days when your gas was low, you would drop Janet Gaynor off at the corner of her street and Sunset Boulevard instead of driving her to her door."

"That's right," Gable said. "I could measure that gas to the last drop."

The next morning Harry Brandt, the Fox studio's publicity chief, called me on the telephone.

"Clark says you talked to Josephine Dillon," Brandt said. "He's wondering about what she said to you."

"Tell him not to worry," I said. "She had nothing but nice things to say about him."

A few weeks later I talked on the telephone with Miss Dillon. She was in a cheerful mood.

"I want to thank you very much," she said. "The mortgage on my house has been paid off, and some men are here right now putting a new roof on it."

"Don't thank me," I said. "I didn't have anything to do with it."

"Well, shortly after you came here to see me," she said, "I heard from Mr. Gable for the first time in twenty-five years. If your visit wasn't responsible, I don't know what was."

Theatrical stock companies, presenting the same players in a different play every week, were thriving in cities all over the country in the late twenties when the movies were making the awkward transition from silent pictures to talkies. In the later Depression of the thirties, when a ticket to the movies was only forty or fifty cents, the talking-picture industry boomed and the stock companies collapsed. In the fall of 1927, when his marriage to Josephine Dillon had broken up, Gable left her and moved to Houston, Texas, to take a steady job with the Gene Lewis Players, a stock company at the Palace Theater, for seventy-five dollars a week. "He didn't need me anymore," Miss Dillon said later. The twenty-six-year-old Gable, now an assured actor, scored a hit in Houston. He soon became the company's leading man, with his pay raised to two hundred and fifty dollars a week. "All the girls in town were crazy about him," Margaret Davis, a friend of mine in Houston, told me recently. "His big ears stuck out, and his hair was too long—almost a Dutch bob—but he had that unique charm and magnetism even in those early days. It put him over here as it did later in Hollywood."

In Houston, Gable became involved with an attractive and wealthy local divorcée, Maria Langham, who did not marry him until four years later, after he became an established Hollywood star. Like Josephine Dillon, Ria, as she was called, was seventeen years older than Gable.

"A lot of people in Houston think, naturally, that Clark Gable broke up Ria's marriage to Langham," Margaret Davis said. "I doubt if even Gable could work that fast. But who knows?"

When I was working on the Gable story in 1955, I was unable to talk with Ria. She had moved back to

Houston from Hollywood after collecting her $300,000 divorce settlement from Gable in 1939, and was still living there. I talked with a man in New York who had known her and Gable well during their marriage.

"When they got married in 1931," he said, "after going together, and actually living together, for about four years, Ria was forty-seven and Clark was thirty, so people assume that he married her for her money. Kindly remember that by the time they got married in 1931, he was already under contract at Metro-Goldwyn-Mayer as a rising star. He had played in a picture with Joan Crawford, and he had made a big hit as the gangster who pushed Norma Shearer around in *A Free Soul*. He didn't need her money. And Ria never had to buy a husband. You never saw such charm as she has. Pictures of her that were in the papers when she was married to Gable never did her justice. She is rather small, with beautiful auburn hair and lovely skin and coloring. Gable married her because she was a very fascinating woman. And she still is. I saw her not long ago at El Morocco with Clarence Bitting, a millionaire with a home at Watch Hill who's been courting her, and she looked wonderful. You know how old she is now? She's seventy-one."

Ria Gable continued to look good for many more years, but she never married again. She died in 1966, at the age of eighty-two, six years after Clark's death.

After a year in the stock company at Houston, Gable got his first big lucky break, the leading male role opposite a talented actress, Zita Johann, in a Broadway play, *Machinal*, which brought him praise from the

New York critics. Ria came to New York with him and rented an apartment there. A few months after *Machinal* closed, Gable went to California to play the leading role in a San Francisco and Los Angeles stage production of a prison drama, *The Last Mile*, in which Spencer Tracy had scored a big success on Broadway. He was planning to return to New York and resume his theater work there when the fall season opened three months later.

"Do you know I never played on the stage again in New York for the rest of my life?" Gable said, recalling that turning point in his career. "Lionel Barrymore saw me in *The Last Mile* and talked Irving Thalberg into giving me a screen test at Metro. It was awful. They had me playing the part of a Hawaiian in a loin cloth with a hibiscus blossom hanging from one of my big ears. It was a scene from *Bird of Paradise* — the first play I ever saw as a kid back in Akron. I was terrible. I heard that when Irving Thalberg saw the test, he yelled, 'Oh, no! Not that! Take him away!' Lionel Barrymore figured that was the end of me in Hollywood. He never expected to see me again. Well, not too many months later, Lionel reports for work on a new Norma Shearer picture, *A Free Soul*. Who does he see in front of the camera, holding Norma in his arms? Me. I saw Lionel standing there, staring at me with his mouth open, so I gave him a casual nod. He was flabbergasted. The last time he saw me, Irving Thalberg was throwing up over a screen test of mine and now here I'm playing a big love scene with Thalberg's own wife. Barrymore couldn't get over it. He kept saying to people, 'And he's taking the whole thing *for granted!*'"

Gable had certainly risen fast to stardom in the previous few months. After flunking Thalberg's screen test and figuring that he was finished in Hollywood, Gable had managed, much to his surprise, to get a role as the villain in a Pathé western, *The Painted Desert*, with Bill Boyd and Helen Twelvetrees. Then came a really big break. Paul Bern, the producer at Metro who later married Jean Harlow and then committed suicide, happened to see *The Painted Desert* and liked Gable's performance. He urged Irving Thalberg to cast Gable in a small but juicy part as a milkman in a Constance Bennett film, *The Easiest Way*. When *The Easiest Way* was seen in theaters, everybody in Hollywood wanted to know the name of the milkman. Thalberg hastened to sign Gable to a contract. Gable did well as a gangster in a Joan Crawford picture, *Dance, Fools, Dance*. "This magnetic man had more sheer animal magic than anyone in the world and every woman knew it," Miss Crawford wrote later about Gable in her autobiography.

Then Gable came on much stronger in a role as a rougher and tougher gangster who mistreats Norma Shearer after she becomes his mistress in *A Free Soul*. He stole the picture from Miss Shearer and two bigger male stars, Lionel Barrymore and Leslie Howard, and went on from there to become the biggest male star of the thirties and forties. When Gable made personal appearances at the Capitol Theater in New York in 1934, the crowds of teenaged girls and older women which massed around the stage door every day and night were so big and unmanageable that the police advised the movie idol to remain in his dressing room from his first performance at noon until after the last show at midnight in order to avoid personal injury. One of the New York newspapers commemorated the event in blank verse:

> *If all the palpitations*
> *Brought on by his appearances*
> *Were placed end to end,*
> *They would generate enough electricity*
> *To light the City of New York,*
> *Or what have you.*
> *His ears stick out.*
> *But who cares?*

But unlike Rudolph Valentino and John Gilbert, the soulful and tender screen lovers of the twenties whose pictures made husbands and boy friends squirm with boredom, Gable's dominating he-man approach delighted men in the audience as it thrilled their women. John Dillinger, that year's Public Enemy Number One, was cornered and shot by the FBI in Chicago in the summer of 1934 because he could not resist coming out of hiding to see Gable play a gangster in *Manhattan Melodrama*. Gaining such popularity among men movie fans while women swooned over his pictures made Gable the biggest box-office attraction in the history of show business. He soon moved up to the five-thousand-dollar-a-week salary bracket and then to seventy-five hundred a week.

"Marion Davies was the one who showed me how to get my first big raise," Gable told me. "She said to me one day when we were working together, 'Go away and get lost. Don't come to the studio.' So I disappeared, and sure enough they came looking for me with a new contract. You know, after I got into the big money, I was working in a picture one day with Jean Harlow and Myrna Loy. I was playing the part of a business executive in a picture called *Wife vs. Secretary*. Some of the titles those days were Godawful. I was doing a scene in an office, at a desk covered with papers. The prop man had put on the desk a bunch of papers from the M-G-M accounting department's file. I picked up one paper and looked at it. It was the daily payroll sheet from a 1925 picture, *The Merry Widow* with Mae Murray and John Gilbert. There was my name among the extras and next to it was my day's pay, seven dollars and fifty cents. I had the sheet framed and hung it in my dressing room to keep me reminded that things weren't always so good."

In the Hollywood of those days, social position depended on salary. A cameraman earning a thousand dollars a week did not mix in the evening with actors, directors, and producers in the three- to five-thousand-dollar-a-week bracket. As the wife of a high-priced star, Ria Gable found herself warmly accepted in movieland's social upper crust, and she enjoyed it. She became a close friend of Gloria Swanson and Louella Parsons and played bridge with the wives of important studio executives. The Gables often entertained at white-tie dinners at their new home in Brentwood and were invited to the important parties and dances.

Getting his first real taste of swanky social life, Gable found that he didn't like it much. He began to spend weekends away from home, duck hunting with Eddie

Mannix, taking sport cars apart and racing motorcycles with Al Menasco, Victor Fleming, and Howard Hawkes. Menasco, a non-social-register type who designed aircraft engines, showed Gable how to remodel automobile and motorcycle engines and became his closest friend. Gable also enjoyed extracurricular romances with Joan Crawford and Loretta Young and other actresses. Finding that he no longer shared many common interests with Ria, and that he had a hearty dislike for her fashionable social life, Gable packed up and moved out of their Brentwood home late in 1935 after four years of marriage. He took a room at the Beverly Wilshire in Beverly Hills.

A few months later, in February 1936, Gable was happily driving to work in an old Ford, painted white and decorated with red hearts. It had been given to him as a valentine by Carole Lombard, who had been at loose ends romantically since her divorce from William Powell three years earlier.

"When Carole fell in love with Clark," Jean Garceau told me, "she changed her whole style of living. Up until then, she went out every night to big dinner parties and nightclubs. On days when she wasn't working, she lounged around in her apartment in a negligee, talking to people on the phone. She thought that outdoor sports were only for idiots. But after her first few dates with Clark, she began to take lessons from an instructor who showed her how to load and fire a shotgun, and how to cast a fishing rod. She was determined not to make the mistake with him that Ria had made — when he was going hunting, she'd go, too. She became the only woman member of his gun club near Bakersfield, and she did her share of the work there, too. Up to that time, I don't think she ever cooked but after she fell for Clark, she learned how to cook with a frying pan over an outdoor fire."

Mrs. Garceau, showing me around on the Gable estate at Encino, led me to the garage and pointed at an old Dodge station wagon. "Mr. Keller of the Chrysler Corporation had that wagon made to Clark's specifications. He and Carole used to go away in it for days at a time on hunting trips. After Carole died, he never drove it again. But, as you can see, he keeps it in nice condition."

Gable and Miss Lombard lived together for four years while he stubbornly refused to pay his wife Ria the $300,000 that she was demanding for a divorce settlement. After Metro-Goldwyn-Mayer advanced him the money for his divorce, Carole bought them the house on a twenty-two-acre farm estate in Encino, a roomy white brick mansion with a sloping roof. The furnishings in the house when I visited it in 1955 had not been changed, Mrs. Garceau told me, since the Gables moved into it in 1939. All of the furnishings and decoration had been selected by Carole Lombard herself. The appearance of the house said a lot about her marriage. It was decorated entirely to suit a man of Gable's tastes. The only room with a feminine look was Carole's own bedroom. The rest of the house looked almost like the home of a bachelor – big sturdy chairs and tables, sporting prints on the pine-paneled walls. The most handsome room was the Early American dining room. On high shelves along one wall was Carole's priceless collection of pink and white Staffordshire china which she had picked up, piece by piece, during her travels. The massive pine table, beautifully finished and polished, came from Gable's previous home in Brentwood. Mrs. Garceau told me that to make it look properly aged, Carole left it outdoors to be rained on for three months and then burned marks on it with lighted cigarettes and slashed and hacked it with knives.

"You wouldn't believe how happy they were here," Mrs. Garceau said. "When they weren't working, they would both get up early and work together around the place. They had three horses, and a mule named Judy, a few cows, and turkeys and chickens. They planted roses and even cleaned out the chicken coops together and they went riding on Clark's motorcycle."

"For the first time in his life, Clark was happy and in love," Howard Strickling, his close friend, said when we were talking about the Gable-Lombard marriage. "He finally had found a woman who was willing to do anything he wanted all day long and still could get dressed up and look lovely and glamorous for him in the evening. He told me one time that she could even make love with him in a duck blind, while they were waiting to get a shot at some ducks, and, let me tell you, there are damned few women in this world who are willing, or able, to make love in a duck blind."

Gable's happy life with Carole at Encino lasted only thirty-four months.

"Eddie Mannix and I got the news first," Strickling said. "They gave us the job of breaking it to Clark because we were the two guys at Metro who knew him best. We chartered a plane at Burbank to take him to

Las Vegas and drove out to his house to pick him up. He and Jean Garceau and Rufus Martin, his house-man, were planning a welcome home party for Carole. As you know, she was flying home from a war bond selling tour—it was only a couple of weeks after the Pearl Harbor attack—and her plane crashed into a mountain near Las Vegas. When we got to Las Vegas, Eddie and I had one hell of a time trying to stop Clark from going up into the mountains to search in the snow for the plane. We had to lock him in a hotel room and sit with him. It was terrible to look at him. He wouldn't talk and he didn't cry. He just sat there, tightened up, trembling and breathing hard, like a caged animal."

Strickling asked me if I had yet met Kay Spreckels, who became Gable's fifth and last wife a few weeks after our interview. I told him that I had dinner with Kay and Clark at his house on the previous evening.

"Then you know how much Kay looks like Carole, and she's got a good sense of humor," Strickling said. "He seems very happy with her, and she pampers him and goes hunting with him, like Carole did. That last one, the fourth wife, Lady Sylvia Ashley, the British café-society countess, looked like Carole, but she doesn't think or feel like Carole. You know, Clark decided to marry her on an impulse one night when he was driving her home from a party at Charlie Feldman's house. She made a wrong move right after the wedding. She asked him to fire Rufus Martin, who has been the houseman at Clark's place since Carole was there. She wanted to get an English butler to replace Rufus. Well, Rufus stayed and Sylvia went. She took a trip to Nassau and when she came home, she found that the locks on the doors of the house at Encino had been changed and her charge accounts were closed. But with Kay Spreckels, it's a different ball game. Kay and Rufus Martin are very good friends, and Kay isn't planning to make any changes in the way Carole decorated the house. She knows, like we all know, that Clark will never get over Carole's death."

Gable was a most interesting personality to write about because the story of his life was a series of sharply contrasting periods of changing tastes, interests, and life-styles. The lumberjack who came out of the Northwest to try his luck in Hollywood during the era of silent movies became a sophisticated and smartly dressed companion of a stylish heiress in Houston and New York. Carole Lombard's lover, and later her husband, was an outdoorsman who seldom went to nightclubs. In 1938, Ernie Pyle, the newspaper columnist, spent a day with Gable and described him coming to work at the Metro studio in a brown beret, a leather jacket, and an old pair of brown duck pants.

During World War II, while he served in Europe as an officer in the Air Force, and for five years after the war, while he tried to recover from the loss of Carole Lombard, Gable changed again. Glumly working in a series of dismal pictures under his Metro contract, he spent almost every night at the big parties and nightclubs that had bored him before the war. He became involved with many fashionable women — Virginia Grey, Anita Colby, Dolly O'Brien, Paulette Goddard, Evelyn Keyes, Joan Harrison, and, for a while, before her marriage to Adolph Spreckels, with Kay Williams.

When I became acquainted with him in 1955, after his divorce from Sylvia Ashley and just before his marriage to Kay Spreckels, he had changed again. No more nightclubbing and no big parties, and no more motorcycles or fast sports cars, either. He dressed conservatively – dark suits, always with a white shirt and a plain black tie. I asked him where he got his clothes.

"The ones I wear when I'm not working are from Brooks Brothers," he said. "They won't let me wear Brooks Brothers suits in front of a camera. They think that Brooks Brothers suits are not snappy enough to please the movie audiences."

During the last five years of his life, when he was not shooting birds Gable spent his free time playing golf well at the swanky Bel Air Country Club and at Palm Springs, where he built a vacation home with extra rooms for his wife's two children from her previous marriage, Joan and Adolph Spreckels. Clark became very fond of the Spreckels children while he was courting their mother.

"They're great kids," he said to me one day, "and you should see how Kathleen handles them. She really makes them toe the mark. Old Kathleen has an awful lot of remarkable stuff in her, a lot of good plain horse sense. I'm hoping that she and I will have a kid of our own. Carole couldn't have children."

But Clark Gable did not live quite long enough to see his only child, John Clark Gable, born on March 20, 1961, three months after Clark died from coronary thrombosis at the age of fifty-nine. A few days later Richard Lang visited the baby and presented to him his father's 1934 Academy Award statuette.

7

SHOR'S

In the carefree and prosperous 1950s, I found myself spending most of my working hours at Toots Shor's bar and restaurant at 51 West 51st Street in the Rockefeller Center section of New York, where the Columbia Broadcasting System's executive office building now stands. In those years Shor's was undoubtedly the busiest celebrity-packed saloon in America. It was also a male chauvinist hangout if there ever was one. Women were politely received at the bar and in the large dining room, but not with the warm roar of welcome ("Harya, crumb bum!") that the big and burly proprietor, a former bouncer in Prohibition speakeasies, showered on his close men friends. Many of the memorable testimonial dinners and birthday parties that Toots staged in his upstairs private banquet hall were strictly stag affairs.

Shor was seldom addressed by his legal first name,

Bernard. The intimate pals who always called him Toots included such show-business stars as Bob Hope, Bing Crosby, Jackie Gleason, Frank Sinatra, Fred Allen, and Pat O'Brien, such sports figures as Joe DiMaggio, Jack Dempsey, Eddie Arcaro, Whitey Ford, Billy Conn, Yogi Berra, Mel Ott, and Mickey Mantle, such sportswriters and columnists as Grantland Rice, Bob Considine, Bill Corum, Red Smith, Gene Fowler, and Jimmy Cannon, and other people such as Ernest Hemingway, Bennett Cerf, Robert E. Sherwood, and Chief Justice Earl Warren. Harry Truman, one of Toots's close friends, dined often at Shor's when he was a senator and later when he was the vice-president. After Truman moved into the White House, Toots dined there often and was an overnight guest.

But Shor was not a celebrity chaser, or at least he never went out of his way to be nice to a celebrity unless he had a warm feeling for him. Many prominent public figures and business or show-business tycoons who came to Shor's often were completely ignored by the proprietor because he felt no particular urge to be friendly with them. One night Louis B. Mayer complained to Toots because he had been kept waiting for fifteen minutes before he was escorted to a table.

"I've waited longer than that over at Loew's State, trying to get in to see one of your pitchas," Shor said to Mayer. "And after I did see it, it wasn't so hot."

On another evening Shor said to Charlie Chaplin, "We ain't got a table for you right now, Charlie. Sit at the bar and do something funny for the folks." That was Chaplin's last visit to Shor's.

While a celebrity like Chaplin was waiting for a table,

he would probably see a comparatively unknown major-league baseball player being seated immediately after he checked his hat. Toots, a passionate sports fan, idolized athletes and sportswriters. On the night of August 1, 1945, Shor was watching at the Polo Grounds when Mel Ott, then the playing manager of the then New York Giants, knocked the five hundredth home run of his career. Toots hastened back to his saloon to arrange a celebration for Ott's arrival there after the game. When Shor came in to the bar, he was told that Sir Alexander Fleming, the discoverer of penicillin, was having supper in the dining room. Toots introduced himself to Fleming and sat down for a chat with the famous medical scientist. After they had talked for a few minutes, a waiter whispered to Shor that Mel Ott had just entered the lobby. "Excuse me," Toots said to Fleming. "I gotta leave you. Somebody important just came in."

Shor's friends often claimed that he was illiterate, a charge that he never bothered to deny. One of his most widely quoted remarks was made during an intermission at the opening-night performance of Michael Todd's modern-dress production of *Hamlet*, starring Maurice Evans, which Todd had talked him into attending. Toots said, "I bet I'm the only bum in the joint that's going back in there to see the rest of it because I don't know how it turns out." One evening Toots warmly complimented Bob Considine for a sports column that Bob had written on the previous day.

"Who read it to you?" Bob asked.

Shor stared silently into space for a moment. Milly

Considine said to her husband, "Bob, you shouldn't talk to Toots like that."

"Don't get excited, Milly," Shor said. "I was quiet because I was just trying to think who *did* read it to me."

Two of Shor's friends who tried, now and then, to broaden his cultural interests were Morris Ernst, the lawyer and author, and dancer Paul Draper. Ernst once sent Toots an autographed copy of his rather heavy book on civil rights, *The First Freedom*. Toots, of course, never opened the book but he sent Ernst a dictated thank-you note which said, "I have read it, and enjoyed it very much. Although you are not a baseball fan, I know you are a good American, and that is enough for me."

Draper once talked Toots, against his will, into attending a concert conducted by Leopold Stokowski at Carnegie Hall. Toots brought Rags Ragland, a sometime movie and stage bit comedian, along with him. After Shor and Ragland were shown to their seats in the crowded concert hall, Toots looked around and said, "There ain't one single bum here that I know." After the first number on the program, there was a long round of applause, with Stokowski returning several times to the podium to take bows. Shor said to Ragland, "Look at that creep taking all them bows! I saw Carl Hubbell pitch a no-hitter one time at the Polo Grounds and the crowd went wild, but he never took even one bow. Let's leave at the half."

Outside Carnegie Hall, Toots and Rags climbed into a taxicab that was parked beside the curb. Shor said to the driver, "Toots Shor's." The driver turned around and stared at him in amazement. "Mister," the cabby said, "I been working this stand for ten years, and this is the first time anybody ever asked me to take him from here to there."

Like Costello's much smaller and less pretentious barroom on Third Avenue, and like most crowded barrooms everywhere, Shor's is remembered for its quotable talk. The proprietor's own wisecrack about the midnight curfew imposed on nightclubs and restaurants to save electric power during World War II was printed on the editorial page of the *New York Herald Tribune*. "Any bum who can't get drunk by midnight ain't trying," Toots said. Back in the years before Mario Puzo gave the role of a godfather a new meaning I once asked Toots to explain the Mafia. He said, "There's this old Italian guy, sitting in the cellar under a run-down, crummy old tenement house over in Jersey. He's calling the shots in the loan shark rackets, the trucking business, the numbers, the bookmaking and everything else." Three of Shor's closest friends were mobsters who employed him in their speakeasies during Prohibition years, Owney Madden, Big Frenchy La Mange, and Longy Zwillman.

Like his friend columnist Bugs Baer, Shor felt that every city in the United States outside of New York was as dull as Bridgeport, Connecticut. He was delighted by Billy Martin's remark after he was traded from the Yankees. At a private party in Shor's, Francis Cardinal Spellman said to Martin, "How do you like it in Kansas City?" Martin turned to Shor and said, "How would *he* like it in Kansas City?" Toots listened one evening to a friend who was praising the steaks served in a certain restaurant in Madison, Wisconsin. "After you eat one of those steaks in Madison," the friend said, "you go to bed that night knowing that you just had one of the best steaks in the world."

Toots said, "And when you wake up the next morning, you're still in Madison, Wisconsin."

Shor was deeply disappointed, but not too surprised, when his favorite baseball club, the Giants, moved from New York to San Francisco. Horace Stoneham, the owner of the Giants, had been suffering from poor gate receipts at the Polo Grounds, which he blamed on the televising of its ball games. A few months before Stoneham decided to make the move, he had told a group of friends at Shor's about watching midnight mass at Saint Patrick's Cathedral on television during the previous Christmas Eve. A spokesman for the archdiocese reminded Catholics in the TV audience that seeing the services on television did not fulfill their obligation to attend mass on that holy day: they were still required to go to mass in a church. After listening to that announcement, Stoneham exclaimed, "Oh, God, I wish the Giants had a gimmick like that!"

Along with Fred Allen and Jackie Gleason, the steady customers at Shor's included such memorable talkers as Jimmy Cannon, Paul Douglas – the stage and screen actor, not the U.S. senator from Illinois – and Robin ("Curly") Harris, the only former newspaper reporter in New York who had worked for both the staid *Times* and the flashy *Daily News*. One evening at Shor's Allen displayed an obituary, mailed to him by Nunnally Johnson, which noted the recent death of a New Yorker named Roy Forkum. "I'm going to show this to Mayor

Wagner," Allen said, "and see if I can get him to put up a plaque in Central Park, dedicating a mall to Roy Forkum's memory. It will have a simple inscription on it, only two words—Forkum Mall."

Another habitué of Shor's was Jimmy Cannon. As a writer on *The Stars and Stripes*, Cannon spent a lot of time with Joe Louis, the heavyweight champion, whom he idolized. He could spend hours recalling Louis's conversational quips. One day in London, Cannon listened to a British journalist questioning Louis about racial prejudice in the United States. "Why are your people so ready to serve in this war?" the reporter asked. "Your government hasn't done much for its Negro citizens." Cannon enjoyed Louis's casual reply—"There ain't nothing wrong with us that Mr. Hitler can fix." While Cannon and Louis were awaiting their discharges from the army at Fort Dix, New Jersey, they encountered a friend who worked as a second at Madison Square Garden boxing matches.

"How is your brother Freddy?" Louis asked. "Was he in the service, too?"

"Freddy?" the Jacob's Beachcomber said. "Freddy was too small to get drafted. Freddy is only about four feet tall."

Louis shrugged, and said, "Small man, get a small gun."

Paul Douglas was one of Shor's closest friends when he scored his first big hit as an actor in Garson Kanin's comedy *Born Yesterday*, playing the role of a loud-mouthed and tough-talking junk-dealing racketeer named Harry Brock. Douglas admitted that he had modeled the Brock character on Shor. While he was appearing in *Born Yesterday*, Douglas lived at the Elysee

Hotel in New York, in a room directly above an apartment occupied by Tallulah Bankhead. "When Tallulah wakes up in the morning," Douglas said at the time, "and roars at her maid for her hairbrush, I jump out of my bed upstairs and start looking for it." Douglas was a spicy talker. One night at Shor's he was discussing an actress whose physical charm he did not admire. He said, "She has a chest like Huckleberry Finn." Complaining about another actress because she lacked the physical strength that her role required, Douglas said, "If I give her a shove, as I'm supposed to do, she'll roll across that stage like a used communion wafer." Before signing a film contract with Twentieth Century–Fox, he turned down a contract with Metro-Goldwyn-Mayer because its payroll at the time included such male stars as Clark Gable, Spencer Tracy, and Walter Pidgeon.

"In a lineup like that," Douglas said, "I'd be playing the part of the guy who carries the relief pitcher's sweater in from the bull pen."

Curley Harris seems to be an intimate friend of almost every prominent person in North America, including Mexico and the West Indies. His wide circle of close pals over many years has included the Kennedy family, Richard Cardinal Cushing, Armand Hammer, Rex Humbard, the TV evangelist, Jimmy Hoffa, Mafia leader Frank Costello, and William Randolph Hearst, Jr., all of whom Curley has served as a public relations counsellor. He and his wife, Patricia, a former Miss America, also write a weekly newspaper column on travel resorts. One of Curley's close friends was John O'Hara, the social-climbing novelist, but they met at

"21," never at Shor's, which was not swanky enough for O'Hara. The snobbish O'Hara's biggest regret was that he was financially unable in his youth to attend Yale, but he did get some satisfaction in later life when he was admitted to membership in the ultraexclusive National Golf Links of America at Southampton on Long Island. Harris and O'Hara, both big, burly, and tough-looking, were often mistaken as plainclothes policemen, much to O'Hara's enraged embarrassment. They once traveled together to Boston to attend the Proper Bostonian society wedding of Nancy Corcoran, C. Z. Guest's sister, to their friend Alfred Wright, a New York sportswriter. The other guests at the reception stared curiously at the two strangers from out of town without saying a word to them. Finally, Eleonora Sears, the grande dame of Boston society, approached Harris and O'Hara with a pleasant smile and said to them, "We have at last figured out who you two fellows must be – you're the detectives guarding the wedding gifts!" Harris laughed, but O'Hara was furious.

Harris once arranged an off-the-record luncheon meeting at Shor's between Frank Costello, who then controlled the nation's slot machine rackets, and an editor of *Life* magazine who wanted to buy a slot machine to play with in his home. It was then impossible to buy a slot machine from anybody except Costello, who explained to the editor that his machines were not for sale. However, Costello added, he would be glad to send a slot machine to the editor's home, free of charge.

Soon after the slot machine arrived, the editor entertained at a Saturday-evening dinner party a group of guests which included his boss at *Life*, who fell in love with the slot machine. After playing the machine, the boss asked if he could take it home, a request that his editorial assistant, feeling the pull of rank, could not deny. Curly Harris was approached once again; could Costello come up with another slot machine? Curly passed the plea on to Costello, who firmly shook his head. "Nothing doing," Costello said. "Only one slot machine to a magazine."

Except on Saturdays, when he was rehearsing and performing in his popular television variety show, Jackie Gleason seemed to spend all of his time in the 1950s at Shor's. He often picked up a few menus and acted as the headwaiter, escorting bewildered customers to their table along a roundabout route that led them through the kitchen. Gleason's casual remarks were sharply witty. One night he handed an ice cube to Sonja Henie, the figure skating star, and said to her, "Do something." When he was a television star, Jackie was earning another $150,000 a year making recordings of soulful love songs, such as "Body and Soul," "I Only Have Eyes for You," and "I'm in the Mood for Love," which he described as "music for lovers only." Even though he is unable to read music, he conducted orchestras of more than fifty musicians and dictated the arrangements himself. "I made a record today with thirty-two Italian mandolin players," he said one evening at Shor's. "While we were making the recording, you couldn't get a haircut anywhere in Brooklyn or Jersey City."

I once wrote a magazine article about Gleason without asking him any questions; I spent an evening with him at the bar in Shor's, listening to his conversations with various people, and reported in the article the highlights of his remarks. At one point, he greeted the wife of one of his friends and inquired about a girl who had been her roommate a few years earlier. "You mean Katherine E. Concannon?" the wife said.

Gleason's eyes popped out widely in astonishment.

"Katherine E. Concannon?" he said. "Is that a girl? It sounds more like the name of a tugboat."

A few minutes later, Gleason was telling the Cardinal's Stan Musial about the neighborhood in Brooklyn where he lived as a child. "I took a couple of pals over there a few weeks ago to show them the tenement house we lived in," he said. "I had a little trouble finding the place. Then we saw two guys getting out of a cab and carrying a television set into a pawnshop. I yelled out, 'I'm home! This is where I come from! Where else in the whole United States of America would you see two guys hiring a cab to bring a TV set to a pawnshop?' The kids in our neighborhood called a cab when they wanted to play baseball. The nearest ball field was over on the other side of Brooklyn and it was so crowded we had to go there by cab at five o'clock in the morning to get the field before somebody else got it. The trip home after the game, also by cab, was something. About twenty-five of us would pile into the cab, all the players on the two teams, some of the spectators, several girl friends, the bats and the bases. And a dime tip for the driver."

Musial said that he had to be running along to keep a dinner engagement. "Get in touch with me next spring," Gleason said to him. "I'll show you how to hold your bat with the label up so it'll last you the whole season without cracking."

A tall stranger with a long white beard sat down on the empty stool beside Gleason's and became involved with him in a long serious discussion about psychiatry and religion. "You've never read Saint Augustine?" Gleason said at one point. "You ought to look into him. He's the one for no-good bums like you and me." Adolphe Menjou, the veteran debonair movie star, gave Gleason a warm greeting. "For what you did in the movies, there was never anybody else who could touch you," Gleason said to Menjou. "You and Edmund Lowe and another guy. Who was the other guy?"

"Clive Brook," Menjou said.

"Clive Brook!" Gleason exclaimed. "That's the guy I was trying to think of! Clive Brook!"

"Best hat wearer in the business," Menjou said. "No other man in the movies or on the stage could wear a hat like Clive Brook."

Some of the goings-on at the old and original Shor's on 51st Street involving Toots and Gleason seem too sophomoric to believe today. One evening they challenged each other to a footrace around the block between 51st and 52nd streets, starting from Shor's front door with the two contestants running in opposite directions. When Toots returned, puffing with exhaustion, to his saloon, he found Gleason sitting calmly at the bar, sipping a drink. Toots stared at him and then remembered that they had not passed each other during the race. "You bum!" Shor roared. "You took a cab!"

Gleason once challenged Shor to a drinking bout,

both of them sipping brandy and soda, which Toots could drink, day and night, without getting tipsy. After a few hours, Gleason pulled himself up from his chair, staggered toward the men's room, and collapsed unconscious on the floor at the entrance to the dining room. Two waiters tried to pick him up. Shor waved them away. "Let the bum lay there for a while so everybody can see him," Shor said.

When the engagement of Grace Kelly and Prince Rainier of Monaco was announced in 1956, Gleason made a bet with Richard Gehman, a magazine writer, that the wedding would never take place. The loser was to pay for a big buffet dinner and an evening of drinking in Shor's upstairs private banquet hall for friends of both the bettors. The payoff party turned out to be a much bigger affair than Gleason had expected, with a bill of more than thirty-four thousand dollars, but Toots, pleased with the entertaining evening, announced that he was picking up the check.

Probably the most memorable of the many stag parties staged at Shor's upstairs dining hall was a celebration of Grantland Rice's birthday on a Sunday evening in November 1954. Rice was not at the party. He had died four months earlier. The array of sports celebrities assembled by Shor to toast his memory would have astonished him. The guests at the head table included Jack Dempsey, Gene Tunney, Johnny Weismuller, Gene Sarazen, Earl Sande, Eddie Arcaro, Lou Little, Hank Greenberg, Tommy Henrich, Yogi Berra, Vincent Richards, and all four of Notre Dame's famous Four Horsemen backfield from the Knute Rockne era of the 1920s—Harry Stuhldreher, Don Miller, Jim

Crowley, and Elmer Layden—who had been given that nickname by Rice. At one point during the evening, I found myself having a drink with Joe DiMaggio. At the time I was writing an article about Yankee Stadium for *Holiday* magazine. I asked DiMaggio what he liked best about playing baseball in that particular baseball park. His rather surprising reply, for some reason or other, has stuck in my mind. "The showers in the dressing room," DiMaggio said. "They're the best showers in the world."

Old-timers at Shor's felt that the Rice dinner was not as grand as an earlier stag party honoring Toot's close pal, Bill Corum, when Corum was elected president of the Churchill Downs racetrack, home of the Kentucky Derby. Each guest at the affair was draped with a blue silk ambassadorial sash. The wine was Dom Perignon. Toots ordered the waiters not to hide the label under a towel. The entertainment was provided by Ethel Merman, Frank Sinatra, Jimmy Durante, and Eddy Duchin.

Miss Merman's husband at that time, Shor's pal Bob Levitt, was then serving in the World War II army as an officer at Fort Hamilton in Brooklyn. The wife of Levitt's commanding general high-pressured him into bringing Ethel, much against her wishes, to a reception and a cocktail party at the fort's officers' mess hall. The bored Miss Merman, sipping a cocktail, was approached by the general's wife who urged her to sing a few songs. Levitt told people at the Corum dinner that Ethel glanced coldly at the general's wife and said to her, "Listen, Cuddles, don't crowd me."

Shor's two closest friends in his later years, next to his devoted Irish Catholic wife, Marian, who was called

Husky by Toots and Baby by everyone else, were Bob Considine and Joe DiMaggio. Milly Considine says that one night when she was feeling unexpected labor pains, Bob telephoned Toots for advice before he called her doctor. Toots once complained that he was unable to reach Considine on the telephone. Bob reminded him that the phone number had been changed to Yukon 6-1100. "That's the number I been dialing, UK6-1100," Shor roared. For many years Shor carried a gold watch chain with a small inscribed plaque that said, "To My Guy Toots—Joe DiMaggio." When DiMaggio was the big star of the Yankees, he spent almost all of his spare time sitting with Toots at Shor's. One day a friend saw DiMaggio running swiftly along 51st Street and stopped him to ask what was up. "I had to go to a Yankee luncheon at the '21' Club," Joe said breathlessly. "Now I've got to get to Toots and explain it to him before he hears about it from somebody else."

One day DiMaggio was stopped on a street by an advertising executive who said to him, "Joe, why did you turn down our fifty-thousand-dollar offer to endorse one of our client's products?"

Stunned, DiMaggio said that he had never heard of the offer.

"But I talked to Toots about it," the advertising man said, "and he told me you wouldn't be interested."

DiMaggio hurried to Shor's and questioned Toots.

"Yeah, I turned that creep down," Toots said. "He isn't our kind of bum."

Although Shor and his many friends did not realize it at the time, his golden era as a convivial host began to decline in 1958 when he sold his lease on the original Toots Shor's building on 51st Street to William Zeckendorf, the real estate speculator, for one and a half million dollars. Zeckendorf promised to build another Shor's at 33 West 52nd Street, next door to "21," a site that held sentimental memories for Toots. It was there that he held his first important job, as the daytime manager at Leon and Eddie's cabaret back in the early 1930s.

The day after he closed his deal with Zeckendorf, Shor handed his two checks, one for one million dollars and another for five hundred thousand dollars, to his accountant, Dick Sherman, and told Sherman to deposit both of them in his checking account at the Irving Trust Company. Sherman was astonished. "Put the money in a saving account," he said, "and you'll earn thousands of dollars in interest on it."

"I don't want those creepy bankers at the Irving Trust using my money," Toots said. "Put it in my checking account so they won't be able to get their hands on it." Shor hated bankers because they were constantly bothering him about his constantly overdrawn checking account. Now that he was rich for the first time in his life, he would get revenge by keeping his new wealth in his checking account where the bankers could not use it.

Toots felt that money was made to be spent or given away, not to be saved or invested, and he despised tight-fisted bankers and business executives who disagreed with that theory. Horace Stoneham once made the mistake of bringing Toots to a meeting that he was having with several bankers to discuss the sale of a hotel that he owned in Florida. The meeting took place in a suite at the Plaza. Drinks were served. One of the bankers handed his glass to Shor and said to him, "Put some ice in my drink." Toots snapped at him, "Put your finger in it and stir it. That'll cool the drink, you crummy banker." A chilled silence came over the meeting. The bankers left the room with no more talk about the sale of the hotel.

Shor's million and a half soon dwindled. He paid off a three-hundred-thousand-dollar mortgage on his 51st Street saloon along with several other big debts, and he sent big checks to many old friends who did not need money, just to remind them that he was still their pal. Most of the gift checks were returned to him but many others were quickly cashed. He and Baby took Virginia Warren, Chief Justice Earl Warren's daughter, on a long and expensive tour of Europe. Jackie Gleason received a picture postcard from Rome portraying the ruins of the Colosseum. Toots wrote on, "I'll work on the rest of it tomorrow."

Shor's friends had warned him to mind his behavior overseas so that he would not give the United States a bad reputation. When the Shor party arrived at the airport in Paris, there was only one available taxicab. "This Frenchman pushes me aside and gets into it with his wife," Toots said later to Art Buchwald. "I bring back my fist to hit him, but Baby starts whistling 'The Star-Spangled Banner' so I let the bum get away." In Paris, Toots visited Maxim's but not Tour d'Argent. "I can't pronounce it," he said later. "Why should I go to places if I can't tell people where I went?"

Toots complained about a story written about his visit to London by a woman reporter on the *Daily Express*. "She said, 'He maneuvered his seventeen stones into London,'" he said. "What kind of a crack is that? It sounds like they kept track of how many times I got loaded. Well, I got stoned a lot more times than seventeen before I got to London."

When Shor returned to New York, he learned that Zeckendorf's plan to build a new Toots Shor's with an attached garage on West 52nd Street had collapsed. After buying the land and excavating a foundation, Zeckendorf ran out of money and found himself unable to complete the project. Toots spent a year trying to find another site. Then he managed to buy the property from Zeckendorf but found himself too broke to construct the building. A mutual friend suggested Jimmy Hoffa's Teamsters' Union Pension Fund. Shor had never met Hoffa. The friend arranged a meeting, and, after looking Shor over, Hoffa quickly agreed to sponsor the loan at the Chase Manhattan Bank.

Shor immediately telephoned Bob Considine, who was vacationing in Honolulu, to announce the big news. Considine reported their conversation in *Toots*, a biography of Shor that he wrote a few years later.

"I got the money!" Toots shouted. "I got the money! I got the money from the Teamsters!"

Considine said without much enthusiasm, "Oh."

"What's wrong with that?" Shor said.

"It's okay, I guess. At least you won't have to worry about a name for the joint. You can call it Toots Shor's Hoffabrau."

"Very funny, you creepy big-nosed bum," Shor said. "All Hoffa's pension fund does is okay me, and I get the dough from the Chase Manhattan."

"And you get Hoffa standing at the bar every day."

"He don't drink," Toots said.

"Suppose he just stands there having a Coke?"

There was a moment of silence. Shor was recalling that Francis Cardinal Spellman's office had once similarly sponsored a mortgage on his old place at 51st Street.

"I'm still not worried," Toots said. "The New York Archdiocese had a mortgage for a while on my other joint, but I never once saw Spelly at the bar."

As Considine wrote later, the ground-breaking ceremony for the new Shor's building on a cold day in October 1960 was the most celebrity-studded opening in New York since *South Pacific*. Among the guests were Chief Justice Warren, James Farley, Jackie Gleason, Jack Dempsey, Baseball Commissioner Ford Frick, Phil Silvers, Billy Conn, Yogi Berra, Bobby Feller, Whitey Ford, and Mickey Mantle. The construction work dragged on for more than a year at a cost of more than five million dollars. Then the opening of Shor's, almost an exact but larger replica of the memorable old place on 51st Street, had to be delayed because of a twelve-week trucking strike staged by its own mortgage holder, the Teamsters' Union. During the opening-night festivities, Groucho Marx watched Jack Dempsey warmly shaking hands with Rocky Marciano, and said, "The least they could do would be to go four rounds for us." Jackie Gleason sent a huge floral piece, shaped like a horseshoe, with six Care packages and a note that said:

Good luck Dear Toots,
On your new domain,

Where joy will reign
As well as tomain.

Gleason was annoyed when he learned that the florist who forwarded his message had misspelled ptomaine. "No wonder Toots was able to pronounce it right," he said. During the festive evening Toots reminisced tearfully about various old pals, especially Ernest Hemingway, who could not be there because they had recently passed on. "The last time I saw Ernie," Toots recalled, "he came in here to pick up a bet I made for him on Ingemar Johansson against Floyd Patterson, when Patterson was the heavyweight champion. Ernie called me on the phone from Spain and told me to put a thousand for him on Johansson. I told him he was crazy but I couldn't talk him out of it. I put the bet on for him at four to one, so he won four thousand dollars. He was the only guy I knew who bet on Johansson. Nobody figured Johansson had a chance because he didn't know how to duck, but as it turned out he didn't need to duck. Poor Ernie. Why would a great guy like that want to shoot himself?"

When Pope Paul VI visited New York in 1965, Cardinal Spellman asked Shor to cater the papal luncheon served to the visiting cardinals and bishops that day at the archdiocesan reception hall behind Saint Patrick's Cathedral on Madison Avenue. "Spelly knew that I'd never speak to him again if he gave that job to somebody else," Shor said. To serve the luncheon, Toots selected a group of eleven captains and waiters who spoke a total of twenty-eight languages. He used plates from his restaurant, inscribed with an interwoven monogram, the letters *T* and *S* imposed on each other. The monogram could be read as *S* and *T*. In fact, when Sonja Henie married Dan Topping, she persuaded Toots to provide her with a set of his plates, which she passed off as her own china. During the archdiocesan luncheon, one of the Italian cardinals picked up a plate, stared at the monogram, beckoned to Jack Barry, one of Shor's headwaiters, and said, "What does this mean?"

Barry said, "It stands for Saint Theresa, Your Eminence."

Burdened with heavy mortgage payments and the soaring prices of food and liquor in the 1960s, Shor soon found himself in deep financial trouble trying to operate his new restaurant on 52nd Street. He also found that carefree and free-spending customers, like the close pals who crowded his old place on 51st Street until dawn back in the 1940s and 1950s, were disappearing from New York's evening scene. Most of them, growing older and living in the suburbs, were catching commuter trains to Long Island and Westchester or New Jersey before the dinner hour. The new athletes, like Joe Namath, with open-collared shirts, talked a hey-man-get-with-it jargon that Toots could not understand. One night he had a bitter argument with Namath. "Get out of my joint, and stay out," Toots roared at Namath, who never returned.

The younger generation of new sportswriters also appalled Shor. "On fight nights, or after a hockey game or a basketball game at the old Garden, you couldn't get near the bar in my joint," Toots said. "Now these young crums cover something at the new Garden, next to Penn Station, or at a ball park, and they rush home, drink a malted milk, and go to sleep."

Becoming moody and irritable, Toots quarreled with old friends, including his onetime idol, Joe DiMaggio, who suddenly disappeared from the Shor scene. Neither Shor nor DiMaggio had much to say about the breakup. It saddened friends of both of them, who remembered Joe appearing proudly at Toots's various upstairs birthday parties with Marilyn Monroe clinging to his arm.

Then, in 1971, the door at Shor's was padlocked for nonpayment of $269,516 in overdue federal, state, and city taxes. "I'll be open again in three weeks," Toots said. But that was the end of Shor's at 33 West 52nd Street. Eighteen months later he managed to open another much smaller Toots Shor's at 5 East 54th Street, between Fifth and Madison Avenues, but that venture soon failed, too.

Toots and Baby sadly moved out from the handsome ten-room duplex apartment at 480 Park Avenue, where they had lived happily with their four children for almost thirty years, and rented a small two-room suite at the Drake Hotel. Toots managed to pay for it by renting the use of his name to a small Toots Shor barroom near Madison Square Garden, which later opened two uptown branches. He seldom visited the place. When his closest pal, Bob Considine, died suddenly in 1975, their friends had some difficulty reminding themselves that there was no Toots Shor's to go to after the funeral at Saint Patrick's Cathedral to drink a toast to Bob's memory. Or, at least, no Toots Shor's where a misty-eyed Toots himself would be raising his glass.

Two years later, the same huge crowd of mourners and a few hundred others from distant places gathered on the sunny but freezing-cold morning of January 25, 1977, at Temple Emanu-El on Fifth Avenue to attend the funeral services of Toots Shor. He had died two days earlier with cancer. One of the speakers, Toots's friend Paul Screvane, said in a eulogy, "He must be the only man who was as close to Longy Zwillman, Big Frenchy, and Owney Madden as he was to Cardinal Spellman, Robert Sherwood, and Harry Truman." Not to mention several thousand other big names and several thousand smaller ones, too.

8

IMPOSTERS

IMPOSTERS HAVE FASCINATED ME SINCE I WAS A youngster in Cambridge, Massachusetts, back in the twenties and thirties, watching the antics of Harvard Square students, the local boys who posed as Harvard undergraduates in order to make out with Radcliffe girls. Johnny Murphy was one of them. He had quit high school to take a job with the city's sanitation department, emptying ash and trash barrels, but in the evening he changed from his overalls to the Harvard student uniform of that era—white buttoned-down shirt with a black knitted tie, tweed jacket, gray flannel slacks, and white buckskin shoes—and spoke with a cultured Groton accent.

At the time I am thinking of, Murphy was carrying on a romance with an innocent Radcliffe girl from the Midwest who thought that he was a Harvard junior named Bruce Kendall. She was also under the impression that his family lived on Park Avenue in New York and spent their summers at Bar Harbor, next door to the home of Atwater Kent. One morning, between her classes, the girl happened to be walking along Dunster Street, near Harvard Square, where she came upon Murphy unexpectedly. He was on an ash truck shaking out a barrel.

"Why, *Bruce!*" she gasped.

Without batting an eye, Murphy smiled and waved to her. "Hello, darling," he said. "This is just an initiation stunt for the Hasty Pudding Club."

Another Harvard-connected imposter, and one of the most famous in modern times, Prince Michael Romanoff, enrolled at Harvard as a graduate student in 1923. That was no small feat because Mike did not have credentials to prove that he was even qualified for the freshman class, let alone for advanced graduate studies. He convinced the dean that his degrees from Oxford, Cambridge, and other European institutions were lost when his suite at the Imperial Palace at Petrograd was looted during the Russian Revolution. Many years later, at his fashionable restaurant in Beverly Hills, California, the prince reminisced with me about his brief stay at Harvard.

Mike recalled that about three months earlier he had made a thrilling escape from the immigration office on Ellis Island in New York Harbor. Every time that he tried to enter the United States in those days he ran into trouble with immigration officials, who contended that he was not an American citizen. They insisted that his real name was Harry Gerguson and that he had been born in Vilna, Russia, six years before his parents emigrated to New York. Mike would admit during these tussles on Ellis Island that he was a Gerguson but maintained that he was born in New York and was, therefore, a U.S. citizen. He told me that during one such dispute late in 1922, he became bored with the investigation and escaped from the island by swimming across the harbor to the Battery, with his cherished blackthorn walking stick clutched between his teeth.

"A policeman pulled me ashore," he said. "I explained to him that I had had too many cocktails. He nodded and walked away. I hastened to make tracks to the interior. I met a benefactor in Minnesota who offered to finance my studies at Harvard. I moved to Cambridge and took rooms on Mount Auburn Street in the area then known as the Gold Coast because it was favored by the wealthier and more socially prominent students. I was getting along famously until one Sunday evening when circumstances forced me to take my evening meal at the college's dining hall. Usually I dined at Locke's in Boston, the only restaurant in New England fit to eat in. But on Sundays Locke's was closed. In the dining hall I spotted a fellow I had seen on Ellis Island. I knew that he recognized me. I knew that the show was over. I went to the dean and resigned from the university. The dean felt badly about it, much more badly than I did. I went off to visit friends in Wichita, Kansas."

Prince Michael never had much to say about the early life of Harry Gerguson. Alva Johnston, who wrote his biography, found evidence that Gerguson lived in New York orphanages as a youngster before World War I. During the war, he worked his way to Europe and stayed there for four years. Nobody except Mike knows for sure where or how he spent those four years, but somewhere, somehow, he picked up an aristocratic-sounding British accent and an intimate knowledge of Oxford and Cambridge universities. One theory, never proven, was that he worked at Oxford as a valet. In 1919, he turned up in Paris as Prince Michael Alexandrovitch Dmitry Obolensky Romanoff. Nobody, however, ever heard him speaking in the Russian language. Johnston reported that in 1926, when Romanoff was serving a stretch in New York's Tombs jail for fraud, a friend brought a real Russian prince, Serge Bagarin, to the jail one visitors' day so that Mike would have somebody to talk with in his mother tongue. Mike refused to speak to the prince, explaining that the Romanoffs had not spoken to the Bagarins in many generations. When I talked with him after he had gone straight as a restaurant proprietor in Beverly Hills, Mike had no regrets about his earlier years as a masquerader. "For what I did, a novelist receives honor and pay," he said. "I gave people a sense of adventure by proxy."

Back in 1951, when I was collecting material for a magazine article about imposters, dramatist and film writer Charles MacArthur told me an entertaining story about how he coached one into landing a fifteen-hundred-dollar-a-week job as a screenwriter at a Hollywood studio. "If he had followed my instructions more carefully, he could have gotten two thousand a week," MacArthur added.

The principal in this case was a not particularly intelligent young Englishman with no literary background and no writing ability. "He couldn't even write a check," MacArthur said. MacArthur himself was working as a screenwriter at the time, but he was spending more time on tennis courts than on film scripts. The Englishman frequented the same courts where MacArthur played and they began to meet for singles matches in the early mornings.

"Let's call him Basil," MacArthur said. "Basil had a habit of looking at his wristwatch every two minutes while we were playing. It drove me crazy. He had a job at an oil company and he was always worrying about being late for work. I was willing to do anything to get him to stop that business of him looking at his watch. It got me nervous. I asked him how much money he was making at the oil company. He said sixty-five a week. I told him that if he'd promise to stop looking at his watch while we played tennis, I'd get him a job as a writer at my studio for two thousand a week."

MacArthur began to bring Basil to story conferences at the studio. Producers eyed him curiously and asked MacArthur who he was. "I told them he was a brilliant young British playwright, the next Noel Coward," MacArthur said. "I said he was just out here for a rest, and not interested in working on pictures. But he's a friend of mine and I wouldn't make a move with a story line unless I asked his advice. Finally the head of the studio called me and asked if Basil could be hired. I said, 'Not a chance.' They arranged a meeting with him behind my back. Instead of holding out for two thousand a week, as I told him to do, Basil got nervous and gave in when the bidding came up to fifteen hundred a week."

Basil held his position as a screenwriter by following a line of MacArthur's strategy: when he was given a story to work on, he sent it back untouched with a note explaining that it was not his type. Then the studio sent him to northern Canada to look into the possibilities of a film about the Hudson Bay Company. "Even in Hollywood, he never spent a dime," MacArthur said. "Up there in the Arctic, drawing fifteen hundred a week, he was able to save a fortune. He came back feeling very cocky. It turned out that either from miserliness or a love of security, the dumb bunny had never given up his sixty-five-a-week job at the oil company. There was a mix-up about his social security deductions. The studio found out about his job with the oil company and fired him a half hour later."

One of the leading characters in my magazine piece about artful pretenders was a bright and pleasant little man from Brooklyn named Stephen Weinberg. While I talked with Weinberg, he interrupted our conversation frequently to urge me to collaborate with him on a book about the story of his whole life. I thought it over and decided against it. The trouble with Weinberg's autobiography was that it seemed too incredible.

Weinberg, also known as Stanley Weyman, Dr. Clifford Weyman, Dr. Sterling Wyman, Lieutenant Commander Royal St. Cyr of the U.S. Navy, and Lieutenant Ethan Allen Weinberg, like the young Mike Romanoff, enjoyed mingling socially with prominent people. One day in 1921 he visited Princess Fatima of Afghanistan at her apartment in a New York hotel, introducing himself as a State Department official. He announced that he had been assigned to escort the princess to Washington for a visit to President Warren G. Harding at the White House. Harding's White House staff did not even know that the princess was in the United States. Weinberg phoned the State Department after checking Her Royal Highness into a suite at the Williard Hotel and made quick arrangements for the meeting with the president. Then he posed smiling with Harding and the princess for newsreel cameramen on the White House lawn.

When Rudolph Valentino died in New York in 1926, Weinberg took charge of his funeral. Hearing that Pola Negri, Valentino's sweetheart and a big movie star herself, was in a Times Square hotel, grief-stricken, he telephoned her and introduced himself as Dr. Sterling Wyman, one of Rudy's old friends. He offered his services.

"The next thing I knew," he told me, "I was in Pola's suite and the newspapers were describing me as her personal physician. So I branched out and took charge of the funeral."

One time when Weinberg was serving a sentence in the prison on New York's Welfare Island for forgery, he smuggled out of the jail letters to several prominent New Yorkers, describing himself as a surgeon who had given up his practice to devote all of his time to serving poor people. He gave his address as 600 East 55th Street. The address sounds like a house in the plush Sutton Place neighborhood, but it happened to be the postal address of the Welfare Island prison. Checks and money orders poured into Weinberg's cell until the prison authorities became suspicious and started to examine his mail.

During World War II, Weinberg was arrested and jailed for operating a school for draft dodgers. For tuition fees ranging from a few hundred dollars to two thousand dollars, he instructed his students in such subjects as the simulation of deafness or feeble-minded behavior. It was charged that about a dozen of the school's graduates succeeded in getting themselves classified as 4-F. In court Weinberg pleaded that he was not all there upstairs. His lawyer said to the judge, "I have been authorized by my client to make it clear that he is definitely nuts. He has delusions of grandeur and would rather fool people than earn money."

Just before I talked with him in 1951, Weinberg had been doing well for the previous few years, working legitimately as a news correspondent for a small news service at the United Nations General Assembly, where he became very friendly with the ambassador from Thailand. He talked the ambassador into giving him an appointment as a special public relations counsel for the Thailand delegation, with diplomatic status. Then he made a big mistake. He sent a long telegram to the State Department, asking if becoming an accredited diplomat for Thailand would jeopardize his U.S. citizenship. The State Department turned the message over to the FBI, which dug up the long police record of Stephen Weinberg, alias Stanley Weyman, Clifford Weyman, Royal St. Cyr, and Sterling Wyman. The exposure of Weinberg made newspaper headlines and he lost his job with the wire service.

I have not heard from Weinberg in recent years. If he is still alive, he is close to ninety years old but, for Weinberg, that would be no problem. He could easily pass himself off as somebody else much younger.

The big problem in writing and editing an allegedly nonfictitious magazine article based on interviews with an imposter is trying to make sure that has told the truth. Somebody who has spent most of his life pretending to be somebody else might be inclined to exaggerate, or fabricate, when he recalls his various masquerades for a listening reporter. The stories told to me by Ferdinand Demara while I was interviewing him for *Life* magazine were carefully checked by *Time*'s large staff of researchers and correspondents all over the United States, Canada, and in Korea, where he posed as a Canadian navy surgeon during the Korean War. The researchers not only found all of Demara's tales to be factually true; sometimes, in his talks with me, he had played down or passed over some of his most impressive accomplishments. At one time, when he was posing as a doctor of psychology, he joined an order of Catholic teaching monks who sent him to De Paul University in Chicago for graduate studies in ethics and philosophy. A *Life* researcher, checking Demara's record at the university, found an interesting detail that he had neglected to mention to me. Although his formal schooling ended at the age of sixteen, when he ran away from home and joined an order of meditative farm-working monks, Demara had no trouble in his later years as an imposter studying and teaching such subjects as psychology, law, and medicine. His scholastic record at De Paul showed that he had received straight A's in rational psychology, metaphysics, cosmology, epistemology, and natural theology. When I confronted him with his high marks, he said, with a shrug, "Maybe the instructors were impressed because they thought I already had a Ph.D. in psychology from Stanford."

Unlike Mike Romanoff and Stephen Weinberg, who were often exposed during their careers of make-believe, Demara's real name and lack of college credits never appeared in newsprint until the Canadian navy announced his discharge because he had used the medical credentials of Dr. Joseph C. Cyr, a general practitioner in New Brunswick, to get himself commissioned as a naval surgeon-lieutenant during the Korean War. Then it was also revealed that in earlier years Demara had posed successfully as a college psychology professor named Robert French, as a doctor of zoology, as a law school student, a hospital orderly, a Trappist monk, and a deputy sheriff. After he was discharged from the navy in Canada, newspapers and news services tried to interview him but he refused to talk. When he returned to his parents' home in Lawrence, Massachusetts, to hide from reporters and curiosity-seekers, *Life* offered him fifteen hundred dollars to tell his story to me and he accepted the deal.

Jay Gold, the editor at *Life* who gave me the assignment, handed me a check for fifteen hundred dollars and said, "Don't give it to him until you're reasonably sure that what he's telling you is on the level." I checked into a hotel at Andover, near Demara's Lawrence home, and invited him and his father, a local movie theater projectionist, to have lunch with me. "This boy is a genius," the elder Demara said. "He can do anything, but he refuses to do it the hard way. Right now we are trying to persuade him to get a college degree and go to medical school, but he won't have any part of it." After talking with Fred Demara for ten minutes, I felt certain that the incredible things he was saying were all true. He was one of the most sharply intelligent and witty people I have ever known. I excused myself for a few moments, went to a telephone booth, and called Gold in New York. "This fellow could do anything," I told Jay. "You could put him in charge of CBS or the J. Walter Thompson advertising agency tomorrow, and he would do a better job than any executives they ever had."

I went back to the table and offered to give Demara his check.

"How long do you want to talk with me?" he asked.

"Maybe for three or four days."

"Then you'd better hold on to the check until you get all of the material that you need," he said. "If you give it to me now, I might disappear this afternoon."

Demara recalled for me one of his first experiences as a deceiver. On a snowy winter day in Lawrence, he found a pair of artificial legs in a trash can, the kind of legs used in store windows to display women's stockings. Fred stuck the two legs into a snowbank beside a busy roadway and hid nearby. Motorists, seeing the legs, stopped their cars and rushed to pull them from the snow. As they drove on, cursing, Fred replaced the legs and waited for the arrival of his next victim.

"I think that was my first crack at fooling people," he

said. "I was about ten at the time. I guess I've been trying to fool people ever since."

Before Pearl Harbor, he left a monastery in Rhode Island where he was studying to be a teaching brother and enlisted in the U.S. Army. Then he went AWOL and joined the navy. While he was in the navy, he decided to give himself a fictitious college background so that he could apply for Officer Candidate School.

"That was my first crack at studying college catalogues to make believe that I had a degree," Fred said. "I was pretty green at it then. I picked Iowa State College, and I threw in a letter from Senator Capper of Kentucky, praising my character. It was a crude job. I was strictly an amateur in those days. The navy caught wise. I decided to leave the service temporarily."

Demara went to Kentucky and joined the Trappist monks at the Abbey of Our Lady of Gethsemane, posing as Dr. French, a psychologist. Then, still using the name French, he moved to Chicago for graduate studies as a Viatorian monk.

"I found myself facing ordination as a priest in that order," he said. "I thought at the time that I had a true religious vocation, but I couldn't see myself being ordained without telling them my real name. So I disappeared. Using French's credentials again, I taught psychology at Gannon College in Erie, Pennsylvania, and at St. Martin's College near Olympia in Washington State."

When I asked Demara how he had managed to teach a subject as complicated as psychology to college students, he seemed surprised. "What's so tough about that?" he said. "I just kept ahead of the class. The best way to learn something is to teach it."

Living in the small town of Lacey, where St. Martin's is located, Demara felt really safe and secure for the first time since he left the navy. He decided to settle there permanently. He was popular at the college and became friendly with the county sheriff, who made him a special deputy so that he could enforce the law on the campus. Demara, in return, made campaign speeches for the sheriff when he ran for reelection. Then one day the sheriff appeared at the college with a warrant for his arrest. He went to the sheriff's office where two FBI agents were waiting for him, charging him with desertion from the navy.

Demara served a year and a half at the U.S. Disciplinary Barracks at San Pedro, California, and then went home to visit his parents in Lawrence while planning his next move. By now he had become an expert in using other people's real names. He decided to pose as Dr. Cecil Hamann, a biologist then teaching at Asbury College in Wilmore, Kentucky, with a doctor's degree from Purdue. Through some method, which he refused to describe to me, Demara managed to get copies of Hamann's academic records from universities and colleges where he studied or taught.

"If you think that's easy, try it some day," he said to me. "Only the other day I had a letter from the registrar at one of Hamann's colleges. He begged me to tell him how I had conned his office into sending me a transcript of Hamann's record. Believe it or not, if you give me ten days, I can produce a complete transcript of anybody's college record. I even managed to get a copy of Hamann's birth certificate, despite the fact that I did not know the name of the town in New York State where he was born. I wrote a tearful letter, a real sob story, to the vital statistics office at the state capital. I told them I had been abandoned by my parents when I was born and I wanted to know my place of birth. I gave them my age and my name, Cecil Boyce Hamann. Back came the information: Hamann was born at Shelby in Orleans County. Then I wrote to Shelby and got his birth certificate."

As Hamann, Demara spent a year studying law at Northeastern University in Boston and working as a hospital orderly. He found the study of law boring. He left Boston and entered the seminary of the Brothers of Christian Instruction, a French-Canadian religious teaching order, at Alfred, Maine. The yen to be a member of a monastic community was still strong. When he introduced himself as Dr. Cecil Hamann, with an array of university degrees, the brothers were overjoyed.

"I was regarded as a big catch," he said. "They rolled out the red carpet and the bells began to ring."

I learned later that a news release, reporting the arrival of Dr. Hamann at Alfred, was published in newspapers at the time. A scientist at Oak Ridge, a former pupil of the real Dr. Hamann, received a package from Boston that was padded with newspapers. While he was unpacking it, he came across a report in one of the papers about somebody with the Hamann name and background joining the religious order in Maine. He mailed a clipping of the item to Dr. Hamann in

Kentucky. The doctor told me that he was determined at the time to expose the imposter but he never actually got around to doing anything about it.

Demara took the religious name of Brother John. He fascinated his fellow brothers with tales of mythical adventures in India, Tibet, and Japan. He helped the seminary to obtain a college charter so that novices in the order would not have to go to the University of Montreal to obtain credits that would qualify them as teachers.

To prepare Demara for his solemn vows the brothers at Alfred sent him to Grand Falls, New Brunswick, to study theology under Brother Boniface, an older man who managed a farm there. He spent hours in the company of a young doctor at Grand Falls, Joseph Cyr, who was treating Brother Boniface for rheumatoid arthritis. Hearing that Brother John had been a physician, Dr. Cyr turned to him for advice. Brother John suggested bee venom. He had read about its use in treating arthritis in one of the many medical journals to which he subscribed. "The bee venom was expensive," Demara told me, "but it worked like a charm." From then on, Dr. Cyr's admiration for Brother John, the former Dr. Hamann, knew no bounds.

"Joe Cyr wanted to get a license in Maine so that he could practice on both sides of the border," Demara told me. "I was due to return to Alfred shortly. I told him I'd be glad to present his credentials to the Maine medical board and say a few kind words about him."

When Demara returned to Maine, he was too busy doing other things to present Dr. Cyr's case to the state medical board. He drove to Boston in one of the monastery's automobiles, and then took a bus to St. John, New Brunswick, where he offered his services, as Dr. Cyr, to the Royal Canadian Navy. He was given a warm welcome. Doctors willing to serve overseas were eagerly accepted by the Canadian armed forces during those Korean War years.

"I told them that if they didn't take me in a hurry, I'd join the Canadian army," Demara said. "That did it. Within two hours they had me on a train to Ottawa. I was commissioned there the next day. They never even bothered to take my fingerprints and I passed the physical exam without taking any of my clothes off."

As a surgeon-lieutenant, Demara was first assigned to a naval hospital in Halifax. There, for the first time in his life, he fell in love.

"I had always kept myself from getting deeply involved with a girl," he said. "I'm a phony, and you can't be a phony and really fall in love. But this time, in Halifax, I couldn't help it. We planned to get married after I did my time in Korea, and then, after I got out of the navy, we would settle down someplace in Canada where I would start a medical practice."

In June 1951, Demara sailed to Korea on the *Cayuga*, a destroyer with twelve officers and two hundred and eighty enlisted men. His first official task on the *Cayuga* presented a challenge that might have shaken a less confident imposter. The captain asked him to pull out a tooth. "I told him to wait until the next day," Demara said. "That night I stayed in my cabin, reading up on dentistry, which was all new to me. In the morning I shot the skipper's jaw full of novocaine and yanked out the tooth. No trouble at all."

Demara's first really serious case came a few months later when three wounded South Korean soldiers were brought to the ship. One of them had a bullet lodged near his heart.

"When I started to operate on him," Demara said, "I couldn't have been nervous, even if I felt like being nervous. Practically everybody on the ship was jammed into the room, watching me."

Conditions for such a risky job of surgery were far from ideal. Demara had only a few surgical instruments and no autoclave in which to sterilize them. His only assistant, the ship's sick-bay attendant, was too nervous to find the vein for an injection of sodium pentothal, which Demara was using as an anesthetic. But Demara performed the operation quickly, as if he had been performing chest surgery for many years. "I kept one basic principle in my mind," he said. "The less cutting you do, the less patching up you have to do later. Cutting and bending back a rib that was slightly splintered, I found the bullet, only a fraction of an inch from the heart. I pulled it out and poured some Gelfoam, a coagulating agent, into the wound and it clotted up immediately. The crowd gave me a cheer. Within a few hours the soldier was sitting up, sipping beef broth. His pulse and his blood pressure were normal and his temperature was 100. Twelve hours later he walked off the ship."

The *Cayuga* made a trip to Japan. When his ship returned to the same area of Korea a week later, Demara went ashore, looking for his patient. He found him in a native hut that the South Koreans were using as a first-aid station. The soldier was feeling well, but

Demara was appalled by the lack of medical care among the South Korean troops fighting in that sector of the front. He obtained permission to spend a few hours a day alone on the shore, doing surgery on wounded soldiers.

The public information officer for the Canadian naval forces in the Far East, Lieutenant R. A. V. Jenkins, was stationed on the *Cayuga*. One day Jenkins heard that a South Korean commanding officer had walked seventeen miles to thank Demara for his services. He decided to put out a release to press correspondents about the unusual Surgeon-Lieutenant Joseph Cyr.

"I tried hard to talk Jenkins out of it but I couldn't persuade him to drop the idea," Demara said. "Then, when he insisted, I tried to make my operations sound as dull as possible, hoping that the correspondents wouldn't use the story. But it was printed in a lot of Canadian papers, and, sure enough, Joe Cyr saw it. Less than a week later, our skipper, Commander James Plomer, called me to his cabin and showed me a radio message from Canada ordering me removed from active duty. He said to me, 'Joe, somebody back home made a mistake. Carry on with your duties and I'll set them straight about this.' But a few days later I was on my way back to Canada. All I could think of was that girl in Halifax. I knew I could never face her after all of this, and the thought of losing her was just about killing me."

While I was working on the Demara article, a *Life* reporter in Korea talked with Commander Plomer about Demara.

"He was a remarkable personality," the commander said. "He had a warm sympathetic regard for all the officers and men and a high perception of human character. As a layman, I cannot judge, but, to my knowledge, he performed his medical duties with considerable skill. The outcome of the whole affair was one of the greatest individual tragedies I have ever encountered."

To make Demara more depressed, an accumulation of mail was delivered to him on a hospital ship in Japan while he was waiting for air transportation to Victoria, where he was to be discharged. In it was a package of food from his girl and several letters from her discussing plans for their wedding.

On the plane trip to Canada, he was shown a news story about his case. As he suspected, the release about his work in Korea had been published in New Brunswick and Dr. Cyr had identified a photograph of the surgeon as that of the man he had known as Dr. Cecil B. Hamann and Brother John. To make matters more complicated, the real Dr. Hamann in Kentucky said that the navy surgeon looked like a man who had been kicked out of St. Louis University for cheating. Demara noticed, however, that there was no mention of his real name in the whole report.

Then, to his surprise, he found no serious charges against him when he reported to the naval authorities in Victoria. The Canadian navy assumed that he had enlisted under a false name for some reason or other, but it had apparently never occurred to them that he was an imposter. He did nothing to change their opinion. His fingerprints were taken in Victoria and then it was established from U.S. Navy files that his real name was Ferdinand W. Demara. He was released from the Canadian navy with all of the pay that was due to him and he was politely asked to leave the country.

Demara took a plane from Seattle to Chicago, where he spent three weeks. "I guess I did a little drinking," he said. "I couldn't get that girl out of my head and I kept thinking about how happy I was in the Canadian navy. I was happier there than I had ever been anywhere else in my whole life. If only that story hadn't gotten into the newspapers, everything would have been all right."

When Demara went back to Lawrence to spend Christmas with his parents, he found hundreds of postcards and letters addressed to him from all over the United States and Canada and from several foreign countries. Some of them from abroad had only his name and "Massachusetts U.S.A." written on the envelopes but the postal officers delivered them to him promptly. He showed me a letter from a nineteen-year-old mother in Detroit, asking him to perform a lung operation on her infant daughter. A lumber camp in British Columbia offered to hire him as its doctor with no questions asked.

After I handed Fred his check, I asked him what he was planning to do next. "I don't know exactly what I'm going to do," he said, "but I have a few things in mind." A few years later a book about his subsequent adventures, *The Great Imposter* by Robert Crichton, was made into a film with Tony Curtis as its star. The last mention of Ferdinand Demara that I saw in a newspaper, several years after that movie was shown, reported that he was serving as a missionary with a religious order in Washington State.

Imposters come and go but none of them will ever quite top Lucy Hicks of Oxnard, California. For thirty years, before and during World War II, Lucy was a well-known and very popular figure in Oxnard, the center of Ventura County's sugar beet country. She was a wise and jovial black from Kentucky who cooked, on special occasions, for the best families in town. At the same time, Lucy reigned as queen of Oxnard's red-light district. She managed a block of brothels where sugar beet farm workers spent their money on Saturday nights. Everybody in town knew all about Lucy's business but nobody thought less of her because of her special profession. The respectable wives in Oxnard still sought her incomparable services in their kitchens and entrusted their children to her care. Lucy dressed their daughters on wedding days. She gave going-away parties, with champagne, for their sons when they went into the service during the war. She prepared barbecues for church suppers. Her tall, bony figure in gay, low-cut gowns with picture hats and high-heeled slippers was a familiar sight at all community gatherings. She contributed generously to local charities. "Just don't ask me where the money came from," she would chuckle. When Franklin D. Roosevelt died, Oxnard newspapers published a comment from Lucy along with statements from other prominent citizens. Everybody thought the world of Lucy Hicks.

A few days after V-J Day there was an outbreak of venereal disease in Oxnard. One case was traced to Lucy's houses. The local doctor who examined her girls apologized to Lucy but informed her that regulations forced him to check on her health, too. Lucy protested but there was no way to avoid it. When the doctor reported his finding, the town had a hard time believing him.

Lucy was a man.

9

BALLPLAYERS, BARRYMORES, AND THE FOIBLES OF FORD

I HAVE WRITTEN TWO BOOKS AND SEVERAL ARTICLES about the Ford Motor Company and both of its Henrys, the founding father and his namesake, the present chairman of the board. One day in the 1950s, when I was writing a series of articles about his family, Henry II invited me to his home at Grosse Pointe Farms, where he was then living with his first wife, Anne, a daughter of a large and wealthy New York lace-curtain Irish-Catholic family named Murray. (A lace-curtain Irish-Catholic family is a family that has fruit in their house when nobody is sick.) When Henry introduced Anne and his three then-young children to me, she shook hands and stared at me with a look of happy excitement. She said, rather breathlessly, "Aren't you the same writer who wrote the Duke of Windsor's memoirs for *Life* magazine?"

"No," I said. "That was another writer with an Irish name, Charles Murphy."

The smile on her face faded quickly. Evidently she had been telling her friends that her husband and his family were being profiled by the same writer who had worked with the duke. Then I was rather startled to see on the piano in the Ford living room, in a large and costly silver frame, a brief and formal thank-you note signed by the duke. Anne had sent him condolences when his mother died. When she received a reply from him, she framed it and placed it on display in her living room.

The framed note reminded me of an entertaining story about the duke and young Henry told to me earlier that same day by a woman who was a close friend of the Edsel Fords, his parents. She described the exciting day back in 1924 when the duke, then the young Prince of Wales, was entertained at Edsel's home in Detroit. The prince was a heart-throbbing romantic figure to most American women at that time. Edsel Ford's mother-in-law, Mrs. William Clay, was dying to get a look at him, but she was too shy to be presented to him. She concealed herself behind a screen in a corner of a second-floor nursery room so that she could get a peek at the prince when he was brought upstairs to be introduced to the Ford children. Henry's younger sister, Josephine, was only one year old at the time. She became sick shortly before the royal visitor arrived, and threw up on the nursery rug. Order was restored moments before the prince was shown into the room. The prince shook hands first with the seven-year-old Henry and asked him how things were going. Henry looked the guest straight in his eyes and said to him, "My sister just threw up, and Grandmother is hiding behind that screen." The woman who told me the story then added to it:

"Young Henry is still a plain, straightforward, and unpredictable man who will tell you exactly what's on his mind. In that way, at least, he's exactly like his grandfather. My husband once took Old Henry to a theater in New York to see a play that was a big hit. When they came out of the theater, he asked Mr. Ford what he thought of the show. Mr. Ford said, 'Those people in that play ought to go out and get themselves jobs and go to work, instead of just hanging around in that theater like that.'"

When I finished the research for the series of articles on the Fords, I said to Henry II, "I'm going to do something for you that I don't usually do with people that I write about—when I get finished with the writing of this piece, I'm going to let you read it. But don't go showing it to all of the vice-presidents in the company."

"Don't worry about that," he said. "I've been helping you with your work on this story for only one reason—we need the publicity it will give us to help us sell more cars. We won't get any publicity from it if it doesn't get printed. If I showed it to our vice-presidents and let them make changes and cuts in it, no magazine would ever print what was left."

The serialized four-part article about the Fords and their motor company was a long one, about twenty thousand words, but after reading it Henry surprisingly suggested only one minor change, a revision of a complicated and rather misleading paragraph describing the formation of the philanthropic Ford Foundation.

The leading personality in the story of the Ford

family, of course, is Henry I, whose introduction of the mass-production assembly line in 1913 brought automobiles into every American village and farm. I first began to dig up a big bag of previously unpublished stories about that Henry's eccentricities in 1952 when his company hired me to write the text in a book of pictures commemorating its fiftieth anniversary. I learned, among many other things that I had never known about Henry, that apparently he and Clara Ford, his wife, never threw anything away. After Mrs. Ford's death in 1950, three years after that of her husband, a group of Ford Company executives brought Robert Bahmer of the National Archives to Fair Lane, the Ford home in Dearborn, Michigan, to see if any of the mansion's contents might have historical value. Nothing had been removed from Fair Lane since Mrs. Ford's death. The first room that Bahmer poked into was a music hall, with a thirty-thousand-dollar organ in it. The hall was piled with boxes of letters and various other papers. Bahmer picked up a letter from one of the boxes. It was a letter from Colonel Robert R. McCormick, publisher of the *Chicago Tribune*, addressed to Ford and dated July 30, 1941. In it McCormick apologized for an anti-Ford editorial that he had published in the *Tribune* in 1916, which had stirred up a famous libel suit by Ford against McCormick's newspaper. Nobody except Ford and McCormick knew of the existence of the apology.

Moving on, Bahmer and the company executives uncovered many more valuable specimens. In a shoe box under Ford's workbench in his laboratory, they found a telegram from Calvin Coolidge thanking Ford for not running against him for the presidency in 1924, and a letter to Santa Claus written by the eight-year-old Edsel Ford in 1901, two years before his father organized their motor company. "I haven't had any Christmas tree in 4 years and I have broken all my trimmings and I want some more," Edsel wrote. "I want a pair of roller skates and a book. I cant think of anything more I want you to think of something more."

More than fifteen hundred dollars in small bills was tucked into various books on the Fair Lane bookshelves. Ford had used the paper money as bookmarks. For many years, Ford's secretary daily handed him an envelope with $200 in cash in it. He carried it in his pocket during the day for use as spending money but he seldom spent it. Getting undressed at night, he would take the envelope from his pocket and toss it into a desk or dresser drawer. Several drawers, filled with envelopes, each containing two hundred dollars in cash, were found in the mansion at Fair Lane after Mrs. Ford's death. Money and banks mystified Ford. One day shortly after his assembly line made him a millionaire he went to a bank where he had an account and drew out from it $150,000 in cash. He counted the money and examined it suspiciously. Then he went to another teller, four windows away, and deposited it. He was just testing.

Henry Ford had many offbeat and strange ideas. On his bathroom's shelf he kept a glass filled with salt water and rusty razor blades and dipped his comb into it every morning before combing his hair. He claimed salted rusty water prevented his hair from falling out. For a long time he was convinced that granulated sugar was ruining everybody's stomach because, under a microscope, it looks like broken glass. One of his chemists made the mistake of showing him that sugar dissolves instantly when a drop of water, or any other liquid, is added to it. Furious because his theory was demolished, Ford fired the chemist. The birdbaths on the lawns of Fair Lane's 1,369 acres had their water electrically heated. Ford had a theory that birds might not fly south in the winter if they had access to unfrozen water. He once had five hundred British birds of various species shipped from London to New York and then brought to Dearborn by train. He sent his secretary, Ernest Liebold, to New York to meet the shipment of birds. They arrived on a Sunday. Liebold had to search all over Manhattan in order to find a bird doctor who could examine the feathered travelers and swear that they were healthy enough to enter the United States. Finally Liebold managed to get the birds through customs and immigration channels and brought them to Dearborn.

"Now what shall I do with them?" he asked Ford.

"Take them to Fair Lane and turn them loose," Ford said.

Liebold did as he was told. Only a few of the birds from England were ever seen again.

The house at Fair Lane had a few valuable paintings, such as Sir Joshua Reynolds's *Portrait of Lady Hamilton as a Bacchante*, but Henry and Clara Ford were not especially moved by or interested in fine art. In his biography of Sir Joseph Duveen, the shrewd art salesman, S. N. Behrman tells of the time in 1920 when five of the leading art dealers in New York—Duveen,

Knoedler, Wildenstein, Seligman, and Stevenson Scott—forgot their differences temporarily and banded together in a joint effort to get Ford interested in the Old Masters. He was too big a quarry to be tracked down by one hunter. The five dealers spent a considerable sum of money collecting and binding in three volumes a set of handsome reproductions of what they considered the hundred greatest paintings in the world. Duveen and representatives of the other firms then made an expedition to Dearborn and presented the books, as a gift, to Ford. He was delighted with the reproductions. As he pored over them, Duveen expressed the hope that someday he might want to own a few of the originals. Ford looked up at him with surprise.

"What would I want with the originals when the ones right here in these books are so beautiful?"

The Ford house at Fair Lane is not as big or as magnificent as the mansions of less wealthy families such as the William Randolph Hearsts or the Vanderbilts, but Ford built it in 1915 with better mechanical equipment for the comforts of living than any other private home in the world at that time. The Ford home drew all of its heat, electricity, and water through an underground tunnel connected to a power plant 296 feet from the house, which, in turn, drew its energy from a dam on the nearby Rouge River. The power plant also provided electric ice-making refrigeration—almost unheard of in 1915—for both Fair Lane and the nearby Ford plant's restaurants and cafeterias, and pumped brine that chilled seven refrigeration systems in the house. Always an independent soul, Ford wanted no truck with public utility companies. The purpose of servicing the house with heat, light, water, refrigeration, a private telephone service, vacuum cleaning, and hot and cold running water, through pipes in an underground tunnel extending from the power plant almost a hundred yards away, was to keep the house as quiet and as free from noise and vibration as possible. In each of the Fair Lane bathrooms, incidentally, there was hot and cold running rainwater as well as regular tap water, for washing hair, and a compressed air outlet for drying hair. Rainwater was caught in deep cisterns under the terraces and then pumped from the power plant to the bathrooms through a separate plumbing system of its own. Ford installed direct current electrical power in his house because his idol, Thomas Edison, preferred it to alternating current. Just as he disapproved of hydraulic brakes, Ford turned up his nose at both oil heat and automatic coal stokers. Until after Mrs. Ford's death in 1950, as incredible as it may seem, the steam-heating boilers in Fair Lane's powerhouse were fired with coke that was shoveled by hand. On a cold day, the firemen shoveled as much as seven tons of coke in twenty-four hours. But each room had a thermostat to control its radiator.

A herd of fifty-eight deer and a flock of peacocks roamed through the grounds at Fair Lane. Three bushels of corn were put out every day for the birds and squirrels. If Mrs. Ford saw a dead bird or a dead animal anywhere on the premises, she launched an investigation as probing as a coroner's inquest. Under such protection, the wildlife at Fair Lane became very independent. One morning Henry went for a walk through his woods before breakfast. Three hours later somebody noticed that he was missing. He was found sitting in the branches of a tree, three miles from his house. He had been chased by a moody buck deer.

In the last two years of his life, after he handed the control of the Ford Motor Company over to his grandson and namesake, the service staff at Fair Lane saw a great change in Old Henry. He slowed down considerably. Days and then weeks went by without his taking a glance at his favorite comic strip, "Little Orphan Annie." But on his last day at Fair Lane, however, Ford seemed in better health than usual. After lunch, his chauffeur, Robert Rankin, drove him around Dearborn. When he returned to Fair Lane, Ford stopped at his power plant where the superintendent, Charles Voorhess, was directing repair work. A few days earlier the Rouge River had overflowed its banks, flooding the powerhouse and extinguishing the estate's electric power. Two auxiliary motors had been brought in that afternoon and attached to the auxiliary turbine. While Henry was watching the work, the lights came on. He said to Voorhess, with a smile, "You won't get sore, will you, if I tell Mrs. Ford I was the one who fixed the lights?"

But the load was too much for the makeshift motors, and that night, at twenty-five minutes past nine, they sputtered and stopped. The home of Henry Ford, with its two hundred and seventy circuits of custom-made direct electrical current, was plunged again into darkness. A few minutes later the twentieth century's master of industrial efficiency left the world as he had entered it eighty-three years earlier—in the flickering light of a kerosene lamp and a few candles.

When I was writing the text of *Ford at Fifty*, the motor company's golden anniversary picture book, I spent several memorable evenings at the Dearborn Inn listening to the entertaining recollections of Philippe Halsman, one of the photographers who worked with me on that project. Halsman was probably the most successful portrait photographer in the world at that time, and he was also a great talker with plenty of interesting stories about the various celebrities who had posed for him. One of his all-time favorites was Anna Magnani, the earthy Italian film star. The first time that Halsman posed Magnani for a picture, he explained to her gingerly that he would be unable to hide the deep lines and dark circles under her smoldering eyes.

"Do not hide them," Magnani said. "I have suffered much to get them."

Halsman told me that most of the women he had photographed, unlike Magnani, were seldom satisfied with his pictures of them. He recalled a picture of Ingrid Bergman that he had taken a few years earlier for the front cover of *Life* magazine.

"I made her look like a girl in a high school yearbook," he said. "She was tanned, exuberant, and smiling. The editors liked it and it attracted a lot of nice comments, but she didn't like it. All she said was, 'I didn't realize my skin looked so leathery.' A few weeks later she gave up her job in Hollywood, left her husband, and ran off to Italy to live with Roberto Rossellini. Then the explanation of her discontent dawned on me. She wanted an image of sophisticated glamour, not a picture from a high school yearbook."

Halsman told me that he usually tried to get his subject involved in a conversation while he was taking a picture, so the person would be less self-conscious. "One time I was photographing Eleanor Roosevelt," he said. "Trying to think of something rather puzzling to say to her, I asked if she knew anything about boxing. The joke was on me. Floyd Patterson was one of her best friends."

One famous subject who flatly refused to be wheedled into forgetting Halsman's camera and insisted that he, not Halsman, should be in command of the picture taking was Winston Churchill.

"You'll take no picture without giving me warning so that I may be prepared for it!" Churchill shouted. "Before you click that thing, you shall count three seconds aloud – count three, two, and one, clicking when you get down to the one."

Obediently, Halsman called off a countdown before each shot of his camera, as if he was firing a missile instead of taking a photograph. The thing that Halsman remembered most clearly about his visit to Churchill's country estate was the prime minister's daily walk to the pool in his garden to feed his fish. At the edge of the water, the old statesman would call out loudly. The fish would rush to him like a pack of affectionate dogs.

During the fish-feeding sessions, Halsman would furtively circle around Churchill, camera in hand, trying to snap him in a candid pose. But Churchill was always careful to watch Halsman out of the corner of his eye. Before the picture could be taken, he would abruptly turn away. Finally, Halsman took a picture of Churchill from behind his back, showing him sitting beside his pool with his familiar head turned away from the camera. It was one of the most widely published and republished pictures that Halsman ever made.

Along with the writing that I have done under my own name, or under pseudonyms, sometimes I have taken ghostwriting assignments, or the writing of "autobiographies" under somebody else's name. One of the most interesting ghosting jobs that I did was a series of articles for *Look* magazine in 1965 under the name of Jackie Robinson, who was ending his career as a baseball star with the Brooklyn Dodgers. Young people may find it hard to believe that ten years earlier, in 1946, when Robinson signed up with the Dodgers and joined their farm team at Montreal for a tryout season, he was the only black player in major-league baseball. When he made his debut as an infielder at Ebbets Field the following spring, Red Smith made his point well when he wrote the memorable line in his advance story that day for the *New York Herald-Tribune*: "If you don't know which Dodger is Robinson," Smith said, "he's the one with 42 on his back."

Several players on the Philadelphia Phillies and the St. Louis Cardinals said that they would refuse to play in home games against the Dodgers if Robinson appeared on the field at their stadiums. They quickly changed their minds when Ford Frick, then the president of the National League, warned that any player trying to stage such a boycott would be barred from baseball for the rest of his life. But there was prejudice, Frick or no Frick. Branch Rickey, the president and general manager of the Dodgers when the club signed its first contract with Robinson, told an illustrative and entertaining story about Clay Hopper, the manager of the farm team at Montreal where Jackie served his season as an apprentice with the Royals in the International League. Hopper was a native of Mississippi and a staunch champion of white supremacy. Sitting beside Hopper on the Royals' bench one day, Rickey watched Robinson make a spectacular fielding play, picking up a fast grounder behind second base and throwing the batter out at first base. Rickey grabbed Hopper's arm and shouted into his ear, "Not another human being could make a play like that!"

Hopper turned around, amazed, and stared at Rickey. "Mistah Rickey!" he said. "You mean to tell me that you really believe a Negro is a human being?" But, Rickey added, Hopper got along well with Robinson during that season and in the fall he told Rickey that Jackie was indeed a real gentleman.

While I was working with Robinson on his *Look* serial, he was moving his family into a new fourteen-room home that he had built in a rural section of Stamford, Connecticut. They were the first and only black family in the town at that time. I was visiting the Robinsons there on the September day when Jackie took his older son, Jackie Junior, then ten years old, to the local school for the first time. I went along with them and watched hundreds of white girls and boys staring curiously at the solitary black boy as he walked toward the school building. I said to his father, "Do you realize that you're putting him through the same thing you went through when you went to your first game at Ebbets Field?"

Robinson stared at me, surprised. "I guess you're right," he said. "You know, I never thought of that?" When young Jackie came home from school that afternoon, he said to his father and mother, "It's a funny thing—I don't know the names of those other boys but they all know my name."

The Robinsons told me that when Jackie Senior first came to New York to play for the Dodgers his salary was so small that he and his bright and charming wife, Rachel, had to take turns eating their meals separately in their hotel's cafeteria because they could not afford a baby-sitter to stay with little Jackie. During Robinson's first season in the National League, when he was the only Negro in big-league baseball, he could have earned a small fortune from commercial endorsements and personal appearances, but Rickey, his mentor and guide, advised him against it. Rickey pointed out that Jackie was being watched critically by millions of white Americans who would have been quick to attack him if he allowed himself to be exploited commercially too soon. But after his first season in Brooklyn, during which he established himself as a big star, his salary went up and so did his outside income. When he retired from baseball, Robinson became a vice-president of the Chock Full O'Nuts fast-food restaurant chain in New York and the owner of a men's clothing store in Harlem. He was also active in various charitable and civil rights works until he died in 1972 at the age of fifty-three. As Gay Talese wrote in a *New York Times* article, the easiest way to identify a traveling major-league baseball club in an airport terminal today is to see a large group of both black and white men strolling together in a corridor. It certainly was not like that in 1947 when Branch Rickey decided to bring Jackie Robinson to Ebbets Field in Brooklyn.

I heard a lot of entertaining talk back in the 1950s when I spent a week at the Lambs Club, the venerable fraternity of the theatrical profession near Times Square, collecting material for an article about the history of the Fold, as its members called their clubhouse. John Barrymore is a character as famous in the annals of the Lambs as Babe Ruth is in the history of Yankee Stadium. Everybody I talked with at the club had a few stories to tell about Jack, as they called him. Emil Friedlander, the theatrical costume dealer, recalled one cold and snowy evening when Barrymore walked into the clubhouse with no shoes on his feet.

"Jack was being entertained in the downtown home of a very beautiful actress," Friedlander explained. "Her husband appeared unexpectedly at the front door. Jack sneaked out down a back stairway and it wasn't until he was walking up Broadway that he realized that he had left his shoes behind him. He came here to the Lambs and, after several drinks, headed back to the actress's house. Her husband, who knew Jack well because he was also in the theater, opened the door and said to him, 'Why, Jack! What brings you here at this hour of the night?' Barrymore roared at him, 'Stand aside! I've come back to get my shoes!'"

Barrymore's father, Maurice Barrymore, and his

uncle, John Drew, were both stalwart Lambs. The elder Barrymore was the author of the most atrocious pun ever heard in the Fold. In the early 1920s Maurice was being needled one evening by the caustic and anti-British Wilton Lackaye about the poor box-office business at a theater where Barrymore was appearing. Maurice protested that the theater, designed as an opera house, was too large for the subtle acting of his leading lady, Madame Bernard Beere. "It's a house for broader effects," he said. Always ready with a comeback, Lackaye remarked that Madame Beere's off-color repertoire could be very broad at times.

"In that theater," Barrymore said, "one can be obscene and not heard."

In the Lambs Club, back in 1906, John Drew, after reading a letter about the then-young John Barrymore's experiences in the 1906 San Francisco earthquake, made a comment, since widely quoted. John had reported that the first tremor of the earthquake knocked him into a bathtub filled with water and that a company of soldiers later ordered him to help with the removal of rubble from the streets.

"It took an earthquake to make my nephew take a bath," Drew said, "and it took the United States Army to put him to work."

One of the most memorable dinners ever staged at the Lambs was a testimonial honoring Frederick Loewe and Allan Jay Lerner shortly after the opening of *My Fair Lady*. Loewe and Lerner had first met each other in the club and formed their partnership. Performers at the banquet included Maurice Chevalier, who made a special trip from Paris for the dinner,

Victor Borge, Bert Lahr, Lauren Bacall, and Laurence Olivier. Everybody in show business tried to get a ticket to the affair. One member of the club who was then living in Florida telephoned George Trampler, then the club's manager, and begged for tickets. Trampler told him that every seat had been sold.

"If I can get just one ticket," the member said, "I'll make a donation of five hundred dollars to the Lambs."

"I just had a cancellation," Trampler said.

One of the interesting characters in my article about the Lambs was the club's elderly bootblack and errand boy, Biagio Velluzzi, known as "Murph." At that time Murph had been working at the club for forty-eight years without ever taking a vacation. He told me that being away from the Fold for even one day would make him unhappy.

When I talked with him, Murph recalled the pleasure he found in shining the shoes of John Barrymore, Irvin S. Cobb, and Ring Lardner. The Lambs was one of Lardner's favorite hangouts. He would sit for hours in the club listening to songs and conversations of other members and never saying much. When he did say something, it was often quoted for months afterward. A fellow Lamb once asked Lardner to read a poem that had supposedly been written by the member's dead brother. After looking at the verses, Lardner said, "Did your brother write this before or after he died?" Another evening Lardner looked at a Shakespearean actor with a wild mane of long hair that hung over his ears, and said to him, "How do you look when I'm sober?"

During the last three years of the *American Weekly*'s lifetime I wrote a column of jokes, wisecracks, and bright sayings of clever adults and outspeaking children for that Sunday newspaper magazine. While I was writing the column, I received in the mail from various publicity or press agents tons of wisecracks and alleged jokes credited to show-business people or mentioning certain nightclubs or restaurants that they were paid to publicize. ("Ronnie Avaricious, the rising musical comedy actor, was telling his friends at Lasagna East the other night about the executive who dictates letters with two secretaries sitting on his lap so that he can avoid the expense of buying carbon paper." Jokes of that ilk.) Arthur Murray, the dancing school operator, was never known to have said anything funny during his whole lifetime but at one time I was getting Arthur Murray jokes almost daily from three public relations agents, two in New York and one in Hollywood. Most of the jokes from press agents were pretty bad and unusable. ("Elsie Vain, the popular singer, saw a Western movie on TV so adult that instead of attacking the army's fort the Indians picketed it.")

Much, much funnier were lines of real-life or un-professional humor, or anecdotes about true happenings, which were told to me by members of my own family or people around our neighborhood, or which came from friends talking about sayings of small children, teenagers, or grown-ups who were not particularly trying to be funny when they made those remarks. A close friend of mine, Louis Mercier, once told me about his ten-year-old daughter saying to him, "If you can afford to take me to Trader Vic's for lunch, why can't you send me to Vassar when I'm ready to go to college?" Or my sister-in-law in Boston, rather embarrassed by the size of her extralarge family, announcing in a loud voice when she is seen with all of them in a public place, "If you children don't behave, I'll tell your mothers." Lines like that seemed to me to be much more entertaining than the straining and self-conscious banter of professional gag writers sitting around the tables at the Hillcrest Country Club in Beverly Hills.

The real humor came from life itself, like Billy Pearson's report on the reaction of his mother after he reported to her on the telephone his winning of the big prize on *The $64,000 Question* TV quiz show. "Hi, Mom!" Billy crowed. "I just won sixty-four thousand dollars!" "I saw you," Mom said calmly. "You need a shave. Why didn't you shave before you went on that show?" Another favorite that sticks in my memory was an exchange between Saul Levitt, when he was a correspondent for *Yank*, and Collie Small, a combat reporter for the United Press who traveled with him in the European combat zones. When, in 1945, the front line of the Allied forces moved for the first time from France into German territory, Levitt and Small ran into the basement of a house to escape from a sudden bombardment of enemy artillery fire. There they found themselves staring at the first German civilians they had seen since the beginning of the war, a woman and two teenaged youngsters who seemed terrified by their presence. Small, thinking excitedly about the report that he would write on the incident, said to Levitt, "Saul, you can speak German! Ask them something!"

"Levitt said, "What will I ask them?"

Small said, "Ask them what's their reaction to all this!"

Fred Corcoran, the golf promoter who invented the Professional Golf Association's tournament tours back in the 1930s, was a gifted talker who recalled countless entertaining tales about his favorite sport. One of Fred's favorite stories concerned the father of the famous Turnesa brothers—Joe, Jim, Mike, Phil, Doug, and Willie—who worked as the greens keeper at the Fairview Country Club in New York's Westchester County back in the twenties. When Turnesa's son and namesake, Joe Junior, was playing against Bobby Jones in the 1926 National Open at a course in the Midwest, the members at Fairview gathered in their club to listen to radio reports on the tournament. For a few hours in the afternoon, on the final day of the tournament, it looked as if Joe was going to be the winner. The members went wild with joy. A group of them ran from the clubhouse to break the big news to Joe Senior, who was on the sixteenth green, working on his knees rooting out a growth of crabgrass. "Mister Turnesa, Joe's winning the National Open!" one of them shouted. "Joe's winning the National Open!" The elder Turnesa glanced at the crowd calmly and turned back to the crabgrass. "Why wouldn't he?" he said. "He's never done anything all of his life except play golf."

Corcoran told me an entertaining story about Walter Hagen that he heard at Sandwich in England where, in 1922, Walter became the first American golfer to win the British Open. On the evening before the final round of that tournament, Walter saw a young boy, about ten years old, putting on the practice green.

"What are you doing?" Walter asked.

"Practicing golf," the boy said.

"What's golf?"

"Come here and I'll teach you how to play it," the boy said. He proceeded to give Walter a lesson.

The next day, when Hagen won the British Open, the boy ran to him on the eighteenth green and announced breathlessly to the people in the crowd that he taught Hagen how to play golf the previous day. Walter assured the smiling spectators that his young teacher was telling them the absolute truth. A few minutes later Walter received his prize money, which then amounted to about five hundred dollars, quite a considerable sum to a professional athlete, or to anybody else, in 1922. He astonished the British fans by endorsing the check and handing it over to his caddy as a tip.

As you must have gathered by now, I have done a lot of writing in Ireland about that island and its people. For some reason that I cannot understand, Irish people of all walks of life in Ireland seem to be much brighter and wittier talkers than people of Irish descent in America, myself included. During my first trip to Dublin, in 1962, I found myself carrying on an interesting conversation with an elderly man who was sitting alone at the next table in the dining room at the Shelbourne Hotel. When I stood up to leave the restaurant, I said to him, "It was a pleasure talking with you." He said, "I would say the same to you, sir, but it would sound repetitive."

A few days later, at an auction sale in a small country town, the glib auctioneer was trying to sell a round black iron cooking pot, used for boiling ham or cabbage over a peat fire. Spotting in the crowd the local Anglican minister, he decided to poke a little fun at the cleric. The auctioneer shouted at him, "Now, sir, this nice little pot would make a grand bell for your church."

The minister's comeback was fast and sharp. "With your tongue in it, Mr. McGrath?" he said.

During a later trip to Ireland, I took my wife, Mary, to my father's birthplace, the small town of Sneem in County Kerry, and introduced her to an old friend of mine, Winifred Hurley O'Connor, who runs a pub there. Mrs. O'Connor was joshing one of her steady customers, a longtime eligible local bachelor, about a recent rumor that he was considering a plunge into matrimony. She poured a round of stout, lifted her own glass of orange crush, and offered him a toast: "May there be a prettier pair of legs than your own under your kitchen table before the next crop of potatoes is dug."

Toasts, of course, are as traditional in Ireland as reciting the prayers of the rosary or betting on horse races. There are a thousand variations of Carl Sandburg's favorite Irish toast, "May the road to hell grow green waiting for you to pass over it," not counting the worn-out old favorite, "May you be in heaven for twenty minutes before the Devil discovers that you're dead." One Sunday in Kenny's bar at Lehinch in County Clare, we heard a farmer addressing his companion over their first drink of the afternoon.

"Here's to you, Padraic," he said. "When God measures you, may he put the tape around your big and generous heart and not around your small foolish head."

A few minutes later an expectant hush fell upon the crowded bar when the manager treated an elderly customer to a pint of stout. Every ear was straining to hear what he would have to say when he lifted his glass.

"If this be a ghost that I see here in my hand before me," he declaimed in booming, measured tones, "I hope it reappears again soon!"

Scraps of casual conversation overheard in Ireland are often more memorable than the carefully contrived witticisms heard in other countries. Two men at the next table in a restaurant at Tralee were discussing the problems of getting ahead in the world. One of them said, "They say it's not what you know, it's who you know, but that's not so at all. It's who knows you." One day I was talking with a friend on a street corner in Dublin. He glanced at a passing funeral procession and said, "Well, there goes another fellow who has given up the cigarettes." Bart Leahy, a friend of ours in Galway, was telling us a few years ago about a man who made a big killing betting on horse races and promptly bought himself a pair of expensive gloves. A less fortunate crony of his, eyeing the new gloves with envy, said with a slight sneer, "Isn't it curious that when a man comes into unexpected wealth suddenly his hands get cold?"

Naturally the talk of the Irish tends to spill over with racial pride. We listened one evening to a lady in Offaly discussing Ireland's history with fire and eloquence. Pausing to pour herself a glass of sherry, she offered an appropriate toast. "Here's to ourselves," she said. "There's none like us." I was reminded of an elderly patriot in Cork who once said to me, "I mind the time when the old Queen Victoria was reviewing her troops. First in the line of march came the Grenadier Guards, a fine-looking body of men, stepping out sharply, but as they passed by the queen, she said nothing. After them came the Coldstream Guards, and they were splendid, too. But as they saluted the queen and swung on by her, still there was not a word coming out of her. Then down the parade ground came the Irishmen of the Royal Dublin Fusiliers. As they marched past the reviewing stand, the queen turned to her prime minister, who was standing beside her, and it was then that she spoke for the first time. She said, 'Jay-sus! Them's *troops!*'"

As Barry Fitzgerald used to say about Ireland, "Ah, the chat!"

10

THE DAY AFTER
V-J DAY

On SEPTEMBER 3, 1945, THE DAY AFTER V-J DAY, I joined a small group of news correspondents and a few curious air force men who sneaked away from Tokyo; against a strict order from General Douglas MacArthur's command, we made a trip to Hiroshima — the first Americans to walk on the streets of that destroyed city after it was devastated by our dropping an atomic bomb four weeks earlier.

Getting to Hiroshima to see what the first atomic bomb had done was the aim of almost every reporter who came to Japan with the first occupation troops. General MacArthur had issued a firm rule against any Americans, or other foreigners, going into that still unoccupied and unpoliced section of the country until after the bombed area had been examined by scientists from the United States. At that time, nobody knew for certain how long the radioactive aftereffects of a nuclear explosion might linger. Some of the scientific experts were speculating on whether or not Hiroshima might be a dangerous place for humans to visit for the next ten or twenty years.

Another big question was what the reaction of people in Hiroshima might be when they saw, for the first time since the bombing, a group of Americans in military uniforms. No United States occupation troops were yet stationed anywhere near Hiroshima. Our party had only about twenty men, and only a few of us, the military personnel in the group, were carrying small sidearms. We imagined what would happen to such a handful of Japanese soldiers appearing in Brooklyn after that borough had been devastated by a Japanese bomb.

But we had learned that Hiroshima would not be inspected by American nuclear scientists for at least another three weeks. That was too long for the impatient newsmen in our group to wait. We were attached to the Strategic Air Force, with Lieutenant Colonel Tex McCrary as the press officer in charge of our group. McCrary had at his disposal a B-17 bomber, refitted as a flying news-writing room with radio operators standing by to put our stories on its wireless radios while we were still in the air. Tex's mission, handed to him by his air force generals, was to see to it that the air force was given most of the public credit for the winning of the war in the Pacific. It did not take much pressure from the correspondents in our group to persuade him to take us on an unauthorized flight to the Hiroshima area. Nobody knew how much damage the bomb had done. An adventurous fellow, Tex himself was as anxious to see the results of the attack as the rest of us, which included the late Clark Lee, the dashing Hearst war correspondent, Homer Bigart of the *New York Herald-Tribune*, Bill Lawrence of the *New York Times*, Jim McGlincy of the United Press, and *Life* photographer Bernard Hoffman. I was then an army sergeant from *Yank*, which was preparing that week to print a special V-J Day edition in a Tokyo printing plant that had been publishing a magazine for Japanese soldiers during the war.

On the afternoon of V-J Day, September 2, after the news correspondents in our group had covered the signing of the surrender treaty on the U.S.S. *Missouri*, we slipped away from Atsugi airport, near Yokohama, in the B-17 and flew some four hundred miles down the coast of Honshu toward Hiroshima. But bad weather forced us to turn back. The next morning, without letting anyone else at Atsugi know where we were heading, we took off again. The weather was still foggy and raining, but this time our skillful pilot, Mark Magnum of Milwaukee, who had flown many bombing missions in Europe, found an opening in the clouds. He somehow managed to land the plane on a small parade ground, or drill field, at a Japanese naval base at Kure, twelve miles from Hiroshima. I still remember Magnum touching his wheels on the parade ground, only a few feet from the water at the edge of the harbor, and bringing the big B-17 to a stop fifty feet from a stone wall. The parade ground was only about two thousand feet long, not much landing room for a bomber.

The astonished Japanese navy men at Kure brought

us to their commanding officer, Vice-Admiral Masao Kanazawa. Luckily for us, the admiral turned out to be an old and close friend of Clark Lee's. They had known each other in Shanghai in the 1930s, when Clark was covering the Japanese-Chinese war for the Associated Press. The admiral told us that he was glad the war was over. "The whole thing was a bad mistake," he said. "You had too many planes." He lent us two old Buicks and a creaky Ford, with drivers, to take us to Hiroshima, and assigned two reluctant English-speaking naval officers to act as our guides and interpreters. The officers tried to be polite to us, but it was obvious that both of them were cursing the admiral for handing them the embarrassing, and perhaps dangerous, task of appearing in Hiroshima with a group of Americans. One of the officers shyly declined to tell us his name. He explained that he had been born in Sacramento, California, and his father was still living in the United States.

Our other guide, Taira Ake, was a medical officer. He asked us immediately if we had brought a formula for treating the victims of the nuclear explosion. He said that people exposed to the blast were still dying at the rate of a hundred a day from destruction of white corpuscles. We explained lamely that the scientists and physicians who might be able to help him would be arriving at Hiroshima within a few weeks. He shook his head sadly and said that too many more victims would be dead by then.

"The men who invented atomic bombs should have invented a cure for the illness," Ake said. "One woman, who had only slight burns on the day of the explosion, died eighteen days later from lack of white corpuscles, and there are many like her. We have tried transfusions, but it does no good."

As we drove toward Hiroshima along the gray fog-shrouded harbor of Kure, a loud and theatrical Japanese sailor in the car I was riding in made a big show out of pointing out to us several half-sunken warships that had been attacked by Grumman dive bombers from U.S. Navy task forces during the closing months of the war. Admiral Kanazawa had told us earlier that three-quarters of all the remaining ships left in the Japanese navy were at Kure and not one of them was now operational. The talkative sailor would point at a bombed ship, making a swooping gesture with his hand and shouting, "Grum-man!" Nodding toward one battered and listing battleship, he shouted, *"Haruna! Haruna-Grum-man!"* The *Haruna* was the Japanese battleship reported to have been bombed and sunk on December 10, 1941, by Colin Kelly, our first publicized navy war hero, off the Philippines. The Japanese navy officers at Kure told us that it was not actually put out of commission until navy pilots pounded it there four years later.

On the outskirts of Hiroshima we began to see houses twisted crazily out of shape by the bomb blast. As we drove farther into the city, with the destruction worse on each block, we glanced at each other questioningly. There was a strong and unmistakable smell of dead bodies rising from the still uncleared debris of the shattered homes. But in the midtown center of Hiroshima, where the bomb had exploded about fifteen hundred feet above the ground, leaving no crater or mark below it, there was not much rubble or debris, no dead bodies – not much of anything except a vast and gaping emptiness.

Hiroshima is flat, built on a river delta. As far as we could see, for about four square miles, everything seemed to be leveled or in ashes, except an occasional concrete and steel-reinforced building with its windows empty and blackened, and, here and there, a brick chimney, a water pipe sticking up from the ashes with its faucet dripping, a few dead trees with their branches bare and leafless. I noticed on one street an iron safe, the only thing left in what was apparently a business office, probably with the bookkeeper's ledger and a roll of banknotes still locked inside it.

"The thing that hits you," I wrote the next day, "is not the destruction but the nothingness."

We had difficulty reminding ourselves that the leveling of Hiroshima had been done not by thousands of incendiary bombs but by a single explosion of one bomb followed by outbreaks of fires that swept through the city for the next two days. When we got out of the cars to walk around, I saw something that summed up the disaster. The Hiroshima fire department's trucks were still standing in the fire station, with parts of their engines scattered on the floor beneath them. The force of the blast had left the fire engines cripples and useless when they were urgently needed, just as the city's hospital was destroyed before the stricken people could go to it for help.

It was also hard to imagine that Hiroshima, now so empty, had been a busy city crowded with 340,000 people only four weeks earlier. In the rain that day we saw very few men and women walking on the streets, or waiting for trolley cars, which had only recently started to run again. Only two public buildings were open for business, the police headquarters and the Bank of Japan, which was sharing its damaged quarters with two other bombed-out banks.

We asked Taira Ake, the medical officer, where the people were.

"In hospitals in other cities, or dead," he said.

Some of the people we did see on the streets stared at us with blank, expressionless curiosity and others turned their backs on us. None of them seemed to show anger, hostility, or any emotion at all. Many carried umbrellas because of the rain. When they came near us, they lowered the umbrellas so that their faces would be hidden from us. I was uncomfortably aware of the air force insignia prominently displayed on the uniforms of our plane's crewmen, who were with us. But as Homer Bigart noted with surprise in his account of the day, "Nobody openly sneered or spat at us, or threw a stone."

Our naval officer escorts drew back nervously when we asked them to stop a few passersby so that we could talk with them about the bombing. "Oh, no, please don't," Ake said. "They won't want to speak with you." But we insisted. Finally the officers approached a group of passing men and women. They backed away from us, explaining politely that none of them had been in Hiroshima on the day of the bombing.

Again and again, as we walked through the city for the next two hours, we received that same answer when we asked somebody on the streets about the bombing.

They said that they were from another town, looking for missing relatives or on a business errand, and none of them had been there on August 6. This eerie absence of eyewitnesses began to impress us as much as the destruction itself. In every bombed city in Europe during the war there were always plenty of survivors who were only too willing to talk about what happened when the bombs fell. But in Hiroshima, as Ake had said, most of the people who were there during the bombing were apparently dead or in hospitals, or determined not to talk about their experience to strange Americans.

The young Japanese lieutenant from Sacramento said, "I know several people who were here during the bombing, but only one of them was not hurt. He was working on the second floor of an office building. He fell through the building to the basement. Everyone else in the building was either killed or injured, but he was not hurt."

Later in the afternoon we found an elderly man and a small boy who had seen the bombing. Like many people exposed to the explosion, the boy's hair had fallen out. With some self-importance, the boy told us that he had thought that "the moon had fallen on Hiroshima." According to Ake's translation, the man was saying such things as "It was terrible beyond imagination." He said that he had heard of two men who were fencing in a garden when the bomb exploded. The fencer facing the flash died immediately, but the other man, with his back turned toward the blast, was only slightly burned on the back of his neck.

Then we located a government official named Hirokuni Dazai who had been in Hiroshima during the bombing and the subsequent fire, surviving with only a minor head injury. Dazai agreed to meet with us for an interview in a motorcycle factory on the outskirts of the city, one of the few buildings in the area left intact.

A weary little man, with his head still bandaged, Dazai described his government job, with some hesitation, as "commissioner of public thought control" in the Hiroshima district. He said that he had returned to his home in Hiroshima from a trip to Tokyo only forty minutes before the bomb exploded. He was standing outdoors, in front of his house, when he saw a strange light moving across the sky.

"It looked like some sort of an electric flash, arc-shaped and bright orange," he said.

Then Dazai was knocked flat on the ground by the concussion of the blast. His house shook, as if rocked by an earthquake, and then fell apart. Some of the beams and rubble landed on him and injured his head. He said that he was surprised to realize later that he had heard no noise whatsoever during the explosion. Other eyewitnesses in Hiroshima said the same thing. Admiral Kanazawa and other officers at the naval base in Kure, twelve miles away, told us that they had heard a thundering roar, followed by a hurricanelike blast of wind that bent trees on the base to the ground.

Dazai had picked himself up and pulled his wife and two children from the ruins of their house. "Our house did not begin to burn immediately," he said, "but I saw great towers of black smoke advancing toward me across the city from the east, south, and north." He left his wife and children with a relative and tried to go downtown to his office. Although the bombing took place shortly after eight o'clock in the morning, the fire that followed it was so intense that Dazai could not get near his office's building until after four in the afternoon. The fire burned on unchecked for most of the next two days, he said, and relief work was impossible with fire-fighting equipment, telephones, electric power, and the local hospital all out of commission. After a long time, he said, the government managed to get some help and supplies to Hiroshima on boats and barges. It took a few weeks before trains were able to reach the city from Tokyo.

Some of the reporters tried to question Dazai, but, as often happens in such group interviews, most of their questions sounded trivial and rather silly. "Did you think there was more than one bomb?"

One of the reporters, with his pencil poised, asked Dazai what he thought of the power of the atomic bomb. The tired little man stared at the reporter for a moment and then said something in Japanese to the lieutenant from Sacramento, who was translating.

"He said," the lieutenant said, "that he believes you Americans have in your possession the ability to destroy everything in civilization."

In our car during the drive back to Kure we spoke of the incredible calmness and apparent indifference shown to us by the people in Hiroshima. The lieutenant from Sacramento, who was with us, listened but said nothing. After a while, one of us asked him if, in his opinion, the people in that part of Japan regarded the atomic bomb merely as a misfortune of war and held no particular resentment against us for dropping it, or, on the other hand, were they concealing hatred. The lieutenant peered at the questioner for a moment through his thick horn-rimmed glasses and said quietly, "They hate you."

When we landed at Atsugi, all hell broke over our heads. General MacArthur's headquarters threatened to court-martial Tex McCrary. The Japanese government filed a strong protest, reminding the Allied command that it could not have been held responsible for our safety in Hiroshima. Nonetheless we wired our stories, envied by all the other American and European correspondents in Japan.

What we had witnessed was unparalleled destruction, the result of only one bomb. It was awesome—and frightening—for there was a question of the long-term effects of radiation on the ability to generate new life. But one morning in January 1946, my wife, Mary, saw an item in the newspaper that provided some hope: a hen in Hiroshima had laid the first egg found in the city since the bombing.